DISTINCTIVE ASPECTS OF BAHÁ'Í EDUCATION

Distinctive Aspects of Bahá'í Education

Proceedings of the
Third Symposium on Bahá'í Education
Birmingham, April 1991

Edited by

Hooshang Nikjoo & Stephen Vickers

© 1993 The Bahá'í Publishing Trust
27 Rutland Gate
London   SW7 1PD

All rights reserved

British Library Cataloguing-in-Publication Data

A catalogue record for this book is
available from the British Library

ISBN 1-870989-46-5

Compiled and edited on behalf of the Bahá'í Education Committee of the National Spiritual Assembly of the Bahá'ís of the United Kingdom. The papers published represent the views of the individual contributors and are not intended to be authoritative statements on Bahá'í educational principle or practice. Taken together, they represent a wide spectrum of understanding and opinion in an exploration of an important topic.

Contents

Preface
Acknowledgements
Foreword

1.	Distinctive Aspects of Bahá'í Education *Ray Johnson*	1
2.	The Nature of Religious Education *John M. Hull*	13
3.	Centring a Secular Education on the Development of Character *Dwight W. Allen*	20
4.	Religious Instruction and Religious Education *Kevin M. Beint*	29
5.	Exploration and Integration of Bahá'í Education *William A. Diehl*	38
6.	Values and Questions - Balancing Acts in Education *Martin Cortazzi*	51
7.	Education and Gender *Sovaida Maani*	65
8.	Gender Education in Society *Joseph Roy Sheppherd*	75
9.	The Importance of the Arts in the Future Development of the Bahá'í Community *Gordon James Kerr*	83
10.	Cultural Imperatives of Bahá'í Education in the UK *Stephen Vickers*	95
11.	The Use of Music, Drama and Art in Bahá'í Education *Alan Woodhurst, John Lester, Carol Khorsandyon*	106

12.	Hot Housing: The Way Forward? *John Parris*	116
13.	Religiously Integrated Education in Northern Ireland *Edwin Graham, Mahvash Graham*	127
14.	Towards a Bahá'í Development Model: The Contribution of the Rural Education and Development Programme of FUNDAEC, Colombia *Michael Richards, Sarah Richards*	136
15.	Festivals and Feasts: Instruments of Community Development *I.S. Narula, J. Jowsey, A. Jowsey*	143
16.	Bahá'í Education for 2½ to 4 Year Olds *Marion Prentice*	151
17.	What can Bahá'ís offer Religious Education in Schools? *George M. Ballentyne*	162
18.	Racial Unity: The Most Challenging Issue in Spiritual Education *Mahzad Mazloomian*	167
19.	*The Children Act 1989* and the Bahá'í Faith *Kathryn C. McGee*	174
20.	SUNWALK: A Model for Moral and Spiritual Education *Roger Prentice*	180

Preface

The Third Symposium on Bahá'í Education took place at Newman College, Birmingham, England, from 3rd to 5th April 1991. Like its predecessors, the symposium was organised by the Bahá'í Education Committee of the National Spiritual Assembly of the Bahá'ís of the United Kingdom. Some eighty scholars, educationalists, teachers and others interested in education, drawn from Europe and North America, participated in the symposium. A number of papers and short presentations were given in Plenary or in interest groups, and the current volume contains a selection of these.

It is widely recognised throughout the Bahá'í world that the systematic development of education - not only of materials and ideas, but perhaps most notably of regional institutions of a Sunday School type - has been, with publishing, the major achievement of the UK Bahá'í community during the past decade. These regional institutions, while ultimately responsible to a single Local Spiritual Assembly, are managed by a Management Committee providing continuity of operation, and opportunities for succession planning and teacher training.

Bahá'í education is not concerned solely with the formal curriculum. The ethos of the school should be to encourage a sense of caring and responsibility, and the way that pupils behave out of the classroom is as important as what they learn in the classroom. Nor is education only a matter for children. Learning is an essential characteristic of any Bahá'í life. This broad definition of education is reflected in the range of topics addressed by the symposium. In addition to practical advice on organising a class, and exploring the nature of Bahá'í education, papers were presented on such seemingly diverse topics as adult education, community development, and the wider legal framework in which education takes place.

The worldwide Bahá'í community faces a common challenge in education. How can we develop a common understanding of the basic Bahá'í educational system and principles so as to be able to develop a curriculum appropriate to a multicultural and multiethnic society? How can we raise our children to be brilliant stars of the future world community? These have been the challenges given to the authors of this volume. We hope that their contributions will provide a platform for future progress.

Hooshang Nikjoo and Stephen Vickers.
(Editors)
Oxford, England

Acknowledgements

We would like to express our thanks to the National Spiritual Assembly of the Bahá'ís of the United Kingdom for their support of the symposium. Our special thanks go to Kevin Proudman, Noushin Proudman, Pervis Reid, Alex Reid, Philip Koomen and Susan Howard without whom the symposium would not have been possible. We would like to thank members of the Organising Committee, Lindsay Thorne (Chairman, Bahá'í Education Committee), Susan Hunter (Director, George Townsend Bahá'í Sunday School, Bangor, N.I.), John Neal (Director, Charnwood Bahá'í Sunday School), Wendi Momen (Chairman, National Spiritual Assembly of Bahá'ís of UK), Gordon J. Kerr (Manager, Bahá'í Publishing Trust) and Katherine Walker (Conference Secretary, Oxford Bahá'í Sunday School). We would also like to express our appreciation to Dwight Allen for his helpful advice and suggestions and to all those who served as session chairmen, discussion moderators and reviewers. Finally, we would like to thank Linda Jasion (Secretary, Bahá'í Education Committee), Rebecca Vickers, Kathryn McGee-Nikjoo, Kathy Irshad and Joy Harrison who helped prepare the manuscript for publication.

Hooshang Nikjoo and Steven Vickers

Foreword

These are moments of great challenge and responsibility in the Cause of Bahá'u'lláh. We must not lose the unprecedented opportunities which are offered to us through the benevolence of Divine Providence - opportunities which may never come again. One of the most intense of these opportunities lies in the field of education. Education is at the heart of Bahá'u'lláh's message for this day, the Day of God. For it is in the Day of God that every human being is given the right to the independent investigation of truth. With that right goes the responsibility to achieve the highest standard of education, a responsibility which rests both on the individual and on society.

Dominant world educational practices are often in direct contradiction to the principles of Bahá'í education. Students are being trained to be *clever* but not *good*. The process of education is passive and dull. Student questioning and dialogue are not encouraged. Not all of the inner and outer senses are used to enhance the process. Fear and criticism, rather than encouragement, dominate. Education in the sciences and humanities is usually considered to be separate from moral and spiritual education. Humility and a prayerful attitude are not encouraged. Reliance on God is unrecognised. Destructive rather than constructive competition is encouraged and rewarded, and competition rather than co-operation is emphasised. The individual is exalted above the group. Music and the arts are not highly valued. The education of girls and women lags behind. Teachers are arrogant in their ignorance, trapped into believing they must be expert in all that they teach. Parents neglect their prime responsibility. Consultation among all participants is missing. Equity is lacking. Excellence is not seen to be an objective for its own sake. Unity and world-mindedness are not focal points. Appreciation of diversity is ignored. Prejudices go unrecognised and unchallenged. Generally speaking, education is both ineffective and inefficient.

As much as we would like to have Bahá'í education fully implemented in the world today, it is not possible or even desirable given the process of development foreordained by God. If Bahá'í education became instantly available to us without effort and without our participation, it would be a contradiction of its own purpose; the training of souls takes place through trial and error. God has created humankind to carry forward an ever-advancing civilisation. Every advancement is both a celebration and a painful reminder of the dual nature of the human being, for we always have the option to ignore spiritual principles and pursue our vain imaginings.

Ours is the privilege of planting the seeds of Bahá'í education, even if not always in the right place, at the right time, or in the right way. From these seeds is destined to grow a spiritual potential for education far beyond anything we can now imagine.

It is in this spirit of inquiry and struggle that the conference documented by this volume was convened. It is one of a continuing series of conferences which may contribute to our understanding of the process of the unfoldment of Bahá'í education for the Golden Age of humankind.

The contexts for the application of Bahá'í principles in education are many. Some of us are professional educators seeking to find ways to improve our practices within old world settings. Some of us are volunteers, teaching in Bahá'í children's schools and trying to apply new spiritual principles to our often overwhelming task. And some of us have the privilege of being on the cutting edge of Bahá'í educational development, administering or teaching in Bahá'í-sponsored schools where our limits are defined only by our perceptions and resources. All of us, touched by the light of Bahá'u'lláh, must admire the efforts of the organisers in bringing together remarkably diverse perspectives. They are chronicled in this volume to make these ideas available for future contemplation and study.

As we read a paper we may see a way to apply its principles immediately, or find a nugget that we can build on, or use the ideas to stimulate our own creative processes. We may disagree with either the premises or the presentation, but our understanding of Bahá'í principles of education will nonetheless be enriched by requiring us to think through our objections and concerns. We must challenge ourselves to rise above the all too popular expectations of reading a book to find a body of expert opinion which we can embrace. Rather, we should celebrate our mutual exploration of unprecedented approaches to the educational process, and give thanks for our opportunity to participate in the development of a significant part of the fabric of the New World Order.

'Abdu'l-Bahá has stated that we create our own reality. How useful this volume may become will ultimately be up to us. The ideas and proposals represented are in all stages of development. A few may catch a glimmer of the light of real Bahá'í education, but most will ultimately contribute only to the process of understanding and further inquiry. And from our current, limited perspectives it is not likely that we will truly be able to discriminate among them. Ideas which, today, seem unreasonable or unattainable may become lynchpins of the new Bahá'í education. Other ideas, familiar and progressive sounding, may simply be temporary diversions in the quest for true Bahá'í education. All are useful to the process of development.

Bahá'í perspectives on moral education are being advanced in a variety of Bahá'í and other settings worldwide, and we can look forward to dramatic new insights in the next decade. One of the most startling developments is the rapid proliferation of Bahá'í sponsored schools around the world at all levels of sophistication from pre-school through to university. They share increasing concern in discovering the essence of Bahá'í schooling, both in spiritual and secular aspects. Bahá'í youth, second generation and beyond, are beginning to give us a glimpse of the power of spiritual education with parents as the first educators. Bahá'í educators are also beginning to forge new relationships between education and social and economic development, linking education to service and reflecting Bahá'u'lláh's admonition that work done in the spirit of service is worship. Bahá'í adult education is also in process of transformation: summer and winter schools, and weekend institutes, are maturing in content, procedure, expectation, and scope; local teaching institutes are combining teaching and deepening at an intimate personal and small group level; and deepening programmes for local spiritual assembly members are contributing to the maturity of Bahá'í institutions as called for by the Universal House of Justice. Education in a Bahá'í context goes far beyond the formal classroom and will continue to incorporate new settings, methods, and instructional patterns, with increasing responsibility shared by all individual believers.

We are rapidly gaining new perspectives on the emerging qualities typifying Bahá'í education worldwide. This volume documents many of the efforts in progress, even as it anticipates new directions made possible, in part, through this consultative effort.

Dwight W Allen
Norfolk, Virginia

Distinctive Aspects of Bahá'í Education

Ray Johnson

"By wonder are we saved."   Plato

I remember Stanwood Cobb telling the story of the first time he met 'Abdu'l-Bahá in Paris in 1913. 'Abdu'l-Bahá asked him what he did for a living and Stanwood said he was a teacher in a school for boys. When asked what he taught in his school, he said Science, Maths, English, and Social Studies - all the regular academic subjects. 'Abdu'l-Bahá asked him if he taught about things of the spirit. Stanwood said, "No, there's no time for all that!" As soon as he said it, he thought, "What have I done?" 'Abdu'l-Bahá said nothing, just looked at him and smiled. Stanwood said that with saying those six words he had condemned all modern education.[1] From that day on, he changed the priorities in his life of service to the Cause of God by putting spiritual education first. Today he is remembered as one who promoted spiritual education above all else.

> *Schools must first train the children in the principles of religion, so that the Promise and the Threat recorded in the Books of God may prevent them from the things forbidden and adorn them with the mantle of the commandments...*[2]

The staff at the Maxwell International Bahá'í School found that they were falling into the same material trap of allocating the vast majority of their time and resources to striving for academic excellence. We knew that spiritual education should have priority but putting the concept into practice was a difficult transition for the staff to make. The staff felt inadequate and had no definitive curriculum to guide them. Yet when they became detached from their perceived inadequacies and relied upon the creative word to guide them, things started changing. It is like putting teaching first on the agenda of the local spiritual assembly. There is always something coming up that seems, on the surface, to take precedence over consultation about teaching. Yet when a community concentrates on teaching, most of the problems seem to diminish. The same thing became apparent in prioritizing spiritual education at Maxwell. When the students prioritized their time so spiritual transformation came first, they began to have more respect for themselves and their peers, and their motivation to strive for excellence in all areas increased. Class disturbances practically disappeared.

> *Training in morals and good conduct is far more important than book learning.[3] Let him improve the character of each and all, and reorient the minds of men.[4]*

Bahá'í educational processes should be structured to create growth opportunities through simulating or creating real spiritual challenges. By confronting spiritual growth opportunities in a supportive environment, the child begins to realize that life itself is continuous movement from crisis to victory. God has given us the freedom to obey the laws and standards of His Revelation. A parent's or teacher's duty is wisely to nurture the child in the skill of making choices while assuming the consequences of whatever choices he or she makes. This training process connects the child's consciousness with the reality of spiritual laws and the consequences of obedience to them. Bahá'í schools have been instructed by the Universal House of Justice to teach the principle of the oneness of mankind.[5] One of several ways that the principle of the oneness of mankind is taught at the Maxwell International Bahá'í School is by ensuring that each dorm room is as diverse as possible in race, culture and nationality. This diversity, which is experienced for the first time by many students, creates all sorts of spiritual challenges. By introducing this social interaction many problems arise, and students learn to confront their feelings while dealing with interpersonal issues. By learning the art of consultation and then applying it in everyday situations, the students begin, out of necessity, to use the spiritual methodology found in the Writings to solve problems and discover truth. This process helps the students to focus on positive responses to problems and realize that there are spiritual principles by which solutions can be found to issues in every situation.[6] Consultation is "a cause of awareness and of awakening and a source of good and well-being".[7]

Addressing the issue of unity in diversity in the students' dormitories results in differences being viewed as personally rewarding and beneficial, as enhanced friendship and closeness follows consultation. For the vast majority of our Western students, in particular, separateness is a cultural norm. The resocialised students soon begin to seek out differences rather than gravitating towards sameness. As the benefits of diversity become an accepted value and a real concern in their daily lives, a reorientation of the students' thinking occurs. 'Abdu'l-Bahá said that "Naught but the celestial potency of the Word of God, which ruleth and transcendeth the realities of all things, is capable of harmonising the divergent thoughts, sentiments, ideas, and convictions of the children of men."[8]

When talking about spiritual challenges, Shoghi Effendi said that it will be through the activities of the youth

> *...that the Cause of our Beloved Master will in future spread all over the American Continent. They have upon their shoulders all the responsibilities for the progress of the Movement; it is our*

duty to rear their spiritual feelings, enlighten their hearts with the light of guidance which has been shed before us by the Master.[9]

Since the children and youth of today have the responsibility of standing at the helm of the Cause, it falls to us to prepare them for this spiritual task and to enlighten their hearts with the light of guidance. This is a real spiritual challenge for educators, parents, and most of all, children and youth themselves.

The North American traditional methods of education are not compatible with the goals of Bahá'í education. They are valueless and concerned only with the material side of the person. Shoghi Effendi explained that "future Bahá'í educationalists...would formulate an adequate teaching curriculum which would be in full harmony with the spirit of the Bahá'í Teachings, and would thus meet the requirements and needs of the modern age".[10] This task is to be "gradually accomplished by Bahái' scholars and educationalists of the future".[11] Now is the future! 'Abdu'l-Bahá wished that children should receive a Bahá'í education so they would not "be beset by sorrows and troubles".[12] We are gathered here at the Third International Symposium on Bahá'í Education to further our knowledge in the distinctive aspects of Bahá'í education so we can gradually create the structure and curriculum necessary for our children not to be beset by sorrows and troubles. For this reason, the International Teaching Centre has asked us again to take up the critical question of how to "assist the children of the world".[13]

Many people today believe that a good school is one in which students constantly have their heads buried in workbooks or textbooks. In the United States, concern about graduating students who could not read or write created the "back to basics" reform movement of the eighties. The emphasis given to students being engaged or "on task" has subsequently defined the approach to school discipline and how we evaluate students. There is an ancient Chinese proverb which says, "If we do not change our direction, we are likely to end up where we are headed." The values and assumptions that are presently shared by the majority in society have created a "deep structure"[14] which shapes our educational system. Eisner[15] talks about schools needing to provide students with the time to create a psychological equilibrium and to nurture their internal powers of learning by recognizing and validating their intuition and inspiration. Are we sure that our present "deep structure", of what we consider to be good education, is more productive in releasing human potential than one that allows students the opportunity to wonder and to meditate?

Though man has powers and outer senses in common with the animal, yet an extraordinary power exists in him of which the animal is bereft ...This is a power which encompasses all things, comprehends their realities, discovers all the hidden mysteries of beings, and through this knowledge controls them. It even perceives things which do not exist outwardly that is to say,

> *intellectual-realities which are not sensible, and which have no outward existence because they are invisible...*[16]

We need to create an environment which provides tasks that elicit and develop respect for wonder and stimulates the imagination. As Bahá'ís we recognize the power of the soul as the source of a person's intuitive and creative thoughts. 'Abdu'l-Bahá tells us we have the power to perceive things which do not exist.[17] Hand of the Cause of God Mr Furutan[18] tells how we complicate things by not believing in our ability to investigate the truth independently. Bahá'u'lláh continually directs us to look within ourselves. He stated that "This is the day when the gems of constancy that lie hid in the mine of men's inner selves should be made manifest".[19] Again He said, "...with your inner and outer eyes contemplate the evidences of My marvellous Revelation..."[20] In the *Book of Certitude* when Bahá'u'lláh spoke to those who wanted to attain the knowledge of the Word of God, He stated, "...wert thou to ponder their outward and inner meaning in thy heart, thou wouldst seize the significance of all the abstruse problems which, in this day, have become insuperable barriers between men and the knowledge of the Day of Judgement".[21] Education should help students to ponder, to perceive, to contemplate, to reach down into their unique beings in order to find perceptions and knowledge that can be manifested in the material world.

Educators are typically unaware of the potential of wonderment. They feel that students have to be engaged in academic exercises that are oriented to stimulate their material senses. By constantly engaging students in this manner we are handicapping them and preventing them from realizing their true potential. Education needs to be structured to provide balance in a student's life. The emotional and spiritual aspects of development need not only to be recognized, but given priority, so as to increase the realization of true learning. Since we know that spiritual education is the first education, we must use the faculty of spiritual learning in intellectual and physical pursuits. We have been conditioned to believe and trust only those things we can feel, touch or see with our outward vision. We have not been educated to use, or trust, our inner vision.

> *O MAN OF TWO VISIONS!*
> *Close one eye and open the other. Close one to the world and all that is therein, and open the other to the hallowed beauty of the Beloved.*[22]

Students at Maxwell memorize a Hidden Word every week as part of the English literature programme. They have weekly worksheets to record their understanding of the metaphors (or spiritual instruction) and sometimes to compare the metaphor (as it is used) with a previously studied Hidden Word. They also relate the Hidden Word to various principles and virtues of the Faith, such as detachment or sacrifice. This exercise stimulates the use of one's reflective and contemplative powers. The

Ministry of Education accepts the use of *The Hidden Words* and *The Seven Valleys and Four Valleys* as poetry for meeting governmental requirements. This enables the teachers to train the minds of our students using a symbolic language which allows the students to view life within a spiritual context.

Recently a Tai-Chi master came to the school to conduct a weekend workshop. It was attended by both staff members and students. After the workshop I was having a cup of tea with the master, and he told me he experienced something unique with our students and staff. He said one of the exercises called *Fox on Water* required the participants to close their eyes and stand on one leg and then the other while carrying out certain motions. He explained that usually at the begining of a course the students would be stumbling and falling down all over the place. However, the Maxwell participants all showed incredible balance. He had never seen such well balanced individuals before. When asked if they did balance exercises, I said, "No, but they have lots of prayers and meditation." He said that they must all have wonderful internal balance in their lives to have done the exercise so well.

If one purchases a BMW and then pulls it around with a team of horses, one is not making very good use of the power and potential latent within the machine. In the same way, when one predominantly uses only the material faculty of learning, one limits one's potential. When we are engaged in reading the Holy Word we are using our outer eyes and material powers of reasoning. When we use our outer eyes and the power of the mind, we cannot engage our inner eye and use the power of the soul to give us spiritual understanding and inspiration. Not until we disengage our minds from material pursuits can we contemplate and ponder the inner meaning of reality. The soul and the spirit are of the next world and are not limited to the restrictions of time or place. This unique aspect of human learning is available to us twenty-four hours a day. We can use the power of our soul to activate our inner senses, or we can choose to keep the door closed and severely handicap our ability to know those things that do not exist outwardly.

Henry Weil, in his book *Drops from the Ocean*, describes how we should use our inner vision as a discerner between right and wrong. We have been given specific guidance on how to perceive the evidences and to find solutions to the abstruse problems of today. Prayer and meditation have been ordained for us to free ourselves from material limitations and to activate our inner vision. The Universal House of Justice tells us that transformation is the purpose of Bahá'u'lláh's Revelation.[23] The goal of transformation is to pattern our lives as closely as possible to Bahá'í standards; an educational process should enhance progress towards that goal. Transformation means constantly improving our ability to make the correct moral and behavioural choices. One of the major distinctive aspects of Bahá'í education is empowering students to develop their inner vision and facilitating this transformation process. This inherent human quality, latent in every individual, is necessary for the transformation process. When we consistently use our inner vision we develop habits of contemplation, and are then more capable of bringing ourselves to account each day and reviewing our progress on personal issues of moral and behavioural choice.

> *Turn thy sight unto thyself, that thou mayest find Me standing within thee, mighty, powerful and self-subsisting.*[24]

When a person says, "I don't know what to do", what he is really saying is that he does not have a reference system for making decisions. As Bahá'ís, we have the bounty of having the reference system relevant for today. That is why Bahá'u'lláh has given us the injunction to read the Writings morning and evening and to bring ourselves to account each day. This command is for our security and well-being. It is one of the tools given to us by the Manifestation of God for surviving in today's crumbling old world order. The Universal House of Justice tells us that "It is particularly difficult to follow the laws of Bahá'u'lláh in present-day Society whose accepted practice is so at variance with the standards of the Faith."[25] It goes on to say that, "If an individual violates the spiritual laws for his own development he will cause injury not only to himself but to the society in which he lives. Similarly, the condition of society has a direct effect on the individuals who must live within it."[26]

Bahá'u'lláh has given us a decision-making strategy so we can determine what to do in every situation. When we are faced with a decision, we are told to go inside ourselves and tell ourselves what it is we must do. Training children and youth to reflect on the standards of the Faith when they are faced with making difficult decisions is crucial as a process of Bahá'í education. By developing habits of contemplation one will consistently review one's spiritual progress and, therefore, will be on a continuous path of spiritual transformation.

> *In most areas of human behaviour there are acts which are clearly contrary to the Law of God and others which are clearly approved or permissible; between these there is often a grey area where it is not immediately apparent what should be done. This is the age in which mankind must attain maturity, and one aspect of this is the assumption by individuals of the course of action in areas which are left open by the Law of God.*[27]

The "grey area" is clearly the blessing of frustration. This is the area of personal choice and, therefore, spiritual growth. Most tests and difficulties come from adjusting our feelings of individual rights and freedoms to the standards of the Faith. As children are trained how to make choices between right and wrong, they are choosing the desire for spiritual growth over the desire for gratification of the self. They begin to experience spiritual happiness and know when they are not happy that they need to reflect on and re-examine a previous choice to see where they have gone off the path. In that way, they will be ready to make a choice more in keeping with the principles and laws of the Faith the next time, and there will surely be a next time!

When we begin making more and more spiritually correct choices, we allow our true nature a chance to surface, positive habits to be formed, and living a Bahá'í life becomes not only preferable but desirable. 'Abdu'l-Bahá said, "There comes a time in the development of character when nobility of expression becomes habitual. We then hardly have to try to be good."[28] Helping young people to acquire spiritual habits for character development will ultimately result in the maturation of the fruit of the tree of humanity. Parents and teachers look forward with anticipation to the ripening of the fruits of their labours. Bahá'u'lláh explained that the fruits of the human tree are "upright character", "virtuous deeds" and "goodly utterance". The parent/educator must prepare the soil, plant the seeds and water the plant with the "sacred Words". If this is done properly, and the plant is well cared for, then the result is the "effulgence of the light of Justice".[29] Children must be guided to the realization that we are in the springtime of the evolution of humanity and are moving from adolescence into maturity. Barbara Ward wrote in the *International Development Review* an article entitled "Where there is no vision, the people perish".[30] Worldwide, children and youth lack vision and purpose in their lives. This is one reason why the International Teaching Centre said in 1988 that we must educate the children and youth today to "...grasp fundamental moral and spiritual principles, deposited within the children".[31] How else can they rescue their peers who lack vision and hope? Education must provide personal meaning and relevancy. To believe that what one is doing has meaning and a connection with a greater goal is basic to the feeling of belonging. One cannot begin to know oneself without feeling that one belongs and is connected to a greater purpose. To have a vision and to help others feel in control of their lives is fundamental to Bahá'í education.

The Universal House of Justice wrote to the Bahá'í Youth of the World in May 1985, explaining how

> *The dark horizon faced by a world which has failed to recognize the Promised One ...acutely affects the outlook of the younger generations; their distressing lack of hope and their indulgence in desperate but futile and even dangerous solutions make a direct claim on the remedial attention of Bahá'í youth, who, through their knowledge of that Source and the bright vision with which they have thus been endowed, cannot hesitate to impart to their depairing fellow youth the restorative joy, the constructive hope, the radiant assurances of Bahá'ulláh's stupendous Revelation.[32]*

Then in the Ridván message of 1989 it said that "A silver lining to the dark picture which has overshadowed most of this century now brightens the horizon." Bahá'í education should give our children and youth the vision that they are part of a global maturation process. They need to feel excitement for this wonderful stage of development that humanity is going through, a painful but necessary process of growth. Understanding this vision is extremely important in how one views life. Individuals who find their lives meaningless and empty are in a vacuum. They are in search of meaning (purpose) for their lives. Once they find meaning, they begin to form a set of personal values which reorient their goals. The International Teaching Centre tells us that "The children of the world at this time have a special destiny before God." We must help them "become an instrument of healing amongst humankind".[33] They have a vision of thousands upon thousands of children rescuing their peers from this decadent phase of human history.

The education that we offer to our children today must give them the skills and attitudes to attract their peers through their activities so that the rescue operation can begin. Religion can provide a spiritual anchor and the security that these young people can find nowhere else. Obtaining a Bahá'í identity must fill the vacuum and give meaning to life. When children and youth grasp this reality then concepts like "peace is not only possible but inevitable"[34] become part of the way they connect their lives with everyday events. A Bahá'í educational programme should not only give them an intellectual understanding but help focus their inner as well as their outer eyes on the dawn that is breaking on the horizon. When children and youth are connected with the Faith so that "their lives reflect to a marked degree the transforming power of the new Revelation they have embraced"[35] then they will have obtained a spiritual vision and know in the depths of their being that their own "human happiness is founded upon spiritual behaviour".[36]

> *Guidance hath ever been given by words, and now it is given by deeds. Every one must show forth deeds that are pure and holy, for words are the property of all alike, whereas such deeds as these belong only to Our loved ones. Strive then with heart and soul to distinguish yourselves by your deeds. In this wise We counsel you in this holy and resplendent tablet.*[37]

The path which gives our material lives spiritual happiness is founded in a life of service. From a child's earliest years a service component is essential to any Bahá'í educational programme. When I reflect on twelve years at the New Era School in India, it is evident to me that the most significant accomplishment there was the integration of service into the curriculum. The Office of Social and Economic Development of the Universal House of Justice said in 1986 that "In the Bahá'í community and in the Bahá'í schools the attitude of service will be taught, its example carried out, its effectiveness demonstrated and its true value nurtured."[38]

> *O people of God! Do not busy yourselves in your own concerns; let your thoughts be fixed upon that which will rehabilitate the fortunes of mankind and sanctify the hearts and souls of men. This can best be achieved through pure and holy deeds, through a virtuous life and a goodly behaviour. Valiant acts will ensure the triumph of this Cause, and a saintly character will reinforce its power.*[39]

Dr Steve Waite wrote on behalf of the Office of Social and Economic Development in India that "It is clear that a Bahá'í school must incorporate a service programme for children from an early age, as it is through the process of building an attitude of service to others that a child will have the opportunity to put into practice those praiseworthy virtues learned in class: hence service is the practical expression of spiritual training."[40]

'Abdu'l-Bahá said that this is the century of altruistic service.[41] Parents and teachers must provide service opportunities for our youngest children as well as for our youth. Do not deny our children and youth the benefits of serving their fellow man. As servitude is the highest station that one can obtain, it seems reasonable that we must instruct our children so they develop an attitude of service. This is one of the pre-eminent features by which Bahá'í education can be dramatically distinguished from other forms of education.

> *Bahá'u'lláh has extended the scope and deepened the meaning of self-expression. In His elevation of art and of work performed in the service of humanity, to acts of worship, can be discerned enormous prospects for a new birth of expression in the civilization anticipated by His World Order. The significance of this principle, now so greatly amplified by the Lord of the Age, cannot be doubted.*[42]

As we examine the distinctive aspects of Bahá'í education, we must not forget that much of the curricular content lies within each individual. We must not only encourage but teach our children to pray and meditate, to contemplate, and to ponder the Words of God so as to discover the hidden gems within them. This Faith of ours has no mullás and no clergy; the truths are there for us to discover independently. Let us break the barrier of passive learning that schools and traditional forms of education have created in our children. Independent investigation is a bedrock principle of this Cause, and we cannot take it for granted that children and youth will automatically wonder and investigate. They have been discouraged from thinking and contemplating, and we must re-establish the burning desire to know those things that God has ordained for the education of humanity.

While children are learning to use their inner vision they must be instructed in religion so as to clarify those things that are contrary to the Law of God and those which are clearly permissible. The right hand of Bahá'í education is training. We are told first to train the children in "behaviour and conduct". This enables the children to "...hold fast to the spiritual perfections", and this resolve protects them so their "good conduct may remain unchanged".[43] This primarily depends on how we monitor the influences to which our children are exposed and how we structure their environment to provide activities that create challenges with a safety net. Children should know that not all failure is bad and that life is full of ups and downs, that one may learn by making mistakes. We cannot abandon them to their own selves and passions but should admonish them and provide good counsel, so they may learn from failure without fear. We cannot refine their character without helping children and youth to clarify the boundaries of moderation.

A Bahá'í education will create the realization that God's greatest gift to us is knowledge. Crucial to a true understanding of this knowledge is a programme of development that enables children and youth to demonstrate "goodly deeds" (through service) and acquire a "praiseworthy character" (through training).

> *This is the century of motion, divine stimulus and accomplishment, the century of human solidarity and altruistic service, the century of universal peace and the reality of the divine Kingdom.*[44]

References

1. Stanwood Cobb, *Thoughts on Education and Life* (Washington DC: Avalon Press) 1975, p 8.
2. Bahá'u'lláh, quoted in: *Bahá'í Education* - a compilation (London: Bahá'í Publishing Trust) 1987, no 15, p 4.
3. 'Abdu'l-Bahá, quoted in: *Bahá'í Education* - a compilation (London: Bahá'í Publishing Trust), 1987, no 81, p 33.
4. 'Abdu'l-Bahá, quoted in: *Selections from the Writings of 'Abdu'l-Bahá*, (Haifa: Bahá'í World Centre) 1978, p 3.
5. Universal House of Justice, *The Promise of World Peace* (Haifa: Bahá'í World Centre) 1985, p 13.
6. Universal House of Justice, in a letter, Haifa, October 1983.
7. Bahá'u'lláh, *Heaven of Divine Wisdom* - a compilation (London: Bahá'í Publishing Trust) 1978, p 2.
8. 'Abdu'l-Bahá, quoted in: *Selections from the Writings of 'Abdu'l-Bahá*, (Haifa: Bahá'í World Centre), 1978, p 292.
9. Shoghi Effendi, quoted in: *Centers of Bahá'í Learning* (Wilmette: Bahá'í Publishing Trust), 1980, p 14.
10. Shoghi Effendi, quoted in: *Bahá'í Education* - a compilation (London: Bahá'í Publishing Trust), 1987, no 139, p 56.
11. *ibid.*
12. 'Abdu'l-Bahá, quoted in: *Bahá'í Education* - a compilation (London: Bahá'í Publishing Trust) 1987, no 48, p 19.
13. International Teaching Center, a letter, Haifa, 5 December 1988.
14. Barbara Tye, *Global Education: From Thought to Action*; ASCD Yearbook, 1991.
15. Elliot W. Eisner, What Really Counts in Schools, *Educational Leadership*; **48**, no 5, Feb. 1991.
16. Bahá'u'lláh, quoted in: *Bahá'í World Faith* - Selected Writings of Bahá'u'lláh and 'Abdu'l-Bahá (Wilmette: Bahá'í Publishing Trust), 1976, p 304.
17. *ibid.*
18. International Teaching Centre, a letter, Haifa, 15 June, 1989.
19. Bahá'u'lláh, *Tablets of Bahá'u'lláh* - Revealed after the Kitáb-i-Aqdas (Haifa: Bahá'í World Centre), 1984, p 88.
20. Bahá'u'lláh, quoted in: *Gleanings from the Writings of Bahá'u'lláh*, (Wilmette: Bahá'í Publishing Trust), 1977, p 325.
21. Bahá'u'lláh, *Kitab-i-Iqán* - The Book of Certitude, translated by Shoghi Effendi (Wilmette: Bahá'í Publishing Trust), 1974, p 123.
22. Bahá'u'lláh, *The Hidden Words*, Persian no 12 (London: Bahá'í Publishing Trust), 1975, p 26.
23. Universal House of Justice, *Ridván Message*, 1989.

24. Bahá'u'lláh, *The Hidden Words*, Arabic no 13 (London: Bahá'í Publishing Trust), 1975, p 27.
25. Universal House of Justice, *Messages from the Universal House of Justice* (Wilmette: Bahá'í Publishing Trust), 1976, pp 105-6.
26. *ibid.* p 106.
27. Universal House of Justice, Letter to an individual, Nov. 1986.
28. 'Abdul'l-Bahá, quoted in: *Thoughts on Education and Life*, S. Cobb, 1989 (Oxford: George Ronald), p 32.
29. Bahá'u'lláh, quoted in: *Tablets of Bahá'u'lláh* - Revealed after the Kitab-i-Aqdas (Haifa: Bahá'í World Centre), 1984, p 257.
30. Barbara Ward, *International Development Review*.
31. International Teaching Centre, 5 December 1988.
32. Universal House of Justice, a letter, 8 May 1985.
33. International Teaching Centre, a letter, 5 December 1988.
34. Universal House of Justice, *The Promise of World Peace* (Haifa:.Bahá'í World Centre), 1985.
35. Universal House of Justice, a letter, 8 May 1985.
36. 'Abdu'l-Bahá, quoted in: *Bahá'i Education* - a compilation (London: Bahá'í Publishing Trust), 1987, no 48, p 19.
37. Bahá'u'lláh, *The Hidden Words*, Persian no 76 (London: Bahá'í Publishing Trust), 1975, p 30.
38. Office of Social and Economic Development of the Universal House of Justice, a letter, 25 December 1986.
39. Bahá'u'lláh, *Tablets of Bahá'u'lláh* - Revealed after the Kitab-i-Aqdas (Haifa: Bahá'í World Centre), 1984, p 86.
40. Steve Waite, *A Charter for Bahá'í Schools*, March 1988, p 14.
41. 'Abdu'l-Bahá, *The Promulgation of Universal Peace* (Wilmette: Bahá'í Publishing Trust), 1982, p 140.
42. 'Abdu'l-Bahá, quoted in: *Star of the West*, Volume XVII, p 161.
43. 'Abdu'l-Bahá, *The Promulgation of Universal Peace* (Wilmette: Bahá'í Publishing Trust), 1982, p 140.

The Nature of Religious Education

John M. Hull

Yesterday, in my office, I had a rather interesting time. I read through a whole lot of press cuttings from newspapers and periodicals in Britain over the last two or three weeks giving a picture of developments in British religious education. Religious education is passing through a time of conflict, which is raising important questions for the relationship between religions in British society and the nature of schooling.[1,2]

Before taking up these points, however, I will try to summarise my own response to the question I have been given about the nature of religious education. I will then relate this to contemporary events. Religious education has three fundamental purposes in our society. First, it seeks to communicate to persons who are not religious a basic understanding of religion. Secondly, it seeks to communicate to persons who are religious a basic understanding of themselves. Thirdly, it seeks to make available, both to the religious and to the non-religious, the benefits of the study of religion. That third aspect we may call the gifts of religious education, which are offered to pupils, and indeed to adults: the gifts of religious study.

The first of these purposes refers to the role of religion as part of the general curriculum. In England and Wales religious education is part of the compulsory provision in schools, required by law.[3] It is part of the basic curriculum, which must be taught to all pupils of compulsory school age, and (in the case of religious education only) beyond the minimum school leaving age. It is taught to pupils who come from religious family backgrounds and to those who do not. Because this first purpose refers to the general educational outcome of this subject, it may be described as making contribution to all pupils *qua* pupils. Young people are here considered not as believers or unbelievers but as students.

Secondly, religious education seeks to offer a self-understanding to those who are religious. Some years ago we might have made sharper distinctions between the task of religious nurture (the fostering of religious faith) and that of religious education in offering a critical perspective on the nature of religion. This distinction, while still useful, is perhaps too sharp. We must recognise, more fully than we did ten years ago, that religious education does have a contribution to make in the encouragement of faith as well as in the education of the secular person. It would be strange if religious education was of benefit to all pupils except those who were religious. Religious education must seek to offer encouragement to those young people who are from religious families. What kind of encouragement will this be? It will largely consist in the affirmation of their identity, offering an opportunity to engage in the critical study of their own tradition along with young people from other traditions. They will thus be able to evaluate their self-understanding. Religious education will make a contribution towards their human development and maturation as religious believers equipped to take a mature and intelligent part in adult society.

The third purpose refers to the contribution of religious studies to the general welfare and educational advancement of young people.[4] In the University of Birmingham we have a project that has to do with the religious education of young children: ***Religion in the Service of the Child***. Central to our approach is the concept of the gift. We take a number of items of religious belief and practice, such as a passage of scripture, a sacred story, a sound such as the Islamic call to prayer, a statue, or an item of devotion such as rosary beads. Of each of them we ask what its gift might be to the imagination of the child. We are developing not so much the children's concepts as their images. Religious education has tended to be too heavy on conceptual development and too light on imaginative development. The gifts that the religious materials have to offer children are not necessarily religious. They may include the provocation of curiosity, the stimulation of questioning, deeper insight into the family backgrounds of other young people, and the knowledge of the lives and backgrounds of other people and other cultures. There may also, of course, be religious gifts. Reference has already been made to the fact that religious education naturally has a contribution to make to those who are religious as well as to those who are not.[5,6]

These then are the three basic purposes of religious education as I see them. In fulfilling these purposes in the school system in England and Wales, to go no further afield, religious education has tended to take a number of different approaches.

First we have what might be called *the transmissional approach,* secondly *the descriptive approach,* thirdly *the personal approach,* and finally *the approach through ambiguity and criticism.*

There is an understanding of religious education which emphasises that its task is mainly to transmit the religious tradition. This approach is currently gaining ground. Indeed some people suggest that children should be taught in separate religious groups in schools, that Christian children should not be taught with children of other faiths, nor should they be taught very much, if anything, about the religion of their neighbours, but Christian children should be taught Christianity. Muslim children should be taught Islam. It is on the basis of such a belief that we find the current interest in relating agreed syllabuses to the characteristics of the local population. In other words, in an area where there are a lot of Muslims you would have an agreed syllabus which contained a great deal of Islamic teaching, and so forth.

I believe that this transmissional approach is mistaken. It would create a situation where we no longer had a community-based religious education which sought for common understanding. We would, on the other hand, have a system which could best be described as parallel instruction. Each child would be taught in separate and parallel groups.[7] Behind this understanding of religious education is a conception of religion which looks upon its mission largely in terms of self-reproduction. This takes us into questions about the nature and destiny of religion itself in our modern world. Is the mission of religion to be summarised in terms of religious reproduction? Or is the mission of religion, in our world today, something greater than mere reproduction?

There is a profound conflict taking place within my own tradition, which is Christian, in many parts of the world today. There are those who believe that the purpose of Christianity is primarily to reproduce itself. Reproduction (the usual word used is evangelisation) would seek to over-populate or out-grow the population of other religions. Its end goal would be the situation where Christianity supplanted and replaced all other religions. This might be described as the re-establishment of Christendom. For some Christians, this is such a fundamental understanding that they find it difficult to conceive of any other kind of Christianity.

There are, however, Christians who take a different view, which is that Christianity does not exist for itself, that the function of the Christian faith in the world has something to do with the destiny of our species as a whole, that Christianity is an instrument in a larger providence. Christians who take this point of view must challenge the transmissional model. That model, conceived in terms of reproduction, becomes little more than a domesticated instrument of religious aggrandisement. We can understand many of the conflicts in religious education in our country at the present time by realising that the transmissional model has become more powerful and is now taking tribalistic and sectarian forms. If unchecked, these trends will separate our religious communities and will lead to the breakdown of dialogue between world faiths.

The second approach is that which describes religion. The technical word for this approach is phenomenological. This movement in British religious education is very influential. It has contributed greatly to the improvements, both in content and method, which we have seen in British classrooms in recent years. The approach is based upon twentieth century methods in the scholarly study of religion. It emphasises that the object of study is the manifestations of religion, the forms of the religious life. Such study is to be objective, descriptive and non-evaluative. The final authority as to religious faith and practice is the believer, and the phenomenological approach has led to a greater respect for and attention to the religious believer. The ultimate aim of the study is to enable young people to appreciate the religious life from the point of view of the believer, to have empathy towards the religious consciousness of others.[8]

The phenomenological approach, for all of its success in establishing an objective social science approach to the teaching of the subject, is unable to take account of one fundamental feature of religion itself. This has to do with the connection between religion and false consciousness, or the intrinsic ambiguity of religion. If the consciousness of the believer is to be taken as the ultimate norm and authority for religion, it must be assumed that believers know themselves and their religion in an unambiguous manner. In other words, the phenomenological approach does not permit an understanding of the role of deception in religion. There seems to be no place for what might be called a 'pedagogy of deceipt'. If we consider the ambiguity, the false consciousness and the self-deception which are such prominent features of religion in our time, then a religious education which fails to grapple with those aspects of religion cannot be completely adequate. The phenomenological approach is an important strand in religious education and should be strengthened. But I also wish to see it employed with other approaches so as to overcome its limitations.

In the personalist and existentialist approach, religious education offers itself as a contribution to the young person's quest for meaning in life. This is the religious education which deals with ultimate problems, with mystery and awareness, that which seeks to provoke an enquiry into values and commitments in living. This is another important strand in the British tradition of religious education.[9,10]

Although it is as important and necessary to the religious education process as the phenomenological method, the personal existential approach has its limitations. In its attempt to enable young people or adults to discover meaning and purpose in their lives, the personal/existential approach tends to become excessively individualistic. It fails to place the quest for meaning within the structural institutional context of modernity. At its worst, the personal/existential approach tends to be expressed in a series of bourgeois asthetic values: kindness to others, doing good deeds and obeying the laws are typical features; while questioning, clear thinking and responsibility place emphasis upon the autonomous citizen. One seldom finds study of justice in the economic order or of the prophetic tradition of social reform, and religious education which does not equip young people to grapple with the great questions of justice in our time is surely deficient. Perhaps this can be a weakness of an approach which concentrates too exclusively on the personal, individual quest for meaning in life.[11]

It is possible to make too much of the so-called problem of the meaning of life. The problem about life is not its meaning but its pain. The question about the meaning of faith in God is seen in a different perspective when God is committed to the enterprise of justice on behalf of the poor and the marginalised of this world. In that context faith in God becomes real.[12] Take faith in God out of that context and no amount of questing will bring meaning back to a life founded on injustice.

As we examine the nature of religion under the conditions of modernity in Western societies today, one outstanding fact emerges: the essential ambiguity of religion. How can it be that religion is associated both with some of the most exploitative aspects of our capitalist tradition and also with those who seek, on behalf of the oppressed, to discover justice and peace? Religion has this two-edged quality. It can be spoken of in personal as well as social terms. Religion functions in people's lives very much the way that sexuality does. It is the source of some of our greatest joys and of our deepest ills. Religion can operate parasitically upon people's lives, leading to regressive forms of fetish-like infantile faith; it can also function as a source of strength, courage and creativity.

Amongst our religious friends we recognise both kinds, those whose personalities appear to be fettered and made infantile by faith, and those whose personalities appear to have grown stronger and more creative through faith. Religion acts as a parasite; it also acts as a launching pad. This ambiguous character of religion, so central to the way it functions in life and society, is something which religious education must take on board.[13]

Let us return in the light of these distinctions to the present controversies. On 18 March 1991 the Secretary of State issued a letter to chief education officers, which was reported in the press on 21 March. In this letter Kenneth Clarke transmitted legal advice which he had received about the interpretation of Section 8.3 of the 1988 Education Reform Act. This Section states that any new agreed syllabus *must reflect the fact that the principal religious traditions in Great Britain are in the main Christian whilst taking account of the teaching and practices of the other principal religions represented in Great Britain.* The legal opinion is fair and balanced emphasising that any agreed syllabus must be specific about the character of the Christian traditions which are to be taught and must be equally specific about the teaching and practices of the other major religions represented in Great Britain. No agreed syllabus, the legal advice says, can be exclusively based on the Christian faith. No syllabus can be legal if *any* principal religious tradition is omitted. This establishes more firmly that world religion syllabuses are now legally required in this country. The letter also points out that religious education is not to urge any particular religious belief or commitment upon pupils. Decisions about the balance of content are to remain at the local level and will be determined by local as well as national circumstances.

Comparison between what the letter says and what the press reported reveals a striking contrast. The headlines said Clarke 'urges emphasis on Christian education' and *'schools told to focus on Bible'*. These descriptions do not correctly represent the Secretary of State's letter. It is no more true that Christianity is to be emphasised than that the teaching and practices of other world religions are to be emphasised. On 4 April 1991 *The Times* and other newspapers reported that the Secretary of State had advised the London Borough of Ealing that its agreed syllabus was unlikely to meet the requirements of the Act. This, however, was because the syllabus is vague. Any new syllabus must be more specific, both in what it says about Christianity and in what it says about world religions. There is no criticism in the Government's letter of the spirit or the balance of the Ealing syllabus; its approach must simply be spelled out in greater detail. To represent the letter as if Ealing was being rebuked because it wasn't Christian enough is to ignore the facts. It is hard to resist the view that a fair and balanced legal interpretation of the Act is being thrown off balance by the influence of a small group of Christians who do not accept the nature of religious education as I have described it.[14,8] Their emphasis upon Christianity at the expense of other religious traditions may force the subject into a position where its role in the creation of understanding and harmony between people of all communities will be undermined.

References

1. Edwin Cox and Josephine M. Cairns, *Reforming Religious Education. The Religious Clauses of the 1988 Education Reform Act*. (London: Kogan Page), 1989.
2. Michael H. Grimmit, 1991, *The use of religious phenomena in schools: some theoretical and practical considerations*. British Journal of Religious Education, 13, 2, pp. 77-88.
3. John M. Hull, *The Act Unpacked, the Meaning of the 1988 Education Reform Act for Religious Education*, (Derby: Christian Education Movement), 1989.
4. Michael H. Grimmit, *Religious Education and Human Development*, (McCrimmons), 1987.
5. Michael H. Grimmitt, Julie Grove, John M. Hull and Louise Spencer, *A Gift to the Child. Religious Education in the Primary School*. (New York: Simon and Schuster), 1991.
6. Michael H. Grimmitt, Julie Grove, John M. Hull and Louise Spencer, *Religion in the Service of the Child: Interim Report*. University of Birmingham, Centre for Religious Education, Development and Research, 1991.
7. John M. Hull, *Studies in Religion and Education*, (Brighton: Falmer Press), 1984.
8. Robert Jackson, ed., *Approaching World Religions*, (London: John Murray), 1988.
9. Edwin Cox, *Problems and Possibilities for Religious Education*, (London: Hodder and Stoughton), 1983.
10. John Hammond and David Hey, *New Methods in RE Teaching - An Experimental Approach*, (Harlow, Oliver and Boyd), 1990.
11. Adrian Thatcher, 1991, *A Critique of Inwardness in Religious Education*, BJRE 14, 1, pp 22-27.
12. Fredrich Schweitzer, 1987, *Progress, Continuity and Change: Three Approaches to the Language Problem in Religious Education*, BJRE 9, 2, pp. 70-77.
13. John M. Hull, 1991 *Religion, Education and Madness - A Modern Trinity* (Inaugural Lecture). School of Education, University of Birmingham.
14. John M. Hull, 1991, *Should Agreed Syllabuses be Mainly Christian?* BJRE (Editorial) 14 1, pp 1-3, 65.

Centering A Secular Education on the Development of Character

Dwight W. Allen

Bahá'ís do not find it at all surprising that the contemporary world is consistently frustrated by the behaviour of its children and youth. Quite simply, children are fundamentally miseducated. From youth gangs and high rates of teen pregnancy to the challenge of parental authority and dropping out of school, the behaviour of children threatens the sense of well being of many societies which have allowed the character education of children to be neglected.

From the Bahá'í perspective, the knowledge of God is the starting point of all effective education. "The fear of God hath ever been the prime factor in the education of His creatures. Well it is with them that have attained thereunto!"[1] "That which must precede all else is to teach them the oneness of God and the Laws of God. For lacking this, the fear of God cannot be inculcated, and lacking the fear of God an infinity of odious and abominable actions will spring up, and sentiments will be uttered that transgress all bounds."[2] "Human happiness is founded upon spiritual behaviour."[3]

As we examine contemporary secular education we can immediately see why it has such difficulty, whatever the detail of its structure and curriculum, because it is not centred on the knowledge of God. But in this spiritual springtime, the bounties and favours of God can also exert powerful, indirect effects on the character education of children, even in secular settings.

In Western, pluralistic, democratic societies a large portion of the values are held in common, as a result of their Judeo-Christian heritage. However, the lack of agreement on a small but visible cluster of values, and in some instances a commitment to the separation of church and state, has often resulted in the neglect of all values as a curriculum focus in the schools of those societies.

These same societies are caught in a maelstrom of change in social structure, much of it destructive and divisive. The primary social unit of the society, the family, is changing and often dysfunctional. Children are caught in a confusion of values between home and school, between peer influences and adult role models which are, themselves, often inconsistent.

How can Bahá'ís help apply principles of sound moral education in secular societies which are unaware of the purpose of life and confused as to the purposes of education? First of all, let us be clear about what we know:

"The foundation principle of a school is first and foremost moral training, character building and the rectification of conduct."[4]

> *These schools for academic studies must at the same time be training centres in behaviour and conduct, and they must favour character and conduct above the sciences and arts. Good behaviour and high moral character must come first, for unless the character be trained, acquiring knowledge will only prove injurious. Knowledge is praiseworthy when it is coupled with ethical conduct and a virtuous character; otherwise it is a deadly poison, a frightful danger.*[5]
>
> *First and most important is training in behaviour and good character; the rectification of qualities; arousing the desire to become accomplished and acquire perfections, and to cleave unto the religion of God and stand firm in His Laws, to accord total obedience to every just government, to show forth loyalty and trustworthiness to the ruler of the time, to be well wishers of mankind, to be kind to all.*[6]

The spiritual goal of life is to reflect the attributes of God as revealed to man by Bahá'u'lláh. For the first time God has provided man the full range of His attributes. Bahá'u'lláh tells us our moral guidance is now complete. Bahá'ís can examine the attributes of God to determine our moral direction.[7] The task is wonderfully complex and fraught with paradox. In a prayer known as the Long Healing Prayer, Bahá'u'lláh invokes God in many negative as well as positive images, pointing to the bounties of life which become recognisable, or even possible, only through comparison and contrast. It will remain our frustration as Bahá'ís not to be able to share the most fundamental principles of character education - the spiritual purpose of life - as we seek to influence secular schools to focus on the character education of children. But that must not prevent us from seeking adoption of aspects of character education which are acceptable to a secular society.

Social agreement on values does not automatically lead to their consideration in schools. Many schools and teachers at present accept no responsibility for developing values. Many educators assert that the teaching of values and ethical concerns are counterproductive to achieving the intellectual objectives of schooling. They see their task to be limited to the education of the mind. A formal commitment to character education as a central concern of schooling at all levels is needed.

What are the values Bahá'ís would seek to teach and have taught in the schools for which there is common acceptance in the broad society? Where there is general agreement we can be more successful in encouraging educational institutions in their consideration. Our immediate objective should be to establish the principle of the importance of character education as a fundamental component of all education. The acceptance of that principle is much more important than the specific components of character education which are agreed upon initially.

Interestingly enough, many of the issues which Bahá'ís would associate with character education, such as discipline and order, while valued, are not thought of as a part of a *curriculum* of character education.

> ...The children's school must be a place of utmost discipline and order, that instruction must be thorough, and provision must be made for the rectification and refinement of character; so that, in his earliest years, within the very essence of the child, the divine foundation will be laid and the structure of holiness raised up.[8]

Principles of Character Education

One of the most important issues is to attend to both intentional and incidental values in the conduct of schools. If character education is to be truly successful, administrators, teachers and all school staff must accept the responsibility of being role models, a responsibility which has substantially eroded over the past century. The school must consciously strive to make all aspects of its programme and environment consistent with the values it has chosen to inculcate in character education, and periodically review its policies and procedures for their effect on the character education of their students.

Effort and struggle are important aspects of character education. "Accustom them to hardship,"[9] counsels 'Abdu'l-Bahá. Character education must begin at home in infancy. Schools should seek to influence the society to mount strong campaigns of parent education. And it is the early years of schooling which are most critical to character education. "It is extremely difficult to teach the individual and refine his character once puberty is passed."[10] "Love and kindness have far greater influence than punishment upon the improvement of human character."[11] "The child's character will be totally perverted if he be subjected to blows or verbal abuse."[12] "The emergence of this natural sense of human dignity and honour is the result of education."[13] Teachers must be modest, even-tempered and forbearing.

Character education must not be seen as a separate *curriculum* but rather the context in which all schooling takes place. "Therefore must the mentor be a doctor as well: that is, he must, in instructing the child, remedy its [sic] faults; must give him learning, and at the same time rear him to have a spiritual nature [in a secular context - a strong character]. Let the teacher be a doctor to the character of the child..."[14]

> *There is thus a great difference between the prevention of crime through measures that are violent and retaliatory, and so training the people, and enlightening them... that without any fear of punishment or vengeance to come, they will shun all criminal acts... [and see] the very commission of a crime as a great disgrace and in itself the harshest of punishments.*[15]

The irony, of course, is that excellence in character will allow the children to achieve excellence in all aspects of secular education:

> *...arousing the desire to become accomplished and acquire perfections.*[16]
> *A child that is cleanly, agreeable, of good character, well-behaved - even though he be ignorant - is preferable to a child that is rude, unwashed, ill-natured, and yet becoming deeply versed in all the sciences and arts. The reason for this is that the child who conducts himself well, even though he be ignorant, is of benefit to others, while an ill-natured, ill-behaved child is corrupted and harmful to others, even though he be learned. If, however, the child be trained to be both learned and good, the result is light upon light.*[17]

A Curriculum for Character Education

There is an abundance of counsel from Bahá'í writings on specific aspects of character education. It would be well for any Bahá'í seeking to work with secular schools to study deeply the attributes of God to gain a perspective of the broad objectives of character education. Of these, many are appropriate to a secular context.[18] It is likely that when Bahá'ís are invited to participate in the process of designing a curriculum for values education, or character education, the process of dialogue will itself be one of the crucial ingredients to the success of such a curriculum. While character education is appropriately a specific curriculum focus, the most important character education will require the entire school to accept the responsibility for character education imbedded in the fibres of its environment and structure, modelled by all its participants and constantly reexamined in its relationships.

Let us examine a brief sampling of the specific curriculum recommendations to be found in Bahá'í writings:

> *While the children are yet in their infancy...let them share in every new and rare and wondrous craft and art.*[19]
> *See to it that the children...will be trained in...humility and lowliness, in dignity, in ardour and love.*[20]

> *The children must be carefully trained to be most courteous and well-behaved.*[21]
>
> *And further, those present should concern themselves with...teaching the various branches of knowledge, good behaviour, a proper way of life, the cultivation of a good character, chastity and constancy, perseverance, strength, determination, firmness of purpose...*[22]
>
> *Let them also study whatever will nurture the health of the body and its physical soundness, and how to guard their children from disease.*[23]
>
> *[They should avoid] materialistic works that are current among those who see only natural causation, and tales of love, and books that arouse the passions.*[24]
>
> *Today it is obligatory for the loved ones of God, and their imperative duty, to educate the children in reading, writing, the various branches of knowledge, and the expansion of consciousness, that on all levels they may go forward day by day.*[25]
>
> *Thus shall they grow and flourish, and be taught righteousness and the dignity of humankind, resolution and the will to strive and to endure. Thus shall they learn perseverance in all things, the will to advance, high-mindedness and high resolve, chastity and purity of life. Thus shall they be enabled to carry to a successful conclusion whatsoever they undertake.*[26]
>
> *Every child without exception must from his earliest years make a thorough study of the art of reading and writing, and according to his own tastes and inclinations and the degree of his capacity and powers, devote extreme diligence to the acquisition of learning, beneficial arts and skills, various languages, speech, and contemporary technology.*[27]

Creating an Environment for Character Education

Effective character education will dictate the creation of a warm, joyful environment for education. It will encourage schools to involve students in decision-making so that students will feel responsibility for their education. Character education will almost certainly transform the school from a passive learning environment to an active learning community. It will encourage group work and its by-products of support and respect. Individual rights will be balanced with common social need and benefit. Attitudes such as a respect for privacy and the integrity of each member of the school community, student and teacher alike, will be taught and practised. Independent investigation within a framework of mutual responsibility will become a standard for teaching and learning. Students will be taught to differentiate between the letter and the spirit of the law, to focus on intentions and to seek mutual support for the fulfilment of those intentions. Imperfection will be understood as inherent to the human condition and accepted both as a part of a student's personal growth and as an expected component of others' behaviour. Not only their peers, but also teachers, parents and other adults will be respected and honoured, and their inevitable faults overlooked or given less importance - if their intentions can be seen to be committed to ever higher standards of conduct and behaviour.

If we take character education seriously, it can provide the key, even in a secular institution, to the transformation of education and become a foundation on which to build many other aspects of educational reform.

References

1. Bahá'u'lláh, *Epistle to the Son of the Wolf*, (Wilmette: Bahá'í Publishing Trust), 1976, p 27.
2. 'Abdu'l-Bahá, quoted in: *Bahá'í World Faith* - Selected Writings of Bahá'u'lláh, 'Abdu'l-Bahá' (Wilmette: Bahá'í Publishing Trust), 1976, p 182.
3. 'Abdu'l-Bahá, quoted in: *Bahá'í Education* - a compilation (Wilmette: Bahá'í Publishing Trust), 1987, no 48, p 19.
4. *ibid.* p 38.
5. *ibid.* p 37-8.
6. *ibid.* p 42.
7. A partial listing of the Attributes of God mentioned in Bahá'í Scriptures is appended to this paper.
8. 'Abdu'l-Bahá, quoted in: *Bahá'í Education* - a compilation (Wilmette: Bahá'í Publishing Trust), 1987, no 43, p 17.
9. *ibid.* no 57, p 22.
10. *ibid.* no 43, p 18.
11. Shoghi Effendi, quoted in: *Bahá'í Education* - a compilation (London: Bahá'í Publishing Trust), 1987, no 134, p 54.
12. 'Abdu'l-Bahá, quoted in: *Bahá'í Education* - a compilation (London: Bahá'í Publishing Trust), 1987, no 97, p 40.
13. *ibid.* no 38, p 12.
14. *ibid.* no 58, p 23.
15. *ibid.* no 41, p 16.
16. *ibid.* no 80, p 32.
17. *ibid.* no 81, p 33.
18. See two appendices.
19. 'Abdu'l-Bahá, quoted in: *Bahá'í Education* - a compilation (London: Bahá'í Publishing Trust), 1987, no 57, p 22.
20. *ibid.* no 62, p 24.
21. *ibid.* no 81, p 33.
22. *ibid.* no 95, p 38.
23. *ibid.* no 93, p 39.
24. *ibid.* no 80, p 33.
25. *ibid.* no 96, p 39.
26. *ibid.* no 97, p 39.
27. Shoghi Effendi, quoted in: *Bahá'í Education* - a compilation (London: Baha'í Publishing Trust), 1987, no 121, p 49.

Appendix I

Some Active Attributes of God Found in the Bahá'í Writings

able	gentle	one
accepter of repentance	glorious	opener
	governor	originator
avenger	grateful	pardoner
aware	great	patient
benefactor	guardian	peace giving
bestower	guide	powerful
compassionate	hearer	praiseworthy
contractor	hidden	preventer
counsel	holy	protector
creator	honourer	provider
death-giver	humbler	reckoner
deferrer	imperious	repairer
distresser	incomparable	responder
dominant	inheritor	restorer
enduring	judge	resurrector
enricher	just	rightly guided
equitable	knower	ruler
eternal	last	seer
exalted	life-giver	self-subsistent
exalter	light	self-sufficient
expander	living	source of faith
expediter	lofty	strong
fashioner	lord	subtle
finder	loving	true
firm	majestic	trustee
first	manifest	unifier
forgiving	merciful	watcher
friend	mighty	wise
gatherer	noble	witness
generous	nourisher	

The Bahá'í Faith teaches that we can know only of the active attributes of God, not His essential attributes. The attributes we know are *God revealed to man*. The true nature of God is totally beyond human conception and understanding. There are many places in Bahá'í writings where Names and Attributes of God are referred to or listed. This list is a synthesis of many sources, and should not be considered comprehensive or exhaustive.

Appendix II

Common Social Values Found in the Bahá'í Writings
A Basis for Dialogue on Character Education in Schools:
Its Principles, Its Curriculum and Its Environment

able	gentle	merciful
aware	glorious	noble
benefactor	grateful	nourisher
compassionate	guardian	patient
counsel	guide	peace giving
courteous	helpful	praiseworthy
deferrer	honest	protector
dependable	honourer	provider
enduring	joyful	self-sufficient
enricher	judge	sharer
expediter	just	strong
firm	knower	subtle
forgiving	leader	true
friend	listener	trustworthy
gatherer	loving	unifier
generous	loyal	wise

There are many ways to list values for purposes of constructing a curriculum.

Religious Instruction and Religious Education

Kevin M. Beint

This paper concerns itself with the distinction between religious instruction and religious education and the importance of that distinction to parents, teachers and institutions responsible for children's classes. It will be based on the premise that religious instruction is an obligation of religious belief and as such is carried out by parents and religious institutions. It has no place in secular schools but is rightly carried out in religion sponsored-schools where, by definition, it has the support of all parents. The premise behind religious instruction is that those who instruct believe they are fulfilling a spiritual obligation by initiating children into a divine cultural heritage. This is as true for Bahá'ís as it is for any other religious belief and its importance must not be underestimated. Religious education, on the other hand, is ultimately aimed at exploring religious issues in open-ended debate with a view to enabling individuals to better understand both their own individual religious quest and contemporary expressions of belief and practice.[a]

Taking the popular notion that religious instruction is, by and large, indoctrination and hence restrictive, and that religious education in modern, secular schools is open-ended and hence freeing, I would like to argue that some form of religious instruction is an indispensable prerequisite to any meaningful dialogue in religious education. From my understanding of the Bahá'í writings on training and education, effective religious education depends upon pupils first acquiring certain skills and attitudes, many of which are attained through religious instruction. In simplistic terms, religious education without religious instruction would most likely be a meaningless and pointless circular debate. If I take the notion that all education should have some tangible result, i.e. lead to change, if only through increased understanding and knowledge, then my argument is that the change effected through religious education should be in the moral/spiritual domain (e.g. increased tolerance and respect for other beliefs). I believe that without a training base, such open debate is unlikely to be powerful enough to bring about lasting and meaningful change in behaviour, particularly in moral decision-making and life skills.

Religious education can be likened to other spheres of education such as mathematics, science and language, but not in every respect. There are many areas where it stands alone as a teaching/learning activity. One comparison is that entry to all spheres of education requires certain skills and attitudes such as listening,

---

[a] courtesy of Northampton County Council RE Advisory Service

patience, concentration, perseverance, discipline, obedience, reading, writing, computation, etc. An ultimate aim of education is that teacher and pupil become equal partners in exploring together ideas and possibilities within the realm of their shared interest. However, the teacher must begin this process with training in relevant skills and attitudes. It is well documented that homes play a vital role in this process, and children who arrive at school with some of the prerequisite skills, especially attitude skills of listening, obedience, perseverance, etc. make the greatest progress. All of this is equally true of science, language, mathematics and religious education. However, schools were not intended to introduce spiritual and moral principles to children for the first time as they so often do reading, writing and computation. Their role was simply to uphold and reflect cultural and religious values. The pluralising of society, the breakdown of family life and the secularisation of culture have left schools under increasing pressure to take over the role of parents and church in fostering moral behaviour and spiritual attitudes. As modern schools are, in the main, secular institutions, a tradition of neutral, secular religious education has evolved which poses many dilemmas because it is so fraught with contradictions and paradoxes. To all intents and purposes religious education in late-twentieth-century Western schools is a square peg in a round hole, an orphan in the curriculum which has lost both its parents, the home and the church.

My argument is that all children need some form of religious instruction both to prepare them for open-ended debate in religious education and to give them a foundation for the moral and spiritual challenges of adult life. What then do I believe is the distinction between religious instruction and religious education in a Bahá'í context? Firstly, in a brief perusal of Bahá'í writings there seemed to be many more references to instruction than to education. This is mainly because a reference to training is usually very specific and so there are many of them covering the whole spectrum of training needs. A short reference to education, however, usually conveys an ocean of meaning. For example, "...train human souls, that their angelic aspect may overcome their animal side".[1]

This is a training requirement which needs to be carried out from the earliest infancy and, if it is missed, then by quite early childhood the individual can encounter many learning and socialisation problems. On the other hand, "...unravel the secrets that are treasured up in the inmost reality of all created beings",[2] is a lifetime's quest. In short, most training/instruction commands pertain to brief, vital periods in the child's early development while education exhortations refer to the process of fulfilling the purpose of human life, which is an endless task.

For the sake of simplicity and to focus debate I have attempted to group some of the training/instruction ideas under the headings of Methodology, Skills, Information and Qualities.

Methodology

How should religious instruction be carried out in a Bahá'í context? The answer is simple to give but very demanding to implement. Its ground rules are: with love and kindness, by example, by heartening and encouraging the child and with regard to refining and rectifying character. It starts from the very beginning of the child's life and continues with perseverance and resolve until the child matures and becomes independent. Corporal punishment and verbal abuse play no part in it but high expectations of behaviour and obedience are essential.

Some of the scriptural passages relevant to methodology are as follows:

> *Love and kindness have far greater influence than punishment upon the improvement of human character.*[3]
> *Train these children with divine exhortations.*[4]
> *Therefore is it incumbent upon the mothers to rear their little ones even as a gardener tendeth his young plants.*[5]
> *That is, it is enjoined upon the father and the mother, as a duty, to strive with all effort to train the daughter and the son...*[6]
> *It is incumbent upon every father and mother to counsel their children over a long period, and guide them unto those things which lead to everlasting honour.*[7]
> *Know that this matter of instruction, of character rectification and refinement, of heartening and encouraging the child, is of the utmost importance, for such are the basic principles of God.*[8]

Skills

In any training it is necessary for the trainer to transmit skills to the trainee. In most educational processes, a wide range of specific skills is necessary for successful progress but in religious instruction qualities are more important than skills. However, certain skills are mentioned, such as reading, writing and speech. I would also include listening for which I have not yet found a reference, possibly because it is subsumed in so many of the training activities that it is left unsaid. As a teacher of many years' experience, I have come to the conclusion that ability to listen with interest and concentration is what sets children apart in the classroom. The skill of listening is born of intensive interaction with parents both at a loving, encouraging level when stories are read at bedtime or family tales recounted and at the level of discipline when obedience is demanded and increasingly complex instructions are given with an expectation that those instructions will be understood and carried out. Inability to listen is a source of so many problems in the learning process, particularly in schools. It is not expected that religious instruction begin with reading and writing and speech. Indeed, it is clearly intended to start at the earliest possible moment, "From the very beginning, the children must receive divine education..."[9] However, Bahá'í children generally experience regular story reading sessions at bedtime and at quiet times of the day and these are accompanied by prayer and the reading of quotations from the Writings with the encouragement to learn such passages by heart, combined with sessions of constructive play. Bahá'í children thus develop a high degree of readiness for such time as reading and writing are taught formally at school. Listening to stories and learning by heart are excellent training for listening.

Some of the scriptural passages relevant to skills in training are as follows:

> *Unto every father hath been enjoined the instruction of his son and daughter in the art of reading and writing and in all that hath been laid down in the Holy Tablet.*[10]
> *It is incumbent upon the children to exert themselves to the utmost in acquiring the art of reading and writing....in every art and skill, God loveth the highest perfection.*[11]
> *Then, so much as capacity and capability allow, ye needs must deck the tree of being with fruits such as knowledge, wisdom, spiritual perception and eloquent speech.*[12]

Information (Content)

Training is content and skill based while education is open-ended and concept based. The Bahá'í writings contain many references to content appropriate for religious instruction. It does not include the customs of previous beliefs. The content includes the oneness of God, the laws of God, observances, Hidden Words, prayers, and sacred rights and responsibilities. Examples of sacred responsibilities are obligatory prayers, daily prayer and reading, fasting, firmness in the Covenant, obedience to Bahá'í laws and institutions. While these are not binding on children, they need to be introduced to them through parental example. Children will then naturally and gradually grow into these rights and responsibilities and follow the laws and observances. It is axiomatic that any instructor must be an excellent practitioner:

> *That which is of paramount importance for the children, that which must precede all else, is to teach them the Oneness of God and the Laws of God.*[13]
> *Schools must first train the children in the principles of religion, so that the Promise and the Threat as recorded in the Books of God may prevent them from the things forbidden and adorn them*

> *with the mantle of the commandments; but this in such a measure that it may not injure the children by resulting in ignorant fanaticism and bigotry.*[14]
> *We have directed that in the beginning they should be trained in the observances and laws of religion.*[15]
> *...these tender little ones have been learning The Hidden Words and the prayers and what it meaneth to be a Bahá'í. There is no doubt that it will yield the desired results; especially is this true of instruction as to Bahá'í obligations and Bahá'í conduct...*[16]
> *...ye gather the Bahá'í children together and teach them the communes and prayers.*[17]
> *...instruct thou God's children in the customs of the Kingdom.*[18]
> *The method of instruction which ye have established, beginning with the proofs of the existence of God...the mission of the Prophets and Messengers and Their teachings, and the wonders of the universe, is highly suitable.*[19]
> *...the things of the spirit, the fundamentals of teachings the Faith, reading the Sacred Writings, learning the history of the Faith...*[20]
> *There is no objection to children who are as yet unable to memorise a whole prayer learning certain sentences only....we should be careful not to introduce into it the customs of our previous beliefs.*[21]

Qualities

The main body of skills transmitted through religious instruction are skills of character and behaviour and as such deserve to be looked at separately under the heading 'qualities'. Perhaps the most challenging and complex issue of Bahá'í religious instruction is the number and scope of the qualities it is intended to foster in the recipient. These qualities form the bedrock on which the child's adult life will be based. All instruction and training should be geared to building these qualities in the child. I have grouped these qualities into:

Purity of character: purity, sancity, detachment, chastity.
Strength of direction: angelic over the animal, shun criminal acts, discipline and order.
Resolve: perseverance, striving/enduring, determination, firmness of purpose, and the ability to cope with hardship.

> *The purpose underlying Their revelation hath been to educate all men, that they may, at the hour of death, ascend, in the utmost purity and sanctity and with absolute detachment, to the throne of the Most High.*[22]

> *...in a divine civilisation the individual is so conditioned that with no fear of punishment, he shunneth the perpetration of crimes...*[23]
> *Good character must be taught.*[24]
> *Thus shall they grow and flourish, and be taught righteousness and the dignity of humankind, resolution and the will to strive and to endure. Thus shall they learn perseverance in all things, the will to advance, high mindedness and high resolve, chastity and purity of life.*[25]

Religious Education

Training is about developing character and spiritual habits so that acting in a spiritual manner becomes an instinct. The spiritual reaction becomes the first reaction, through prayer, detachment, perseverance, discipline, respect and reverence. With these qualities as habits the child is able to make the fullest response to education. Education is a process of interaction. The educator's role is to share knowledge, give good counsel and explanation, facilitate understanding and enable the formulating and testing of hypotheses and reasoning. The response to education is to reveal latent treasure, to evolve wisdom, increase perception, unravel secrets, and contribute to unity and harmony. Religion and, in particular, belief are at the heart of some very fundamental questions. At the level of the individual's religious quest these questions include: what is God like, how does prayer work, why do cruelty and injustice exist, what happens after death, etc. At the level of studying contemporary expressions of belief a wide range of issues warrant discussion: religious strife, laws and prohibitions, expressions of belief in music, art, literature and architecture, rites of passage, etc.

Over the last thirty years or so religious education in schools has moved towards an exploration of these issues with the aim of promoting understanding and tolerance in a multi-faith society. However, recently the government reacted to this trend by legislating that religious education in schools should be broadly Christian in character. It is an ill-informed decision borne of a desperate desire to reinstate some form of religious instruction in an increasingly secular and pluralistic society. The first problem will be to find enough committed Christian teachers with the skills, knowledge and motivation to carry out the task. The second problem will be to motivate a school population alienated from the underlying assumptions and belief system of what the teachers are trying to transmit. It demonstrates that at the highest level of political decision-making the dynamic relationship between religious instruction and religious education is not fully understood.

In a Bahá'í school, as in any other religious educational establishment, the teachers have a mandate from the parents to carry out both religious instruction and religious education. However, it is important that all the participants - parents, teachers, pupils and administrators - know which is which and what their purposes are. Some scriptural passages relevant to the concept of education are as follows:

> *Regard man as a mine rich in gems of inestimable value. Education can, alone, cause it to reveal its treasures, and enable mankind to benefit therefrom.*[26]
>
> *Bend your minds and wills to the education of the peoples and kindreds of the earth, that haply the dissensions that divide it may, through the power of the Most Great Name, be blotted out from its face, and all mankind become the upholders of one Order, and the inhabitants of one City.*[27]
>
> *Man is even as steel, the essence of which is hidden: through admonition and explanation, good counsel and education, that essence will be brought to light.*[28]
>
> *O Lord, help Thou Thy loved ones to acquire knowledge and the sciences and arts, and to unravel the secrets that are treasured up in the inmost reality of all created beings.*[29]
>
> *Wherefore must the loved ones of God, be they young or old, be they men or women, each one according to his capabilities, strive to acquire the various branches of knowledge, and to increase his understanding of the mysteries of the Holy Books, and his skill in marshalling the divine proofs and evidences.*[30]

Thus it is possible to distinguish clearly elements of training and opportunities for education in Bahá'í homes and Bahá'í schools.

Examples of elements of Bahá'í instruction/training for inclusion in Bahá'í school curricula include: Bahá'í laws, Bahá'í concepts of God, manifestations and progressive revelation, obligatory prayers, qualities of good character, observances, memorising of scripture.

Examples of concepts that can be explored as education in the curriculum of a Bahá'í school: how prayer works, the nature of the soul, the wisdom behind religious laws and observances, the relationship between religion and science, understanding the equality between men and women, the use of metaphor in scripture.

I have tried to argue that from my understanding of the Bahá'í writings there is a clear and important distinction between the processes involved in religious education and religious training. Religious instruction is at the heart of moral training and in establishing identity within a religious tradition. This process is as important in the Bahá'í Faith as it is in any other established religion and the

Bahá'í writings unambiguously point to the 'what', 'how', 'when' and 'why' of instruction. Homes carry out instruction from the earliest possible moment because it is part of the belief system of one or both parents, and a religion-sponsored school can carry on the instruction process which reinforces the belief/value system of the home and gives the child a wider religious identity and stronger sense of culture. Religious education, on the other hand, is a process of deepening and widening religious understanding by exploring questions and sharing ideas. An example of religious education would be to explore the layers of meaning in a scriptural metaphor. The object would be that each participant could offer insights. There are no correct answers, only new understandings. Education is part of a evolutionary process whereby conclusions serve a time, a place or a circumstance and insight will continue to supersede insight. I hope I have been able, therefore, to demonstrate that without religious/moral training beforehand, participation in religious education can only have limited value because the participant will have too few reference points on which to build understanding, thus the message of the education is unlikely to bring about lasting or meaningful change in behaviour.

References

1. 'Abdu'l-Bahá, *Some Answered Questions* (Wilmette: Bahá'í Publishing Trust), 1981, p 235.
2. 'Abdu'l-Bahá, quoted in: *Bahá'í Education* (London: Bahá'í Publishing Trust), 1987, p 8.
3. Shoghi Effendi, quoted in: *Bahá'í Education* - a Compilation (London: Bahá'í Publishing Trust), 1987, p 54.
4. 'Abdu'l-Bahá, *The Promulgation of Universal Peace* (Wilmette: Bahá'í Publishing Trust), 1982, p 53.
5. 'Abdu'l-Bahá, *Selections from the Writings of 'Abdu'l-Bahá* (Haifa: Bahá'í World Centre), 1978, p 125.
6. *ibid.* p 127.
7. *ibid.* p 134.
8. *ibid.* p 137.
9. *ibid.* p 127.
10. Bahá'u'lláh, *Tablets of Bahá'u'lláh* (Haifa: Bahá'í World Centre), 1978, p 128.
11. Bahá'u'lláh, quoted in: *Bahá'í Education* - a compilation (London: Bahá'í Publishing Trust), 1987, no 20, p 5.
12. *ibid.* no 9, p 3.
13. *ibid.* no 14.

14. *ibid.* no 15, p 4.
15. *ibid.* no 26, p 6.
16. 'Abdu'l-Bahá, quoted in: *Bahá'í Education* - a compilation (London: Bahá'í Publishing Trust), 1987, no 50, p 19.
17. *ibid.* no 55, p 21.
18. *ibid.* no 64, p 24.
19. *ibid.* no 77, p 30.
20. Shoghi Effendi, quoted in: *Bahá'í Education* - A Compilation (London: Bahá'í Publishing Trust), 1987, no 119, pp 48-9.
21. Shoghi Effendi, *Unfolding Destiny of the British Bahá'í Community* (London: Bahá'í Publishing Trust), 1981, no 153, p 446.
22. Bahá'u'lláh, *Gleanings from the Writings of Bahá'u'lláh* (Wilmette: Bahá'í Publishing Trust), 1977, no 81, p 157.
23. 'Abdu'l-Bahá, quoted in: *Bahá'í Education* - a compilation (London: Bahá'í Publishing Trust), 1987, no 41, p 16.
24. *ibid.* no 43, p 136.
25. 'Abdu'l-Bahá, *Selections from the Writings of 'Abdu'l-Bahá* (Haifa: Bahá'í World Centre), 1978, p 125.
26. Bahá'u'lláh, quoted in: *Bahá'í Education* - a compilation (London: Bahá'í Publishing Trust), 1987, no 4, p 1.
27. *ibid.* no 5, p 2.
28. *ibid.* no 10, p 3.
29. 'Abdu'l-Bahá, quoted in: *Bahá'í Education* - A Compilation (London: Bahá'í Publishing Trust), 1987, no 29, p 8.
30. *ibid.* no 30, p 8.

Exploration and Integration of Bahá'í Education

William A. Diehl

The Bahá'í Writings on education are extensive, comprehensive and inspiring. The Faith emphasises the importance of education and assigns to educators a lofty station indeed, as, for example, indicated in this quotation from 'Abdu'l-Bahá:

> *The education and training of children is among the most meritorious acts of humankind and draweth down the grace and favour of the All-Merciful, for education is the indispensable foundation of all human excellence and alloweth man to work his way to the heights of abiding glory.*[1]

While the Writings are inspiring and motivating to educators, they are also enormously challenging. The challenge that educators who are also Bahá'ís have is two-fold. First, educators must read, digest and understand the many aspects of education covered in this Revelation. Second, educators must put this knowledge and understanding into action to integrate the principles, ideals and different facets of education into educational programmes, into the upbringing of children, into every aspect of individual and community life. These are by no means sequential; the process of integrating knowledge into practice develops understanding as much as understanding produces better integration.

The Importance of the Paradigm Shift

As most of us have probably found, the understanding of Bahá'í principles and ideas of education is no easy task. It is not just that the Writings are voluminous on the topic. More so, it is because the Writings call on us to change the way we view most aspects of education; they are the vehicle for what amounts to a paradigm shift in our understanding of just about everything, including education.

One of the problems with a paradigm shift in our thinking is that we still have the same words as our tools for description. We are called upon to view reality, and the purposes and processes of education that are based on that reality, in substantially different ways, yet we are constrained by having to use the same words. So words like *education, learning, teacher, transformation, discipline, potential, spiritual* and so on take on quite different meanings in a new paradigm. (For example, does the local school system use the word "education" to describe what 'Abdu'l-Bahá described above, namely, that it is the indispensable foundation of all human excellence that allows students to work their way to the heights of abiding glory?) Part of the challenge in even understanding the Writings about education, then, involves moving away from the definitions we learned from our cultural and ideological backgrounds and moving towards the definitions and understandings used in the Writings. Our understanding is intimately linked with our ability to move into a new culture and ideology. This process is nicely summed up in a letter written on behalf of Shoghi Effendi:

> *There is no limit to the study of the Cause. The more we read the Writings the more truths we can find in them and the more we will see that our previous notions were erroneous.*[2]

The Guardian is describing the process of working through a paradigm shift. It involves learning to see things in a new way, to find new truths and discard old ideas because these old ideas have lost their relative usefulness given the new paradigm.

The more I have worked in trying to explore and integrate Bahá'í education, the more vital this idea of *paradigm shift* becomes. This concept of radically changing the way we understand and organise the world is found throughout the Writings. It is a core part of the *transformation* that Bahá'ís strive to attain. It is what the Universal House of Justice calls for from the peoples of the world when it writes in *The Promise of World Peace*:

> *As the need for peace becomes more urgent, this fundamental contradiction [between the desire for peace and the uncritical assent given to the proposition that human beings are selfish and aggressive] ...demands a reassessment of the assumptions upon which the commonly held view of mankind's historical predicament is based...*[3]

or when the Universal House of Justice asserts that "World peace is not only possible but inevitable."[4]

Part of this paradigm shift is what 'Abdu'l-Bahá is defining when He writes that "I desire distinction for you" and states all the ways we are not to be distinguished, but that we "must become distinguished in all the virtues of the human world".[5] Many of the admonitions and statements in the Writings, when looked at as part of a fundamental paradigm shift, take on deeper meanings and assume a qualitatively different purpose.

The purpose is partly to lead us to change our basic assumptions about ourselves and our world, to change our perspective. This in turn changes our understanding, our values, our connections with others, our personal and spiritual development. The change is profound.

Two further examples of *paradigm shifts* will illustrate the impact of this concept. However, the shift which the Writings, quoted above, call upon us to make is, of course, far more profound than the following examples.

The first is one of the classic examples, namely that of Galileo. Galileo became convinced of, and then popularised, the Copernican theory that the planets revolved around the sun. This theory enabled Galileo and other scientists of his time to look at the universe in a different way, a way that made more sense, a way that could be explained elegantly and was amenable to making predictions and discoveries. This was also a fundamental change in the perspective of the times and was so threatening to the prevailing views about who human beings were and how they related to the universe that Galileo was opposed by, and made to recant by, the Catholic Church (on the grounds of *vehement suspicion of heresy*). The shift, of course, was primarily in one factor - on the question of whether the earth was the centre of the universe or not. By shifting that one assumption, our understanding of the universe and our place in it was forever changed.

The other example is from the field of literacy. Researchers, such as Michael Cole and Sylvia Schribner,[6] have found that people from pre-literate societies organise the world differently from people who are literate. As an example, a person is shown a group of small figures --- people, animals, houses --- of differing colours and the person is asked to group the objects. Most of us, most people who are literate, group the objects either by type (all the animals, all the people, all the houses) or by colour (all the blue objects, etc.) People from a pre-literate society will group the objects in what seems to be an illogical way (a blue house with a green man and a white animal, for example). When asked to explain, the person will tell a story - the blue house reminded him of his brother's house and one day his brother left his house and came across a cow, which belonged to this neighbour man, and so on. The objects tend to be grouped in story fashion, apparently because this kind of oral tradition is the accepted way of grouping, organising and remembering information. The point is that it seems that the acquisition of literacy, in and of itself, changes the way we organise the world. This change is fundamental and represents a paradigm shift. The proposition of some of these researchers is that Gutenburg's printing press did not empower people simply by making written material more easily available; it also caused a change in the way the masses of Europeans organised their categorised perceptions and interactions. This change is what empowered the masses and led to the Reformation and the great revolutions of the 18th century. An appreciation of the empowerment of people through access to written language can perhaps be gained by considering that often one of the first acts of a despot often is the burning of *undesireable* books.

These two simplified examples illustrate the significance of a paradigm shift. Again, what the Writings require of us is far more profound and far-reaching. I stress this concept of *paradigm shift* because it is critical, I believe, to the topic of exploration and integration of Bahá'í education. We are talking about exploring and trying to integrate a change so fundamental in how we view and use education that many of the words we use and take for granted acquire meanings that we can only begin to grasp.

The Importance of Action

The importance placed on action in the Writings is of equal importance to the idea of a paradigm shift.

> *It is incumbent upon every man of insight and understanding to strive to translate that which hath been written into reality and action...*[7]
>
> *Chant the Words of God and, pondering over their meaning, transform them into actions.*[8]

Again, this call to transform words into actions is not simply an admonition; it requires a fundamental change in how we learn and how we educate. There is a spiralling process implied in these quotations. The quotations do not just suggest or admonish us to transform the Word into action. They say it is incumbent, it is to be done, and imply that the striving to act is part of the process - of understanding, of insight, of gaining knowledge from pondering. The process could be simplified to the idea that through understanding we know how to act, and through acting, we understand.

This idea of translating the Word into action is repeated often and in many ways in the Writings. I became especially aware of this while working with Melanie Smith on trying to develop materials to help Bahá'ís improve their reading of the Writings. In reading and study skill techniques, stress is often put on doing things before reading (like previewing or asking questions) and doing things after reading (like summarising or reflecting). The Writings describe a parallel system of preparing yourself (as through prayer, or asking for guidance), then reading the Writings, then reflecting (e.g. pondering) and then acting on your understanding. The action is, it appears, a critical component of reading the Writings. In fact, the Writings tell us to take action before and after reading the Writings.

One of the powerful influences changing American education is new research on learning from the cognitive sciences. This research is challenging many sacred cows and is based on the idea that intelligence and expertise are built out of an interaction with the environment, not in isolation from it. *Action* is thus emerging in American education as a key component of learning.

Another concept that is related to action and is being stressed more in American schools is the concept of *modelling*. Modelling, or demonstrating through words and deeds and even emotions, is being viewed increasingly as the most powerful of educational tools. Simply put, if you want someone to learn something, model it. It is striking that this Revelation is blessed with the personage of 'Abdu'l-Bahá who is often referred to as *the Perfect Exemplar*. Through word and deed, 'Abdu'l-Bahá is this model, this powerful educational influence. The exploration and integration of Bahá'í education, which is the topic of this paper, reflects the action element. Exploring and integrating imply taking knowledge and acting on it. This paper will discuss a few of the elements in these exploration and integration processes that seem especially important in this new paradigm, in the Revelation of Bahá'u'lláh.

Two Aspects of Integration

When we talk about the integration of these elements of Bahá'í education, we can talk about at least two different types of integration. First, there is the effort to integrate the Writings about education into Bahá'í-sponsored classes and activities. Second, there is the task of integrating the Writings about education into secular educational programmes. The latter may mean translating the concepts in the Writings into a secular system. It may mean seeing and articulating the aspects of an educational endeavour that may or may not be in keeping with the Writings. This latter task is part of our challenge in emerging from obscurity, of reaching people of prominence in education, of winning ever-widening acceptance of the Revelation. It requires us to overcome what I sometimes see as a fear of appearing unscientific or parochial or naive.

We know that, armed with the Writings, we are none of these, yet there is a continuing reluctance (beyond the wish not to proselytise) to assert the validity of Bahá'í educational principles in secular settings. The emerging power of the Bahá'í community and its insights on education were evident to me last year when I attended the North American Conference on Literacy. The keynote speaker for this conference, organised by the International Reading Association and a score of other groups, was Dr Dwight Allen. Dr Allen presented concepts clearly from a Bahá'í perspective (although the name *Bahá'í* was not used) to a most receptive audience. At the same conference, the United Nations Non-Governmental Organisations, which took a lead role in the Year of Literacy, were represented by one of their number - the Bahá'í International Community, a community that is more and more singled out in such ways because it is truly a grassroots, international, progressive network.

The non-Bahá'í speakers at this conference were also remarkable. Thomas Sticht, the U.S. representative to UNESCO's committee on literacy, spent his entire session showing all the proof from literacy campaigns that the best way to educate a people is to educate the women, the mothers. This concept of the *intergenerational nature of literacy* is almost revolutionary in the field, yet most Bahá'ís know about and fail to realise the significance of the teachings about educating women.

Even the U.N. definition of literacy contains many points that are very similar to the Bahá'í ideas about the purpose and process of education:

> *Literacy is defined as the set of knowledge, qualities, skills, attitudes and capacities that enable individuals to preserve self-esteem by assuming both control over their own growth, and by becoming mature participants in a process of social change that will lead to a more peaceful, just and harmonious society.*[9]

Note how encompassing this definition is and how it stresses the many uses of literacy and the desired, noble outcomes. This definition is a dramatic shift from *literacy as the ability to read or write a simple sentence* and demonstrates a movement in the world towards the fundamental truths in the Bahá'í teachings.

In describing some key elements in the exploration and integration of Bahá'í education, it is important to look at the integration of ideas into Bahá'í-initiated programmes and the possible integration of parallel kinds of ideas found in secular education.

Some Key Elements in the Exploration and Integration of Bahá'í Education

In the last ten years I have been involved in efforts toward active exploration and integration of Bahá'í educational ideas. First, I have been involved in trying to develop literacy programmes and training that reflect an integration of Bahá'í ideas of education. Second, I have been director of the Louhelen Bahá'í School and have worked at integrating these ideas into conferences and into a residential college for Bahá'í students from around the world. From these experiences, certain key elements and issues stand out.

A few of these key elements and issues will be explored. Rather than discuss many issues, I will concentrate on a few and try to discuss them in the light of three questions: What shift in perspective/paradigm is required of us? How is this idea integrated in Bahá'í educational programmes? What are similar trends in secular education?

A Context - The Louhelen Residential College

Integrating Bahá'í education with individuals and in a community has been a particular challenge in the Louhelen Residential College (LRC). The LRC was established four years ago by the National Spiritual Assembly of the Bahá'ís of the United States in response to plans drawn up by the Louhelen Council. The Council plans, in turn, were based on letters from Shoghi Effendi to Louhelen in which the Guardian outlined the long-range development of the School into the "ideal Bahá'í university of the future..."

The LRC has had 20 to 26 students each year. About half have come from other countries; some are international students and some children of American pioneers. Of the remaining students, half are from disadvantaged backgrounds - from inner cities, the deep South or Native American reservations. The student body, though small, is very diverse. This year, for example, there are students from eight different countries, there are 14 different languages spoken, and there are students of almost every racial and socio-economic background.

The students live at Louhelen and are enrolled in degree-earning programmes at one of two colleges in the nearby city of Flint. At Louhelen, students take part in Bahá'í study classes and deepenings and teaching activities, they receive tutoring or counselling support, they take part in community-development activities, and they assist with the operation of the School through service.

Since the students live, work, study, deepen and socialise together, it is a very intensive and extensive experience in Bahá'í community life. The diverse backgrounds of the students make it an ideal workshop for integrating the Bahá'í teachings about education and community into practice.

The students have almost had an identical experience in the first month of being in the LRC. Students come with an expectation of what a Bahá'í community looks like and acts like. They come determined also to look and act like their ideal Bahá'í. By the end of a month or so, these students are disillusioned. The community is not perfect. They cannot maintain their appearance of perfection.

At this point, the real education begins. A number of elements have proven to be key in this education.

Education is for the Mind and Heart

Education traditionally refers to developing or training the mind. The Writings shift this emphasis to both the mind and the heart:

> *The priniciples of the Teachings of Bahá'u'lláh should be carefully studied, one by one, until they are realised and understood by mind and heart...*[10]
> *The heart must needs therefore be cleansed from the idle sayings of men, and sanctified from every earthly affection, so that it may discover the hidden meaning of divine inspiration, and become the treasury of the mysteries of divine knowledge.*[11]
> *The understanding of His words and the comprehension of the utterances of the Birds of Heaven are in no wise dependent upon human learning. They depend solely upon purity of heart, chastity of soul, and freedom of spirit.*[12]

This is a clear shift in our thinking about education. This idea is integrated in Bahá'í education through our use of, and modelling the use of, the Creative Word. Partly this is using the Creative Word for intellectual understanding, but far more this is drawing spiritual insight, heavenly power, divine assistance, grace and other spiritual bounties through use of the Word. This is also integrated in Bahá'í education when we help the friends learn to discipline and structure their spiritual lives (e.g. to pray and meditate each day; to bring themselves to account each night) so that they learn the additive effects of learning with the heart.

The notion of learning with heart and head has some parallels in secular education. Interest has grown in the last few years in the area of *moral development*. Research about how moral development occurs, programmes to teach moral development, the training of teachers in this area, have all increased. Recently, researchers in this field have even begun to talk about the *spiritual* components of the process; it seems the academic climate is finally becoming amenable to discussing the importance of, and the development of, a spiritual education.

Being a Bahá'í is a Process, not a Product
(Or, Bahá'í communities are workshops, not museums.)
What shift in perspective/paradigm is required? The realisation that all the members of a community are in different stages of becoming Bahá'ís seems to be a significant element. This change in perspective - which for some can be a radical change - changes all the relationships in the community. The interdependence of the community increases as the Bahá'ís see their role not as judging others but as fighting their own spiritual battles and helping other people with theirs. Another part of the change in perspective is one of seeing tests as opportunities for growth, not as shortcomings. The following quotation from Shoghi Effendi illustrates these elements:

> *If we could but perceive the true reality of things we would see that the greatest of all battles raging in the world today is the spiritual battle. If the believers like yourself, young and eager and full of life, desire to win laurels for true and undying heroism, then let them join in the spiritual battle - whatever their physical occupation may be - which involves the very soul of man. The hardest and the noblest task in the world today is to be a true Bahá'í; this requires that we defeat not only the current evils prevailing all over the world, but the weaknesses, attachments to the past, prejudices, and selfishnesses that may be inherited and acquired within our own characters; that we give forth a shining and incorruptible example to our fellow-men.*[13]

How is this idea integrated in Bahá'í educational programmes? We have found that helping the Bahá'ís focus on fighting their own spiritual battles, and realising that others' battles are equally difficult and offer equal opportunities for growth, are important. Full and frank consultation is the best tool for achieving this realisation. Modelling is another tool, and it occurs when one of the friends, usually an older person, shows how he/she deals with and learns from a personal spiritual battle. Or it occurs when the Writings or stories of 'Abdu'l-Bahá are used, to find new ways of approaching a test or difficulty. Once attitudes change in the community, once the community talks about its problems and tests as opportunities for growth, not as setbacks, and uses the Creative Word as an active agent for growth, the community becomes a very nurturing and supportive place.

What are similar trends in secular education? Clearly, the concept of modelling has gained enthusiastic acceptance in many educational quarters. Notions such as mentorship and apprenticeship can have some parallel aspects. And the growing stress on problem-solving and critical thinking has some application to the idea of using problems for growth.

Being a Bahá'í Community is a Process

What shift in perspective/paradigm is required? M. Scott Peck in *The Different Drum: Community Making and Peace*[14] identified stages in community building that seem to describe the experience of the LRC and other intense Bahá'í communities. First, there is a pseudo-community, where everyone agrees to pretend that there is unity and love and community. Problems are ignored. *Negative feelings* are denied. There is no growth. Then, there is a period of chaos as the pseudo-community is challenged for what it is. This phase would seem necessary if, in fact, the community is struggling to understand and use a new paradigm. Then comes a period of disillusionment, of having left behind the old community paradigm and not yet having established a new community paradigm. The fourth stage is a new community where consultation is used to resolve problems, where unity and diversity exist, and so on.

These stages describe a process, and one that repeats itself. As soon as a sense of true community is established, some other concerns or issues arise that are ignored or denied, then met with chaos and then are resolved in an even greater sense of true community. These stages are helpful because they can be used to label and understand the key part of this shift in perspective, namely that building a community does not yield a product; it is a process, and it is a process that works if the principles of the Faith are applied. Especially for the younger students, this idea that they are part of a never-ending process, not part of a community that is or will be perfect, is a real shift in perspective.

Although the process repeats itself, each time the community is stronger, more able to move through the stages and, most importantly, more trusting in the process of developing a community.

In Bahá'í education, the development of community is critical. A safe community promotes individual growth, exploration and learning. Additionally, learning the new ways of being and behaving that are taught in the Writings includes learning the process of community building; this is one major goal in Bahá'í education. The goal might be summarised as educating how to make a community so united, so *family-like*, that every member feels in their mind and their heart that "the injury of one shall be considered the injury of all; the comfort of each, the comfort of all; the honour of one, the honour of all."[15]

Consultation is a Key Tool

What shift in perspective/paradigm is required? Although Bahá'ís take the word and idea of consultation for granted, especially since it is used so often in the Writings, true consultation represents a significant change in how we view and interact with each other. It requires a shift away from the competitive and hierarchical models of human interaction that are so strongly reinforced in our schools, businesses and even families. It also requires a change in view - the purpose of human interaction is not to dominate or subvert, elevate or diminish; the purpose is to gain understanding, to assist in personal and community growth, to increase the power of insight and action. Additionally, consultation is powerful in educating; here, the shift is away from the model of teacher-learner and towards the model of learner-learner. The educational power is illustrated by Bahá'u'lláh's statements:

> *The heaven of divine wisdom is illumined with the two luminaries of consultation and compassion...*[16]
> *...Say: No man can attain his true station except through justice. No power can exist except through unity. No welfare and no well-being can be attained except through consultation.*[17]

How is this idea integrated in Bahá'í educational programmes? Bahá'í programmes, like the LRC, actively promote learning and practising consultation, deepening on consultation, critiquing consultation, learning with consultation. In every area, wherever possible, consultation is used. This empowers the students and they *shoulder the responsibility* developing the School into a Bahá'í university as envisioned by the Guardian. The uses and power of consultation, as outlined in the Writings, cannot be overemphasised in developing community and in education.

What are similar trends in secular education? Perhaps because the changes in the world in this age are so far-reaching and profound, educators in secular programmes have embraced more and more ideas and processes that are akin to consultation. Peer teaching, reciprocal questioning and cooperative learning, to name but a few, are gaining a strong following in public schools. Likewise, training and development in business and industry are stressing *quality circles* and *participatory learning* and *management by consensus*. Bahá'í insights and practice in consultation could clearly be useful in these endeavours.

Service

What shift in perspective/paradigm is required? Farzam Arbab, in a paper on *Literacy, Culture and Empowerment*[18] presents the two dominant ideologies that shape education - the *western liberal tradition* with its emphasis on individualism and the *Marxist* with its emphasis on society as a sum of individuals, all isolated spheres, each free to do as he wishes within the sphere, with each sphere touching others only at the boundary of harm to each other's freedom. The Bahá'í perspective is not, Arbab says, somewhere between these two extremes. Rather, it is valid to say that the Bahá'í discourse on the individual and society always has and always will be carried out on a plane that transcends the traditional discussions of the subject.[19] The educational process is seen as one in which the individual strives to know himself and understand the purpose of his life - to know and to worship God. This knowledge leads him not to individualism but to understanding the interconnectedness of all things and the need to renounce his own will and accept the will of God. "To know and love God" points immediately to service and to the sacrifice of personal liberty for the good of all, but the motivating force now comes from the knowledge that the individual believer gains about his or her own innermost reality.[20] 'Abdu'l-Bahá said:

> *The divine ideals are humility, submissiveness, annihilation of self, perfect evanescence, charity and loving-kindness. You must die to self and live in God. You must be exceedingly compassionate to one another and to all the people of the world. Love and serve mankind just for the sake of God and not for anything else. The foundation of your love toward humanity must be spiritual faith and divine assurance.*[21]

This quotation highlights how service is part of the paradigm shift in the Writings. Of course, service is mentioned in many places and clearly is a key in education, community development and personal growth. Service is integrated in Bahá'í education directly and indirectly. In many Bahá'í programmes service is part of the requirement or expectation for individuals in the community. Bahá'í classes often have service activities and Bahá'í families often make service part of their life.

But service can also be indirect. Students who study hard in order to be good at their profession and serve others better are, in fact, engaged in service. 'Abdu'l-Bahá stressed this idea in the three cardinal principles of a university education:

First: Whole-hearted service to the cause of education, the unfolding of the mysteries of nature, the extension of the boundaries of pure science, the elimination of the causes of ignorance and social evils, a standard universal system of instruction, and the diffusion of the lights of knowledge and reality.
Second: service to the cause of morality, raising the moral tone of the students, inspiring them with the sublimest ideals of ethical refinement, teaching them altruism, inculcating in their lives the beauty of holiness and the excellency of virtue and animating them with the excellences and perfections of the religion of God.
Third: Service to the oneness of humanity; so that each student may consciously realise that he is brother to all mankind, irrespective of religion or race. The thoughts of universal peace must be instilled into the minds of all the scholars, in order that they may become the armies of peace and the real servants of the body politic - the world...[22]

Conclusion

The work of exploring what *Bahá'í education* is and then working to integrate this understanding into the development of individuals, families, communities and societies is exciting and truly pioneering work. The Faith requires a paradigm shift in how we view all aspects of ourselves, our communities and the world. Education is the tool and the process of bringing about this paradigm shift.

It is active work. Bahá'í education has action as an integral part of the process. Action is part both of the learning process and of an educational tool when used to *model.*

Bahá'í education involves many elements. This paper discussed five of these elements: educating the mind and the heart; the process of being a Bahá'í; the process of building a Bahá'í community; consultation; and service. These elements were discussed in terms of how they represent a shift in perspective, how they are integrated into Bahá'í education and similarity into other educational settings. While these five are by no means an exhaustive list of the elements of Bahá'í education, they illustrate the challenges and opportunities in the exploration and integration of Bahá'í education.

References

1. 'Abdu'l-Bahá, quoted in: *Selections from the Writings of 'Abdu'l-Bahá* (Haifa: Bahá'í World Centre), 1978, no 103, p 129.
2. Shoghi Effendi, quoted in: *The Importance of Deepening* - a compilation (London: Bahá'í Publishing Trust), 1983, p 93.
3. The Universal House of Justice, *The Promise of World Peace* (Haifa: Bahá'í World Centre), 1985, p 3.
4. *ibid.* p 1.
5. 'Abdu'l-Bahá, *The Promulgation of Universal Peace* (Wilmette: Bahá'í Publishing Trust), 1982, p 190.
6. Michael Cole and Sylvia Scribner, in: *Language and Thought/Language and Reading*, Harvard Educational Review, 1978.
7. Baha'u'lláh, *Gleanings from the Writings of Bahá'u'lláh* (London: Bahá'í Publishing Trust), 1977, p 250.
8. 'Abdu'l-Bahá, *Selections from the Writings of 'Abdu'l-Bahá* (Haifa: Bahá'í World Centre), 1978, p 86.
9. International Task Force on Literacy, *Definition of Literacy*, 1990.
10. 'Abdu'l-Bahá, *Paris Talks* (London: Bahá'í Publishing Trust), 1971, p 22.
11. Baha'u'lláh, *Kitáb-i-Íqan* (The Book of Certitude), translated by Shoghi Effendi (Wilmette: Bahá'í Publishing Trust), 1974, p 70.
12. *ibid.* p 211.
13. Shoghi Effendi, letter of 5 April 1942, quoted in: *Excellence in All Things* - a compilation (London: Bahá'í Publishing Trust), 1981, p 15.
14. M. Scott Peck, *The Different Drum: Community Making and Peace* (New York: Simon and Schuster), 1987.
15. 'Abdu'l-Bahá, *The Promulgation of Universal Peace* (Wilmette: Bahá'í Publishing Trust), 1982, p 168.
16. Bahá'u'lláh, *Tablets of Bahá'u'lláh* (Haifa: Bahá'í World Centre), 1984, p 126.
17. Bahá'u'lláh, quoted in: *Consultation* - a compilation, p 3.
18. Farzam Arbab, *Literacy, Culture and Empowerment*, unpublished paper, Feb. 1990, (private communication).
19. *ibid.* p 30.

Values and Questions - Balancing Acts in Education

Martin Cortazzi

Introduction

A balanced programme in education has variety, moderation and appropriateness. It has a carefully chosen range of aims, content, methods and activities which complement each other to meet learners' short-term and long-term goals. It avoids extremes; it is relevant to learners' current and potential development. This paper is organised around the question: What kinds of balance are there? *Eight* kinds of balance are considered. Behind these there are three underlying points relating to values and acts: (a) It is useful to strive for a systematic balance between the education of individuals in Bahá'í values and collective action in organised classes designed to deepen the understanding of adults and children. (b) It is productive to seek a balance between acting according to general principles in education and acting to promote the development of Bahá'í values. (c) It seems valid when considering Bahá'í values to take cognisance of values from other religions, philosophies and cultural systems; this may confirm, extend, or revise ideas, or simply show continuity.

Education means more than children's learning - it goes from the womb to the tomb, and, since this world is the womb of the next, it goes beyond, threading through the loom of eternity. Life is a spiral curriculum. Education spirals outwards across the generations: those of us engaged in education are teaching teachers, in the sense that children will teach their peers and future generations. We have much to balance.

Balancing Virtues

Balance is necessary in all things - even in virtues. This is probably a culturally specific concept, but it has been around for a long time. Plato taught that the balance of virtues is the decisive element in a good and happy life. Confucius stressed the Golden Mean, the way of central harmony, to be central in our moral being and to be in harmony with all people: "To go too far is the same as not to go far enough."[1] Bahá'u'lláh speaks of *the Middle Way* and of the need for moderation in all things, even in the exercise of virtues. "If a thing is carried to excess, it will prove a source of evil."[2] To avoid this, our concept of moral and spiritual development must include the need to balance one virtue with another.

Each virtue needs to be controlled by others - otherwise it is no longer a virtue as Confucius said:

> *Courtesy uncontrolled by the laws of good taste becomes laboured effort, caution uncontrolled becomes timidity, boldness uncontrolled becomes recklessness, and frankness uncontrolled becomes effrontery.*[3]

Take the example of **will** and **obedience**. It is vital for children to develop their own willpower and parents and teachers need to help children to do so. This development of volition is important for setting immediate and long-term life goals, for sustaining motivation and for developing a sense of identity. Yet unbridled willpower rapidly becomes intolerant and selfish, a domination of others - unless it is balanced by further virtues such as obedience or consideration. So children need to learn to respond to the will of others in appropriate contexts: to parents or teachers, to the majority, and ultimately to God. The problem, of course, is how to know one's own will, how to know God's will, how to know the difference between our will and His, and how to help children to develop their willpower yet still have a sense of obedience. Reflection on examples like this leads inevitably to questions: Balancing what? When and how can we balance conflicting demands? Is balance for children imbalance for adults and vice versa? What kinds of balance are there? Eight kinds are considered below.

1. Equal Static Balance

Apparently, educational balance means that two things are equal and it may seem that once balance is attained it is somehow fixed forever. In fact, it is hard to see how such a balance *could* be static for very long, particularly in today's world. Circumstances alter, contexts change, the understanding of teachers grows. Today's balance is tomorrow's equilibrium upset - if only because the learners themselves develop. On a global level, humanity is learning rapidly but is still trying to employ old balances. Taking a long view, we can dismiss the idea of balance ever being equal and static. Rather, balance is the continual adjustment of things which are shifting.

2. Equal Shifting Balance

Educational concepts are in a shifting balance, as on a pair of scales. By moving the objects or altering their weight the balance can be adjusted. This metaphor seems to be the common mental model for balancing activities and ideas in education. Over time, such aspects as the following should be balanced:

| broadening ideas | deepening thinking |
| knowing and using facts | developing imagination |

knowing objectively	feeling intuitively
consolidating the known	encountering the new
understanding the past	envisaging the future
developing individually	living collectively
learning intellectually	behaving morally
having willpower	showing obedience
acting vigorously	reflecting carefully
questioning critically	accepting humbly
being flexible	being firm
being serious	having fun

The list could be greatly extended to include many pairs of factors associated with learning, understanding, behaving and becoming. Ultimately the list would cover a catalogue of *general education* principles, on the one hand, and of *virtues*, on the other - two key features in Bahá'í education which themselves need to be balanced. To balance all these in school programmes and in our lives is daunting indeed. A solution is to see that some, at least, can be balanced by seeing them in a hierarchy and giving priority to developing those aspects of learning, or virtues, which appear near the top of the list.

3. Hierarchical Balance

Potential virtues and capacities which it is desirable to develop in education can be analysed in terms of a balance between *knowing* and *loving*.[4] These can be seen as being at the top of a hierarchy of values. Core values should play a key role in education. *Faith* will be high in this scale, since through faith "man's highest station... is attained".[5] Faith means a loving of the unknown or unknowable and feeling an attraction or capacity to approach it. *Truthfulness* will also be high in this pyramid of values: it means knowing the truth and loving it sufficiently to speak it under difficult circumstances. Knowledge is a core virtue because it generates other virtues: "through its employment and exercise...the development of the virtues of mankind is made possible".[6] Love is similarly "the cause of development to every enlightened man,[7] "the source of all the bestowals of God".[8] Such a hierarchy makes sense when our capacity to know and love is seen as the generating impulse underlying creation.[9] Children should be taught to analyse values, situations and events in terms of knowledge and love, to understand how people use these capacities and how the values function in society.

Alternatively, we might see the hierarchical order of values balanced at the top by *love* and *justice*: love as the central value of personal ethics and justice as the central value of the world social order.[10] All other values can be analysed as forms of these and are subordinate to them. This makes sense because justice is "the best beloved of all things"[11], the essence of all that Bahá'u'lláh revealed;[12] it includes the element of investigation with one's own eyes,[11] and is allied to equity, "the most fundamental among human virtues".[13] Near the top of the hierarchical balance will be other foundation virtues:

sincerity   *the foundation-stone of faith*[14]
truthfulness   *the foundation of all human virtues*[15]
patience   *without patience the wayfarer on this journey will reach nowhere and attain no goal*[16]

Other key qualities, according to Bahá'u'lláh's *first counsel*, will be purity, kindness and radiance.[17] These can all be seen in terms of balances between love and justice.

Further reasons for focusing on these core attributes in Bahá'í education emerge when we observe how purity, radiance and patience feature in 'Abdu'l-Bahá's list of qualities required for consultation[18] and how faithfulness and sincerity are included in the list of qualities sought in those elected to membership of assemblies.[19]
Again, teachers can take situations and events embodying dilemmas from local or far-off communities, from the media, from biographies or learners' lives and together with children try to analyse the full facts of the situation, see how values are involved and discuss the difficulties of applying them.

Having such a list of values and attitudes in a syllabus is not going to help education if the process of the classroom or community life do not also mirror them. **Content** and **process** need to be balanced. The above considerations must therefore be complemented by practical questions about core values which teachers must ask themselves when evaluating the classroom or community processes.[20]

Respect
Are people (children, adults or teachers) being listened to seriously? Are their views being taken into account? To what extent is each individual participating in decision-making? Are people having their confidence in themselves supported? To what extent are we explicitly encouraging respect for disadvantaged or minority groups?

Justice
To what extent are people encouraged to give expression to any sense of having been unfairly treated? Is any such expression taken seriously and responded to constructively? Are learners helped to make any protest constructive? Are there mechanisms for dealing with perceived injustice which all members recognise as fair?

Truthfulness
To what extent is hypocrisy present and what forms does it take? To what extent is it possible for people to express truthfully their feelings for each other?

Keeping Promises
How far do people carry out what they said they would do? To what extent are the (unspoken or unwritten?) contracts in the learning environment understood, discussed and adhered to? To what extent is cooperative activity encouraged?

These are challenging questions, if we are truthful. Additionally, we may put these questions to learners in classrooms as part of an effort to give them greater awareness of the social and moral learning environment and give them more responsibility for their own education.

Many aspects of shifting or hierarchical balance seem contradictory. Sometimes there is a tendency to feel compelled to choose between one or other value in a pair. This may be a false choice, resulting from the Western tendency to think *either - or*. This tendency should be balanced by a more Eastern style of thinking *both - and*. This suggests a balance of polarity.

4. Polarity

In the balance of polarity in education apparently conflicting demands are in tension.[21] We might believe that we have to choose between one or other pole in a pair of values, but careful reflection shows that both are in fact necessary. Polarities are important as pairs, at either end of a continuum of possibilities. Experienced teachers oscillate between the tensions of the two poles according to the demands of the situation. They are never able to adhere to only one end, as the following examples show.

Individual - Class
Teachers recognise individuals, yet teach whole classes. Because of the demands of the class, they cannot meet every need of every child. When there are problems with one child many teachers find it useful to focus back on the needs of the whole class. This polarity can be elaborated:

Individual - Class and Outstanding - Grey
Often some outstanding children (those who are *bright*, *slow* or *troublesome*) dominate the teacher's attention and dictate the pace, style and management of classroom work. Apparently some children never stand out as individuals in their teachers' eyes. These are 'grey' children who work quietly but are easily overlooked or forgotten. It is the outstanding children who dominate the teacher's consciousness of how the class is, i.e. the balance of the teacher's perception and attention is inequitable - it does not take *all* children into account. (Are there equivalent perceptions in - or of - Bahá'í communities by members of institutions?)

Humour - Seriousness

Education is a serious business, but there is always humour when children do or say incongruous things, or when things go wrong. After laughter, a teacher needs to restore seriousness, but humour is a key element in enjoying teaching. Conventionally, teachers complain about the difficulties, which is one element of camaraderie: the serious pole. Much teaching *is* a hard struggle so the sharing of any enjoyment and humour with colleagues is an important second pole of teachers' collegiality. Humour reminds us of the difference between our aspiration and our performance, and "laughter is spiritual relaxation";[22] perhaps this is why Bahá'u'lláh says that through His people "the countenance of the world hath been wreathed in smiles".[23] We should be relaxed about Bahá'í education and enjoy it.

Individual - Collective

These two poles express cultural orientations to communication. Most Westerners have absorbed cultural values which stress individual development and the right to individual self-expression. Many oriental cultures, however, put far more emphasis on a collective awareness of the group. A Westerner using the individual pole is likely to state the main point quickly, will be fairly direct and will feel free to disagree with others in a group. Someone from the East, in contrast, is more likely to give a general background to establish collective harmony and understanding within a group before making the main point. In a mixed group, Westerners listening for an oriental to make a main point swiftly may not hear one immediately and may have switched off by the time the point is actually made, so that they may miss it or believe there wasn't one. The Eastern style, with more hints and allusions, contrasts with Western directness. Either style may be frustrating to those using the other pole. The collective orientation makes it difficult for Easterners to disagree openly with others; instead, people will discuss things without expressing opinions until it is clear from hints what most people feel. Only then will opinion be expressed - as a group opinion; anybody still disagreeing will not flout collective harmony by expressing disagreement. Westerners in a mixed group may wrongly conclude that if others do not express an opinion it means that they have none. Easterners may wrongly conclude that the Westerners are rude, insensitive, domineering and inconsiderate.

Both styles are useful - in their own cultural context; both styles are dysfunctional - when they are opposed to each other in cross-cultural situations. Awareness of both is necessary; attempting to balance the two is likely to lead to growth of understanding. Talking about such examples or using them in role playing would be valuable to promote awareness of cultural styles of communication as preparation for world citizenship.

A number of challenges to maintaining balance can be interpreted in terms of polarity: the notions of conflict, diversity, change and differences in perceptions may turn out to be necessary elements in a wider balance of polarity.

5. Systematic Balance

How to keep more than two things in balance is a problem. Where more than two things are in a systematic relationship with each other, adding an extra element changes the relationship of all the others, not only to the new element but to each other. An example of a system in balance can be seen by examining the relationship between *knowledge* and *action*.

These have long been seen as complementary in China: "Knowledge is the crystallisation of the will to act, and action is the task of carrying out that knowledge; knowledge is the beginning of action, and action is the completion of knowledge"[24] and in medieval Europe: "Take heed to give your words the voice of power. You ask, what is that? It is that your words harmonise with your works, that you be careful to do before you teach". (St Bernard of Clairvaux, 1101-53). There is a middle step, however, as 'Abdu'l-Bahá indicated: "Knowledge is the first step; resolve the second step; action, its fulfilment, is the third step".[25] "The attainment of any object is conditional upon: first, knowledge; second, volition; third, action".[26]

Knowledge - Resolve - Action

So we should teach children to know their own resolve and act on it, balancing theory and practice through resolution. To develop this children need to be free to make choices. They need to know how to choose.

Recent discussion in teacher education about the links between theory and practice has emphasised that much professional knowledge is the kind of knowledge-in-action of knowing what to do in situations when they arise, a practical intuitive knowledge not usually articulated,[27] but which teachers can draw out through reflection on classroom events.[28] Systematic reflection on classroom experience is seen as important input to advance our understanding of theory. This suggests a recurring cycle of: **knowledge - resolve - action - reflection** or, since we can teach children to do this: **plan - do - apply - review**. All the elements in the system are important and all affect each other. That this is also a systematic spiritual balance is suggested by 'Abdu'l-Bahá's comment that "the spiritual life is symbolised by simplicity and contemplation, combined with usefulness and well-directed activity".[29] We should contemplate the usefulness of our activity - perhaps through using questions.

Asking Questions

In most classrooms most questions are asked by the teacher. If questions lead to learning, children should be encouraged to have their own questions, as an important part of learning. "Half of knowledge is the question; the other half is the answer".[30] If we deprive children of the opportunity to ask questions, we deprive them of the opportunity to acquire half of knowledge. Socrates proposed that someone charged with the upbringing and education of children should make a law that they should devote themselves especially to the technique of asking and answering questions.[31]

Teachers should not only ask children questions, but should also ask themselves. If teachers aren't asking and learning, how do we suppose children should be asking and learning? There should be room for doubt in education.

This point was made in medieval Europe by Peter Abelard (1079-1142): "The first key to wisdom is constant questioning. By doubting we are led to enquiry and by enquiry we are led to the truth", and by Chu Hsi (1130-1200), the most influential Chinese philosopher since Confucius: "I used to tell students to think and to seek points of doubt. But I have come to understand that it is not fruitful to start out with the intention of findings things to doubt. Just study with an open mind. After working hard at a text, there will be places which block your path and cause you perplexity. That's where doubts naturally come up for you to compare, to weigh, to ponder over."[24] The suggestion is that teachers should ask themselves questions about the systematic generation of knowledge in the classroom. Furthermore, teachers should encourage learners to ask similar questions. *Children need to verbalise their experience and to have the experience of verbalisation.* This applies to children's experience of learning.

Knowledge
What do I know already about the topic? What kind of answers do I need? What do I plan to learn?

Resolve
What do I want to find out? How important is it to learn or understand this topic? Do I really want to make the effort?

Action
How am I going to go about learning this? What answers do I have? How worthwhile are they? What will I do with the answers?

Reflection
(After a lesson). What did I actually do in the lesson? How well did I learn? Was it worthwhile? How do I go about evaluating it? What will I try next time? What new questions do I have? To what extent am I refining the process of knowing - resolving - acting - reflecting?

Similarly, questions can be posed about the systematic balance between aspects of classroom tasks. It is important to think of what children will be learning in terms of tasks: "Unless we embody the material to be learned and remembered in a task that makes sense to the child, one that includes objectives he can realise and that draws his attention naturally to the elements we wish him to take in, our imperatives to concentrate, memorise and learn are bound to fail".[32]

For any task, the teacher could examine the systematic aspects of goals, input, activity, teacher's and learners' roles, and the setting.

Goal
What should the learners be learning, doing, feeling, communicating in this task? To what extent are the goals of the task obvious to the teacher? To learners? Is the task appropriate to the age and level of knowledge of the learners? What beliefs about the nature of learning and the nature of Bahá'í values are inherent in the task? Is the task likely to be interesting and motivating to learners?

Input
What form does the input take: tape, picture, story, text, game, experience? How useful or realistic is it?

Activities
What activities are appropriate: drawing, matching, comparing, sequencing, ranking, completing gaps, problem-solving, responding to a text, role-playing, using puppets, interviewing, exchanging information, generating ideas, sharing experiences? Can the activities be sequenced? Do the activities allow learners to communicate and cooperate in pairs or groups? Do the activities reflect Bahá'í values?

Roles
How much control does the teacher have over the learning, the content, the communication? Is the teacher talking too much? How will the learners contribute to the learning? Do the learners' roles allow for a variety of learning strategies?

Setting
Will the learners work individually, in pairs or groups, in a whole class or several classes? Is it appropriate to involve members of the community? Is the setting confined to a classroom? Is the learning confined to the lesson?

Similar questions might be applied to the handling of a text in the classroom, in order to approach a balanced discussion:

Knowing
What do I think the text is about? What do I know about the topic already? What do I want to know about it? What might others want to know? What do I think the words of the text mean? What does the text imply?

Seeing
How does this text fit in with my picture of the Writings as a whole? How does it affect how I see myself and the world?

Feeling
How do I feel about this? How would others of a different background feel?

Saying
What other ways are there of saying what the text says? Is there anything special or interesting about how the words are used?

Acting
What would putting this text into practice mean? What are the results? How can I do so? In these ways, reading will be on the lines (looking at literal meaning), between the lines (looking for implication), beyond the lines (looking from personal experience and expectations, and looking towards a global context). A part of reading many Bahá'í works will be to notice how things are said, which includes the use of metaphors.

6. The Balance of Discovery

A metaphor compares the familiar with the unknown, balancing the concrete with the abstract or the material with the spiritual, e.g. *the Sun of Truth* compares the physical sun with the Revealer of religious Truth. Using a metaphor is not merely poetic decoration, rather it is an important way of thinking. Often the use of such phrases leads to the discovery of many other meanings. Through reflection, contemplation and the exercise of volition we are led to find new aspects of knowledge for ourselves.[33] Metaphors are thus *bridges to reality*, as the classical Arabic saying has it. They have an important teaching function. Indeed, there are metaphors for the educational process itself in the Bahá'í scriptures: teachers are gardeners,[34] or doctors.[35]

In many texts, Bahá'u'lláh uses tiers of metaphors to build up pyramids of knowledge. It is the reader's task to climb these steps towards higher understanding. The Kitáb-i-Íqán, for example, shows how metaphors are keys to understanding past Scriptures: *sun, moon, stars, clouds, city, riches* and so on, have rich symbolic value, and in the past the *tenor* (the Truth) has parted company with the *vehicle* (the Sun), so that the literal alone (the sun) is understood. Bahá'u'lláh restores the balance of discovery by explaining the link (the Sun of Truth). Yet in the course of His explanation in the Íqán, the whole texture is itself woven with other unexplained metaphors. This second layer demonstrates the continuing validity of the first by constantly offering both tenor and vehicle as food for further thought:

the cup of the love of God, the cup of divine knowledge, the cup of His singleness ... A third layer of metaphors is seen in more than fifty terms for the *Manifestation* - itself a balance-to-discovery metaphor: *these sanctified Mirrors, Birds of Eternity, Treasuries of His holy names, Channels of God's immortal utterance* ... A fourth layer might be seen in the Names of God...

In our efforts to help children understand such writing it is important to realise two points: the use of metaphor is basic to thinking, and metaphors are extremely common in everyday speech. Children's own speech is full of metaphors - often they create their own, unnoticed by adults. Teachers' speech also sparkles with metaphors. A brief look at some of them illustrates how metaphors may lose their balance. Consider how primary teachers describe the moment of learning:[21]

it all clicked	it seemed to click
it's clicked in his mind	there was a click
the light dawns	he saw the light
her face lit up	daylight has dawned

These are frequent and typical examples of teachers' everyday descriptions of learning. The mechanistic metaphor (learning is a click) and the visual image of light (learning is light dawning) are arguably important parts of the teachers' everyday thinking about children's learning. However, they seem to embody limited, unexplained, uninformed views of learning expressed in cliches, where one might have supposed that teachers would have given more thought to the fundamental question of how children learn. Overused metaphors can be *barriers* to reflection just as much as they can be *bridges* to reality - it depends on whether and how they are seen. Yet metaphors are crucial for the expression of cultural values: "The most fundamental values in a culture will be coherent with the metaphorical structure of the most fundamental concepts in the culture."[36] To help children understand fundamental Bahá'í values, and their expression in Scripture, it is clearly vital to engage them in the conscious use of metaphors, perhaps using drawings, charts, models, drama, puppets and other means to approach allegory, parables, and other kinds of symbolic language.

7. Dynamic, Interactive Balance

Children's talking is an important part of their learning. It is not just that their talk reflects learning, rather as they try to express what is to be learned they come to understand it. Thought comes into existence through words. It may be that the consciousness of values - our awareness of what we believe about living and how to go about it - is born through talk, with ourselves and others. Words may be the midwives of deeds. Was it E.M. Forster who said, "How shall I know what I think until I see what I say?". By saying what they tentatively think, children may come to understand through seeing the effect of what they say on others, getting others' response to their ideas, causing them to reflect on their saying and therefore on their thinking. "In speech and art individuals do not simply share what they possess; it is only by virtue of the sharing process that they attain what they possess".[37] Teachers also come to understand by explaining, as Jerome Bruner recounts: "I went through it once and looked up to find the class full of blank faces - they had obviously not understood. I went through it a second time and they still did not understand it. So I went through it a third time, and that time I understood it".[38]

Thus, in the end, a Bahá'i curriculum is at the tip of the tongue; it is created in the balance of talk and expression between teacher and learner. That this is a dynamic, interactive balance is suggested in the work of Vygotsky.[39,40] In contrast to the influential Piagetian view, which emphasises learning as a matter internal to the individual mind, Vygotsky saw concept development as firstly a social affair, which is only later internalised in the mind of the individual. He saw ever-shifting patterns of talk and growth as being a major means to the release of greater potential, not just realising potential but creating it. The adult may talk through activities or problems, scaffolding the child's talk and activity by providing more capable assistance, later helping less, handing over more and more initiative to the child till the vicarious consciousness which was first provided by the adult has become internalised conscious knowledge of the child. What the child can do or say *with* an adult today is what he or she will do or say *alone* tomorrow. The adult's talk and activity is aimed at what the child can do now *plus* a bit. It is working in this zone of the plus, where new knowledge and understanding is created, which is important. As this zone is constantly moving, the balance is held by a continual dynamic shifting, with a constant focus on the child's tomorrow. If, as many psychologists think,[33] this is not only how language is acquired but also how thinking and learning skills are acquired, there is reason to suppose that this process will greatly assist children to acquire values.

8. The Balance of Transcendence

An eighth kind of balance in education, which is stimulating for Bahá'í teachers to consider, was repeatedly shown in the conversations of 'Abdu'l-Bahá. He consistently broadened others' vision by giving spiritual counterparts to their immediate situations and activities. He showed others how to transcend their immediate environment by having spiritual goals, which he expressed through extended metaphor. One example illustrates the point: When someone pointed out warships in the harbour of Alexandria, in 1912, 'Abdu'l-Bahá replied, "I desire that you may see the divine ships. These ships are the blessed sails traversing the sea of Divine mercy; their propellers are the powers of spiritual love and their captains are the inspiration of the Holy Spirit. No ship is ever wrecked in this sea; its waves are life-giving. Each one of the friends of God is like unto an Ark of Salvation. Each ark saves many souls from the storms of troubles. The future centuries and cycles are like the sea on the surface of which these arks glide blissfully toward their spiritual destination" [41].

Instead of war, his transcendent vision saw with awe: not warships, but worship. Most people understand backwards (looking to the past), but live forwards (to the future). However, the balance of transcendence encourages a forward-looking understanding of our potential.

Conclusion

This paper has stressed balancing Bahá'í values in education and the importance of asking questions. Asking questions is a major way to monitor and maintain the balance of our actions in education. Asking questions needs to be balanced with another neglected activity: listening to the answers and following them. It is sometimes said that the Bahá'í Writings have all the answers. If so, I only wish that we had all the questions...

References

1. Confucius, *The Analects*, translated by D.C. Lau (Harmondsworth: Penguin), 1938, pp 11-15.
2. Bahá'u'lláh, *Tablets of Bahá'u'lláh* (Wilmette: Bahá'í Publishing Trust), 1984, p 69.
3. Confucius, *The Analects*, translated by D.C. Lau (Harmondsworth: Penguin), 1938, pp 8-11.
4. Daniel Jordan, "Becoming Your True Self", *World Order*, 3, 1, pp 43-51.
5. The Báb, *Selections from the Writings of the Báb*, tran. by H. Taherzadeh (Haifa: Bahá'í World Centre), 1978, p 89.
6. 'Abdu'l-Bahá, *The Promulgation of Universal Peace* (Wilmette: Bahá'í Publishing Trust), 1982, p 31.
7. 'Abdu'l-Bahá, *Tablets of 'Abdul-Bahá Abbas*, Vol III (Chicago: Bahá'í Publishing Society), 1916, p 526.
8. 'Abdu'l-Bahá, *The Promulgation of Universal Peace* (Wilmette: Bahá'í Publishing Trust), 1982, p 15.
9. Bahá'u'lláh, *Gleanings from the Writings of Bahá'u'lláh* (Wilmette: Bahá'í Publishing Trust), 1983, p 65.
10. Udo Schaeffer, *The Imperishable Dominion* (Oxford: George Ronald), 1983, p 213.
11. Bahá'u'lláh, *The Hidden Words*, translated by Shoghi Effendi (London: Bahá'í Publishing Trust), 1975, p 5.
12. Bahá'u'lláh, *Tablets of Bahá'u'lláh* (Wilmette: Bahá'í Publishing Trust), 1984, p 157.
13. Bahá'u'lláh, *Gleanings from the Writings of Bahá'u'lláh* (Wilmette: Bahá'í Publishing Trust), 1983, p 203.

14. 'Abdu'l-Bahá, *Secret of Divine Civilization* (Wilmette: Bahá'í Publishing Trust), 1975, p 96.
15. 'Abdu'l-Bahá, quoted in: *The Advent of Divine Justice* (Wilmette: Bahá'í Publishing Trust), 1976, p 26.
16. Bahá'u'lláh, *The Seven Valleys and the Four Valleys* (Wilmette: Bahá'í Publishing Trust), 1971, p 5.
17. Bahá'u'lláh, *The Hidden Words*, translated by Shoghi Effendi (London: Bahá'í Publishing Trust), 1975, no 1, p 5.
18. Shoghi Effendi, in a letter, 5 March 1922.
19. Shoghi Effendi, in a letter, 30 January 1923.
20. D. Wright, *Moral Competence, An Exploration of the Role of Moral Education in F.E.* (London: Further Education Unit), 1989.
21. M. Cortazzi, *Primary Teaching, How It Is* (London: David Fulton), 1991.
22. H. Ahdieh and E. Hopson, *'Abdu'l-Bahá in New York* (New York: Spiritual Assembly of the Bahá'ís of New York), 1987, p 20.
23. 'Abdu'l-Bahá, *The Advent of Divine Justice*, op.cit, p 76.
24. Moore, C. (ed.) *The Chinese Mind* (Honolulu: University of Hawaii Press), 1967, p 15.
25. 'Abdu'l-Bahá, *'Abdu'l-Bahá' in London*, (London: Bahá'í Publishing Trust), 1982, p 46.
26. Star of the West, **4**, p 57.
27. D. Schon, *The Reflective Practitioner* (New York: Basic Books), 1983.
28. A. Pollard and S. Tann, *Reflective Teaching in the Primary School* (London: Cassell), 1987.
29. 'Abdu'l-Bahá, quoted in: *Star of The West*, **1**, 8, p 5.
30. Abu 'Uthmana l Makki - in a Hadith.
31. Plato, *Plato's Republic*, VII, 534.
32. P. Woods, *How Children Think and Learn* (Oxford: Blackwell), 1988, p 61.
33. John Hatcher, *The Purpose of Physical Reality* (Wilmette: Bahá'í Publishing Trust), 1987.
34. 'Abdu'l-Bahá, quoted in: *Bahá'í Education* - a compilation (London: Bahá'í Publishing Trust), 1987, p 27.
35. *ibid.* p 130.
36. G. Lakoff and M. Johnson, *Metaphors We Live By* (Chicago: University of Chicago Press), 1980, p 22.
37. E. Cassirer, *The Logic of the Humanities*, Ernst 1961, p 113.
38. J. Bruner, *The Process of Education* (New York: Vintage Books), 1963, p 88.
39. L.S. Vygotsky, *Mind in Society* (Cambridge-Mass: Harvard University Press), 1978.
40. L.S. Vygotsky, *Thought and Language* (Cambridge-Mass: MIT Press), 1986.
41. 'Abdu'l-Bahá, quoted in: *Star of the West*, **8**, 8, p 104.

Education and Gender

Sovaida Maani

Introduction

For all its indispensability, education has been and continues to be one of the most misunderstood and misapplied concepts of our time. Even the so-called *civilised* nations of the world belonging to the ranks of the *first world* countries continue to wrestle with and be baffled by the seemingly endless and insoluble problems presented by their attempts to forge an educational system that will produce the sorts of individuals so desperately needed to shoulder the ever-increasing burdens of present-day society rather than be crushed by them.

In the inner cities of the United States, for instance, a teacher attending class is forced to contend not only with the tasks of inculcating certain knowledge into his/her students but is also faced with the awesome and frightening responsibility of dealing with armed children who are more than likely to be dealing in drugs and who at any time may turn violent and kill anyone whom they perceive to be a threat to them. As a result of such potential and dangerous exposure, fewer and fewer would-be teachers are willing to assume the responsibility of attempting to *educate* the children of these inner cities. Apart from the dangers, remuneration is far from satisfactory and the end reality of all this is that the business of teaching has been left to those who are perhaps less qualified and less motivated than they should be to be entrusted with such a delicate task as the moulding of the future generations into whose hands the reins of the destiny of this entire planet must inevitably fall.

Redefining Education

In attempting to understand why we have run up against such formidable barriers, and to find means of tearing these down, we would do well to start with a re-examination of the basics. Our starting point should be the very definition of the concept with which we are grappling. That concept is *education*. The original meaning of the word was "to draw out and cause to flourish the innate potentialities that lie hidden within each human being".[1] This is a profound concept that is supported by numerous statements in the Bahá'í Writings. Bahá'u'lláh says: "Regard man as a mine rich in gems of inestimable value. Education can, alone, cause it to reveal its treasures, and enable mankind to benefit therefrom."[2] As one ponders this beautiful metaphor, one is struck by a number of thoughts. One of these is the tremendous effort, dedication and faith that is required for the successful mining of gems. Cutting through the rocks and the gravel is an arduous task involving patience, determination and a willingness to put up with a lot of undesirable dirt (namely, the negative attributes of the child) in order to finally reach the gem that makes all the hard work seem worthwhile. Another realisation is that discernment is needed even to recognise a gem when one finally happens upon it. This subject will be touched upon later. Yet another realisation is that the role of education is not, as we have come to expect, to implant gems within human beings, but rather to uncover those existing gems that are innate and inherent within each individual. The very fact that human beings, man and woman alike, were created in the image of God means that we are all potentially able to mirror forth our Creator's attributes.

To reiterate the foregoing, Bahá'u'lláh in the same passage says: "Man is the supreme Talisman. Lack of a proper education hath, however, deprived him of that which he doth inherently possess."[2] 'Abdu'l-Bahá sheds further light on this idea with his following statement:

> *Man is even as steel, the essence of which is hidden: through admonition and explanation, good counsel and education, that essence will be brought to light. If, however, he be allowed to remain in his original condition, the corrosion of lusts and appetites will effectively destroy him.*[3]

This statement adds a new dimension to our understanding of the concept of *education*. All at once, the urgency of the need for proper education is made apparent, for in neglecting truly to mine for gems we risk not only the onset of a wistful longing for a gem that might have been ours, but we are also now faced with the potential of severe harm accruing both to the individual thus neglected - caused by the corrosion of his true self - and to those around him who will also be affected by the spread of the rust. As we know from experience, once rust sets in, it must be dealt with swiftly and effectively or else it spreads among materials of similar properties with which it comes into contact. Finally, 'Abdu'l-Bahá likens a child to a plant which He says:

> *...will grow in whatever way you train it. If you rear it to be truthful, and kind, and righteous, it will grow straight, it will be fresh and tender, and will flourish. But if not, then from faulty training it will grow bent, and stand awry, and there will be no hope of changing it.*[4]

Once again the dangers of allowing improper education to go unheeded, are brought forcefully to our attention. Once a plant has hardened, it is very difficult and dangerous to its existence to attempt to straighten it, if crooked. In fact, too much force exerted at once will cause it to break. While it is still young and supple, however, it can be trained to grow in whatever direction the gardener pleases without the risk of injury.

To What End Should We Develop Potential?

Having established that education entails none other than the drawing forth of already existing hidden potential within a human being, the question becomes to what end we should strive to elicit this potential. The Guardian of the Bahá'í Faith sets the stage for us with his following statement:

> *...Bahá'u'lláh considered education as one of the most fundamental factors of a true civilisation - this education, however, in order to be adequate and fruitful should be comprehensive in nature and should take into consideration not only the physical and the intellectual side of man but also his spiritual and ethical aspects.*[5]

This paragraph presupposes the truth that is gradually beginning to be grasped, particularly in recent years, that the individual affects the society in which he or she lives and that society in turn affects the individual. Therefore, in order to create the kind of civilisation that best addresses our needs and concerns in this day, we must begin by educating the individual members of our society to display the sorts of characteristics that will redound to the benefit of the whole. Once the whole has been thus benefitted it, in turn, provides the environment that is conducive to further individual growth.

On the individual plane, there are two fundamental elements at play here. The first involves the development of intellectual and mental capabilities including the acquisition of knowledge, arts, crafts and sciences. Bahá'u'lláh, in *Epistle to the Son of the Wolf*, says:

> *Knowledge is as wings to man's life, and a ladder for his ascent. Its acquisition is incumbent upon everyone. The knowledge of such sciences, however, should be acquired as can profit the peoples of the earth, and not those which begin with words and end with words.*[6]

This element of the individual's development allows him to be a useful member of society allowing him to contribute his share to the interdependency of the whole. Without such knowledge and skills a man is *but a barren tree*,[7] and such a tree, as Christ said, was fit only for the fire.

The second element at play in the development of the individual is the ethical and spiritual element. The inculcation of ethical values and, more importantly, a sense of discernment, enabling the individual to distinguish for himself/herself the difference between proper and improper use of knowledge, is essential, for without this type of discernment, the fruits derived from scientific knowledge and technological advances become dangerous weapons in the hands of an immature humanity. Fire can constructively be used by a wise person for heat and light; alternatively it can be used to destroy and burn. It is, inherently, neither good nor bad. It is the use to which it is put that yields positive or negative results. The spiritual development of the individual encompasses the ethical aspect, for it is through spiritual nurturing that we instil within the individual the mechanism and balance wherein he/she weighs the propriety of his/her intended actions, thus eliminating the need to drum into him/her a long list of rights and wrongs.

Over and beyond this, however, the spiritual development of the individual is founded upon the bedrock of the following truth: that one's purpose in this life is none other than to prepare oneself for the next life. Just as the babe within the mother's womb must develop its limbs and organs in order to make the most of its opportunities in this life and to partake of its enjoyments to the fullest, so also must we on this earthly plane develop the spiritual limbs without which we will be handicapped in the afterlife. These spiritual limbs, the Bahá'í Writings tell us, are none other than certain qualities that must be mined like gems and polished to perfection. They include such qualities as dignity, self-discipline, humility, detachment, self-sacrifice, love and faith. The supreme importance of the acquisition of these spiritual characteristics and its place within the scheme of things, is made very clear from the following paragraph from 'Abdu'l-Bahá in which He says, talking about the development of these virtues:

> *This is the primary consideration. If a person be unlettered, and yet clothed with Divine excellence, and alive in the breaths of the Spirit, that individual will contribute to the welfare of society, and his inability to read and write will do him no harm. And if a person be versed in the arts and every branch of knowledge, and not live a religious life, and not take on the characteristics of God, and not be directed by a pure intent, and be engrossed in life of the flesh - then he is harm personified, and nothing will come of all his learning and intellectual accomplishments but scandal and torment.*[8]

To the degree that we develop our understanding of our true purpose in life and learn that a life spent solely in the acquisition of wealth, prosperity and power is a life misspent, and that fighting for the material things of this life is a serious squandering of precious energy, we will put aside our childish inclinations towards wars, which have so sorely afflicted our planet, and will strive to establish the peace longed for over the ages, thus establishing the optimum environment within which humankind can develop its potential as a collective unit.

Education when viewed in this light leads us to perceive the untold damage and havoc wreaked on our society because of the separation of church and state. Little wonder that we find ourselves, despite our tremendous scientific and technological advances, in such a proverbial pickle.

Mistakes of the Past

There seem to be a number of spiritual laws that we, as a race - the human race - continue to insist on flouting, regardless of the disastrous consequences that ensue time and again. One of these is the law that says that every human being is a continuum and a blend of his/her various aspects: emotional, spiritual, mental and physical. As soon as we try to isolate one of these elements and make it the sole basis upon which we conduct our lives, the result is imbalance, for we are attacking the very unity and oneness of our own beings. So, also, in attempting to draw out the hidden gems latent within another human being, we must be careful not to over develop one aspect at the expense of another. For instance, if we teach a child to rely solely on logic to the exclusion of its intuition, then we are perforce narrowing its sights and depriving it of the creative and guiding spark which intuition has to offer and which has so often been the genesis of the greatest inventions and discoveries in all fields, e.g. scientific, musical, literary and artistic.

Another principle that seems to be consistently ignored is that all human beings are born with varying degrees of capacity. Some are prone to excellence in mathematics, others in music, etc. Each mine treasures within it different gems. This principle applies also on a broader scale to the genders, male and female. Certain attributes come more naturally to women than they do to men. These are often referred to as *feminine qualities* and are laughed upon as symptoms of weakness. They include alertness, intuition, tolerance, compassion, nurturing, service, understanding and love. Because they are more difficult to draw forth in men, the mining process being more painful, they have simply been ignored. Not content with simply ignoring them, we, as a society, have gone a step further and have devalued them to the point of convincing ourselves that they are actually undesirable qualities and that to betray a hint of possessing them is tantamount to an unabashed confession of weakness. We have indulged this incredibly ignorant attitude at great expense to ourselves individually and as a world community, for by ignoring these qualities which are a vital part of the continuum that goes to make up our very beings, we have caused imbalances, neuroses and a destruction of the integrity of the whole both on an individual and collective level. We have chosen, in our ignorance, to focus upon, promote and encourage the development of those traits which are regarded as *masculine* such as aggression and competition, and have thus distorted our own realities and created untold misery within the family unit, in the workplace and in the realm of world politics. In short, we have destroyed both our inner and outer peace. The Bahá'í Writings are very clear and emphatic regarding this matter. 'Abdu'l-Bahá says:

> *The world of humanity consists of two parts: male and female. Each is the complement of the other. Therefore, if one is defective, the other will necessarily be incomplete, and perfection cannot be attained. There is a right hand and a left hand in the human body, functionally equal in service and administration. If either proves defective, the defect will naturally extend to the other by involving the completeness of the whole; for accomplishment is not normal unless both are perfect. If we say one hand is deficient, we prove the inability and incapacity of the other; for single-handed there is no full accomplishment. Just as physical accomplishment is complete with two hands, so man and woman, the two parts of the social body, must be perfect. It is not natural that either should remain undeveloped; and until both are perfected, the happiness of the human world will not be realised.*[9]

In the past, not only have certain traits been considered *feminine* and hence frowned upon, but women themselves have been often considered inferior. For instance, there was a time when women were not considered to be on the same level as human beings in India, Persia and throughout the Orient. For certain Arab tribes, the word for woman was the same as the word for donkey and a man's wealth was measured by the number of these collective animals of burden that he possessed.[10] This sort of behaviour, 'Abdu'l-Bahá explains, can be attributed to the fact that "the world in the past has been ruled by force, and man has dominated over woman by reason of his more forceful and aggressive qualities both of body and mind".[11] He does, however, also emphasise that the new age will be "less masculine, and more permeated with the feminine ideals - or, to speak more exactly, will be an age in which the masculine and feminine elements of civilisation will be more evenly balanced".[11]

In its recent Statement on Peace, the Universal House of Justice asserts that: "Only as women are welcomed into full partnership in all fields of human endeavour will the moral and psychological climate be created in which international peace can emerge".[12]

This link between the achievement of peace and the education of women and their entry into all fields of human endeavour is a potent and important one. In the same passage the Universal House of Justice explains that the achievement of full equality between the sexes is one of the most important prerequisites for peace. The injustice currently perpetrated against half the world's population, they further explain, "promotes in men harmful attitudes and habits that are carried from the family to the workplace, to political life, and ultimately to international relations."[12]

'Abdu'l-Bahá also stresses this link between the development of women and peace by saying that women must be accorded the same educational opportunities as men, so that they may occupy the same positions in the social and economic spheres. Once this happens, He says, the world will attain unity. He further explains that the education of women will be a *mighty step* towards the abolition of war, as they will use all their influence against it. Women after all bear, rear and painstakingly educate their children and will therefore refuse to have their sons sacrificed on the battlefields. "In truth", He says, "she will be the greatest factor in establishing universal peace and international arbitration. Assuredly, woman will abolish warfare among mankind".[13] This balancing is necessary since "man is more inclined to war than woman".[14]

This understanding of the link between the drawing forth of feminine elements and a balancing thereof with the masculine elements is beginning to pervade the literature of our times. In the field of psychology, the principle of the existence of a male and female side as parts of each person's personality (man and woman alike), is becoming well-established. Any time one of these parts begins to dominate the other, or there is an excess of one over the other, psychological imbalance results which affects the way the individual views and perceives his/herself, which then in turn affects his/her interaction with those around him/her, which in turn affects society in general. The effect of this imbalance which starts with the smallest unit of our social order can be likened to the ripple effect produced when a stone is thrown into a body of water: each ripple produces another, wider and more far-reaching and encompassing in scope.

One of the most fascinating courses of study recently embarked upon is the study of human history and evolution within the framework of the relationship between the two halves of the human race. In her book *The Chalice and the Blade*, Riane Eisler postulates her theory of *Cultural Transformation* that proposes that a study of our history as a race reveals that in any given period in the history of a people, there were one of two basic models in operation governing the relationship between men and women. The first of these she calls the *dominator model* which inevitably entails the ranking of one half of humanity over the other. The second of these models she refers to as the *partnership model* in which social relations are based on the principle of linking rather than ranking and in which the diversity between the two sexes is a cause of strength and is not equated with either inferiority or superiority. Her historical analysis demonstrates quite clearly that the way in which we structure the most fundamental of all human relations (which forms the basis for the continuation of our species) has a profound impact on all our institutions and values and determines the direction and course of our cultural evolution, particularly whether it will be peaceful or warlike.[15]

Among the myriads of interesting examples she gives is the following which she draws from Randolph Trumbach's *The Rise of the Equalitarian Family*. Trumbach shows that while France, Russia and Germany suffered violent antimonarchic upheavals in the eighteenth and nineteenth centuries, England by contrast, was spared such upheavals. This he attributes to the fact that important changes were brought about in the men who governed England by virtue of the rising power of women in the families of the British ruling classes, making these men more ready to accept important social reforms such as the move to parliamentary government, with the monarch remaining only as titular head while by contrast, the Russian, German and French kings continued to rule as despots.[16] Thus, a whole nation was saved from the ravages of bloodshed by virtue of the fact that women were given the opportunity to make their presence felt at all levels of the social structure and feminine ideals were allowed to pervade and thus save the day.

Riane Eisler points out that we currently stand at a critical juncture in the history of our race and have the free will to decide which path to pursue - that of destruction or that of peaceful coexistence. Shall we continue upon the path of our domination-oriented society which has brought the globe so perilously close to the brink of potential self-annihilation or shall we adopt a partnership model and set about the task of building a new world order?

The Solution

If we are to opt for the path of least resistance which entails letting go of our stubborn ways that have become entrenched within us and our communities for such a long time, our best guarantee for long-term success is to develop an educational system that will ensure not only that our sons and daughters both receive the same education, but that both the masculine and feminine qualities in each will be developed to the same extent. If we do this, we will save ourselves from falling into the old trap of encouraging the development of solely masculine characteristics in our men and barely tolerating feminine characteristics in our females. The more multifaceted the gems that are uncovered in our mining for and polishing of the gems of human potential, the more lustrous and beautiful the resulting jewel.

Let there be no mistake that the Bahá'í Writings *presuppose* an equality of capacity between men and women. 'Abdu'l-Bahá makes this very clear in several statements, including the following: "In the world of humanity... the female sex is treated as though inferior, and is not allowed equal rights and privileges. This condition is due not to nature, but to education."[17] Later in the same passage He reiterates this in the context of scholarship by saying: "If women received the same educational advantages as those of men, the result would demonstrate the equality of capacity of both for scholarship". Thus, the key to achieving the balance of masculine and feminine ideals, and hence a peaceful world, is the affording of equal education and opportunities to both men and women.

Here we see the interplay of an important psychological principle that has hitherto been used to disadvantage women: we humans tend to live up to whatever standard of expectation is set for us; as the standard changes, we adjust our performance accordingly. This means that even if a person has an inherent capacity that is, say, equivalent to that of a bucket, but we set for that person a standard of expectation of only a thimbleful, chances are that that individual will not fulfil anywhere near their God-given capacity. 'Abdu'l-Bahá acknowledged the potency and significance of this principle when He said in this regard:

> *In brief, the assumption of superiority by man will continue to be depressing to the ambition of woman, as if her attainment to equality was creationally impossible; woman's aspiration toward advancement will be checked by it, and she will gradually become hopeless. On the contrary, we must declare that her capacity is equal, even greater than man's. This will inspire her with hope and ambition, and her susceptibilities for advancement will continually increase. She must not be told and taught that she is weaker and inferior in capacity and qualification. If a pupil is told that his intelligence is less than his fellow pupils, it is a very great drawback and handicap to his progress. He must be encouraged to advance by the statement, You are most capable, and if you endeavour, you will attain the highest degree.*[18]

In order to avoid perpetration of such a devious injustice, it is absolutely essential that in setting the curricula that embody our standards of expectation for achievement, the same curricula, embodying the same standards, be applied for both males and females. Moreover, these curricula should encourage the adoption not only of traditionally male-oriented subjects such as sports and the acquisition of scientific knowledge, but should also include moral, ethical and spiritual training and standards. They should also place as much emphasis on the development of female qualities such as compassion, intuition and service in *both* sexes, as on the development of male qualities. 'Abdu'l-Bahá affirms the principle propounded by Bahá'u'lláh that the curriculum for men and women should be the same. He says:

> *He [Bahá'u'lláh] promulgated the adoption of the same course of education for man and woman. Daughters and sons must follow the same curriculum of study, thereby promoting unity of the sexes. When all mankind shall receive the same opportunity and the equality of men and women be realised, the foundations of war will be utterly destroyed.*[19]

This concept is part of a larger concept that lies at the very foundation of the Message of Bahá'u'lláh who, as the Divine Physician, has brought the remedy for mankind's present-day ills; that world order can be founded only on an unshakable consciousness of the oneness of mankind.[12]

The longer we wait to implement the mechanism which will allow human potential to be equally developed across the board, the longer we delay our own individual and collective birthright - which is to soar to the highest pinnacles of glory attainable for man - for 'Abdu'l-Bahá makes it very clear that the world of humanity has two wings, one being women and the other men. Not until both are equally developed can the bird fly. Moreover, true prosperity and success are impossible to all until both are equally strong.[20]

References

1. Herman Kahn and Anthony Weiner, *The Year 2000* (New York: Macmillan), 1967, p 189.
2. Bahá'u'lláh, *Gleanings from the Writings of Bahá'u'lláh*, (Wilmette: Bahá'í Publishing Trust), 1983, p 260.
3. Bahá'u'lláh, quoted in: *Bahá'í Education* - a compilation (London: Bahá'í Publishing Trust), 1987, no 10, p 3.
4. 'Abdu'l-Bahá, quoted in: *Bahá'í Education* - a compilation (London: Bahá'í Publishing Trust), 1987, no 92, p 37.
5. Shoghi Effendi, quoted in: *Bahá'í Education* - a compilation (London: Bahá'í Publishing Trust), 1987, no 128, p 52.
6. Bahá'u'lláh, *Epistle to the Son of the Wolf* (Wilmette: Bahá'í Publishing Trust), 1976, p 26.
7. Bahá'u'lláh, quoted in: *Bahá'i Education* - a compilation (London: Bahá'í Publishing Trust), 1987, no 9, p 3.
8. 'Abdu'l-Bahá, quoted in: *Bahá'í Education* - a compilation (London: Bahá'í Publishing Trust), 1987, no 79, p 32.
9. 'Abdu'l-Bahá, *The Promulgation of Universal Peace* (Wilmette: Bahá'í Publishing Trust), 1982, p 134.
10. 'Abdu'l-Bahá, *'Abdu'l-Bahá on Divine Philosophy* (Boston: Tudor Press), 1916, pp 81-3.
11. J. Esslemont, *Bahá'u'lláh and the New Era* (London: Bahá'í Publishing Trust), 1974, p 141.
12. Universal House of Justice, *The Promise of World Peace* (Haifa: Bahá'í World Centre), 1985.
13. 'Abdu'l-Bahá, *The Promulgation of Universal Peace* (Wilmette: Bahá'í Publishing Trust), 1982, p 108.
14. ibid. p 284.
15. Riane Eisler, *The Chalice and The Blade* (New York: Harper & Row), 1988.
16. Randolph Trumbach, *The Rise of the Equalitarian Family: Androcratic Kinship and Domestic Relations* (New York: Academic Press), 1978.
17. 'Abdu'l-Bahá, *Paris Talks* (London: Bahá'í Publishing Trust), 1961, p 161.
18. 'Abdu'l-Bahá, *The Promulgation of Universal Peace* (Wilmette: Bahá'í Publishing Trust), 1982, pp 76-7.
19. ibid. p 175.
20. 'Abdu'l-Bahá, *Selections from the Writings of 'Abdu'l-Bahá* (Haifa: Bahá'í World Centre), 1978, p 302.

Gender Education in Society

Joseph Roy Sheppherd

Introduction

I would like briefly to address two interesting and interrelated elements of human society: the psychological phenomena of gender perception and the process of social education. As a Bahá'í anthropologist, I personally find that these are intrinsically interrelated in very subtle and complex ways. However, among my fellow male colleagues in the teaching profession, this subtlety and complexity seem to go unnoticed with regard to gender and education. They seem to overemphasise the one, underestimate the other and never relate the two. It is often frustrating for me to try to explain to them how I feel. In my view, our personal attitudes towards gender and our understanding of the importance of education clearly affect the propagation of the cultural values we hold and the social norms we share. This is manifestly obvious to me, but when I express this opinion, these colleagues fail to see it this way at all. They tend to take for granted the concept of social division by gender and appear to believe that male superiority is a basic natural condition. Of course, this being the last decade of the twentieth century, they would never openly admit to this, especially in the presence of females, but their behaviour still reflects an age-old underlying tacit belief in a hierarchy of gender. It seems that not all dinosaurs are extinct. The trouble, I suspect, is that they see only differences and not similarities. It is for this reason that I will not make the same mistake and focus in this paper on the physiological differences of gender. The differences are all too obvious and have become, in my opinion, quite clichéd in how they are used to justify gender rôles. I will try, instead, to look at some of the causes which have resulted in today's gender rôles.

Gender Rôles

Humans are a sexually dimorphic species with each gender having a few distinct biological functions. We must understand that the physiology of our species delineates only these biological functions and nothing else. Gender rôles, like all social rôles, are the creations of human culture and are non-biological in origin. What we often forget is that social rôles require a reciprocal human counterpart, for example, the rôle of a daughter or son indicates the existence of a parent, the rôle of a student implies a corresponding teacher. This reciprocity usually denotes two different levels of social hierarchical status. This is why the concept of gender rôles is so misleading; it presupposes a hierarchical status and places women below men.

If the rôle of the daughter or son is obedience towards the parent and the student's rôle is acceptance of the teacher's instruction, then a rôle of deference is inferred upon women towards men. The result is a non-egalitarian relationship between the two genders. We have used the excuse of our sexual dimorphism to justify the social rôles we have evolved. *Men are bigger and stronger*, I hear people say, *Women are weak and helpless. It is natural for men to dominate and control society*. We must recognise that it is our belief in the significance of these physiological differences and not the differences themselves that has led us to the gender rôles we have today. It is not the individual's ability which determines the rôle, but society's collective cultural sense of propriety. The continued imposition of these rôles has become a deep-rooted social habit and now forms the basis of our perception and appraisal of gender. It has become an erroneous social feedback system, a circle of false legitimisation. With great determination and effort, however, this condition is reversible, but first we must understand how it is habituated.

Within society, most of the psychological perceptions and attitudes we hold are perpetuated by a universal process of cultural development. This is basic anthropology. Our most fundamental conceptional beliefs, our social values and behaviourial norms are actually transmitted from generation to generation in a very specific way. Firstly, all of these are learned by the individual members of a society. No one is born with beliefs, values or norms; they are all learned. From the earliest years, they are learned in formal and informal settings from the words and actions of our parents, older siblings, relatives, playmates and teachers. As the individual grows older, they are shared with peer group and reinforced through interaction with fellow members of the same society. In a word, societal peer pressure. The sharing of the same beliefs, values and norms is important to the functioning of a society. They are what make it work. Finally, they are subtly transformed and modified by the individual before they are transmitted again on to the next generation. Each of these four elements of cultural development - learning, sharing, transformation, and transmission - is vital to the perpetuation of gender rôles. They are also vital to the mechanism of change, because no social change endures unless it comes from within this process. If this process of cultural development is consciously understood by people like us who want change, then it can be employed as the best means of correcting some of the misconceptions we have acquired about gender. It is perhaps the only way to dismantle gender rôles because it can change gender attitudes.

Gender Attitudes

Gender attitudes lie at the root of our gender rôles. They stem from the subtle beliefs we have about *appropriateness* and *propriety* and together with our emerging system of beliefs concerning *possibility*, they form our gender expectations about what should be done by whom and therefore what can be done by whom. Gender attitudes are for the most part socially invisible. They exist as feelings and unless they are manifested in social behaviour among one's peers, remain unseen. They also remain unheard as mute emotions because young people are usually not articulate enough to describe them to themselves or others. In the subconscious mind, they remain vague, fuzzy-around-the-edges kinds of feelings of rightness and wrongness with regards to gender. It isn't until they are verbalised by parents and other authority figures that they become values for the young individual. This articulation solidifies beliefs into values. Unfortunately, as teachers and parents, we sometimes resort to prescription rather than description of gender rôles. We didactically prescribe rôles we feel are appropriate, instead of describing rôles objectively and thereby empowering the child to see what is really happening socially. We transmit our own gender attitudes to children who can do nothing but learn them. Unlike beliefs, values are not private and personal. They soon become seen socially in the form of behaviour. Behaviour is socially moulded, through positive and negative social sanctions, and with it the values, until they are aligned with the approved norms of behaviour. These norms of behaviour are what we share within our society. They are our culture.

But we can change our culture; transformation is part of the process. Historically, however, the one mistake most unsuccessful social reformers have made is attacking the norms of behaviour within society while not adequately addressing the underlying beliefs or values of those they wish to change. In some respects, the advocates of gender equality have followed the same tactics. They have seen sexist behaviour and tried to eliminate it because it was visible. Perhaps this is why there has been such slow progress towards gender equality. As teachers and educators, we are the best-placed social reformers. We should understand that it is the unseen gender attitudes that are the real culprits, and if we are not to make the same mistakes as past reformers, then the first place to look for these is within ourselves. It is important to understand that sexism is ingrained within all of us. It is not a natural condition but a learned one, and we have all learned it. No one is immune. To be part of the solution instead of part of the problem, we must understand that the delimiting disposition of our own expectations concerning gender will be passed on and continue to cause a strange kind of visual agnosia which blinds the mind to real potential, unless we consciously do something about it. This is where the transformational element of the process of cultural development comes to our rescue. An individual's transformation of the culture is a integral part of this anthropological process. It is ultimately individuals who weigh the appropriateness of what they have learned and shared within the society and who then decide what they will transmit on to the next generation in the form of words and deeds.

The formal structure of the classroom and the informal setting of the home are both necessary for education towards new gender attitudes. They are both essential to the dynamics of cultural propagation, in which beliefs, values and norms are consciously transmitted from generation to generation, from teacher to student, from parent to progeny. We must strive to provide the kinds of social surroundings which are conducive to acquiring new gender attitudes so that the children can learn new values and then share them with their peers in the form of new norms of behaviour. It is in this way that gender rôles will eventually disappear. But before we can begin the process of cultural transformation we must first weigh the appropriateness of what we have. How can we know what we want until we know what we've got?

Gender Prejudice

One of the things we've got is a strange toleration of sexism. I find that most people speak about sexism in a disturbingly dismissive way. To me, sexism is nothing less than gender prejudice. People seem to use the word sexism quite causally without really thinking about what it means. If they were to compare sexism to racism then perhaps they could see just how bad it is. As forms of prejudice, sexism and racism have a lot in common: sexism is based upon the same types of supposition, presumption and ignorance which mark racism; racist behaviour can be identified by acts of social elitism and segregation, as can sexism; and both sexism and racism continue to exist only because people tacitly countenance them. It is important to recognise, dispassionately, that in social terms, machismo and feminism are both forms of sexism. The kind of feminism I am referring to is that which divides and separates women from men. It is ironic that in an effort to combat macho attitudes they have simply created another strain of gender prejudice. Feminism is the result of women's understandable impatience with men. It is hard to come to terms with the knowledge that change takes generations to be successful. I can relate to these feelings but in its impatience, radical feminism has marginalised women to the point that they are sometimes treated by men like a different species. They have become so unrecognisable to some males that they have come to view the other gender as alien to their own. This is perhaps why these men have become dismissive of their own sexism. Strangely, these people can somehow dismiss being accused of sexism but could not tolerate being called a *racist* or a *bigot*. To them, these are ugly words, while *sexist* still lacks the social condemnation of *racist*. The basis of racist attitudes is something anthropologists call *ethnocentricism*. It is the inability to perceive anyone else's culture but one's own. If members of one racial society see something they don't understand in another race, they will try to explain it in terms of their own culture, missing completely the complex structure of the other. Perhaps there is a kind of *gendrocentricism* which is at the root of sexism. Perhaps people with sexist attitudes are actually unable to perceive the social dynamics of the other gender.

Gender Equality

Our personal perception of equality is not unlike our discernment of love; if we cannot readily see any social evidence of it around us, then we don't feel we have any. Gender equality is no different. Unfortunately, its absence is more obvious than its presence. In fact, all we have is absence. We have no clear social example of what equality really looks like. All we have is an abstract concept in the form of an ideal. Gender equality is something we have certainly never had, so perhaps our expectations need to be re-examined philosophically before we can begin to know where to look socially for an example. From talking to people, so far as I can tell, there are at least three philosophical kinds of gender equality: absolute, subjective and relative. It is strange to note that when most people speak fervently of the equality of the sexes, it is in absolute terms. Their sentences are loaded with emotive superlatives and moral imperatives. Socially, however, absolute gender equality is very unrealistic. In society, there is no absolute anything. It is an idealised condition which employs metaphors and similes to describe itself. In the end, it is still defined in abstract terms. Abstractions are of human intellectual origin and I am not sure that this kind of equality can exist outside the human mind in the current social world. The second kind of gender equality is subjective, in which people compare their own personal condition with what they perceive as more beneficial circumstances. The trouble is that equality is a condition we desire only with our superiors. No one attributes inferiors with an enviable situation and seeks equality with them. This is perhaps why the struggle for equal rights and privileges is usually a struggle by women to become equal to men, rather than the other way around. The third type of gender equality is relative. It is relative both historically and culturally and recognises that what was perceived as socially appropriate in the past and what is presently viewed as culturally correct elsewhere in the world is relative to the social needs of the people at that time and in that place, and not seen as right or wrong in absolute terms. To me, this is the most realistic and insightful of the three, because it describes the real world and lends itself to the process of change and sustained progress. With this kind of philosophical outlook, which takes into consideration the passage of time and the social diversity in the world today, we are able to examine what we have socially with what we used to have, and not resort to seeing equality as a goal or an end, but as the means to something more subtle and complex and perhaps even greater. It allows us to regard gender equality as a process rather than a product. It gives gender education a rôle in our society.

Gender Education

At last, we come to the subject of this paper: gender education in society. As an anthropologist, I have tried to examine what I see as some of the important issues which underlie gender perception in the world today. As a Bahá'í, I would now like to address the rôle education has in changing these perceptions. 'Abdu'l-Bahá puts the relationship between these two into perspective: "In the world of humanity... the female sex is treated as though inferior, and is not allowed equal rights and privileges. This condition is not due to nature, but to education. In the Divine Creation there is no such distinction. Neither sex is superior to the other in the sight of God."[1] And again He writes: "Daughters and sons must follow the same curriculum of study, thereby promoting unity of the sexes. When all mankind shall receive the same opportunity of education and the equality of men and women be realised, the foundations of war will be utterly destroyed. Without equality this will be impossible because all differences and distinctions are conducive to discord and strife."[2]

In these two passages, 'Abdu'l-Bahá states three important facts: gender inequality is the result of miseducation rather than nature, there is no gender superiority or hierarchy in the sight of God, and the gender attitudes which have led to what we call sexism are one of the foundations of war.

Education is a major element of culture, and the social expectations and behaviour of a people are culturally transmitted both formally as a result of schools and informally as child rearing. To give an example of how this can affect gender education, I would like to use a closely-related analogy. Sex education and gender education are quite different, but historically they have a lot in common. For a long period of time sex education was seen as inappropriate for the classroom and was omitted from the curriculum of schools. It was left to the parents to educate their children, or not, about sex. The result was that peers and older children did most of the educating. Subsequently, enormous misconceptions were transmitted from generation to generation and sexual ignorance was perpetuated until sex education was legitimised and formally introduced into the school and home. I fear that it is the same with gender education. If not addressed formally and accurately by teachers and parents, it will be learned wrongly from uninformed sources. Gender education cannot be left to chance. We have a great responsibility. Teachers and parents not only teach children but also the next generation of teachers and parents which the children grow up to be.

In conclusion, I would like to offer a few observations and suggestions towards a more appropriate form of gender education in society:

1. We must understand that, clearly, it is the quality of both parental and academic education that is to blame for the gender attitudes we hold. Children mirror the social values of their elders. Particularly at fault is religious education. It, more than anything else, has failed successfully to communicate the reality that to God there is no distinction of gender.

2. We must understand that our present beliefs about gender are a learning deficiency, a perceptional handicap to social potential.

3. We must strive to equip our minds with new belief patterns so that we can cease teaching children that there is a particular way in which each gender thinks. It is still quite common to hear people say that women think differently and feel differently to men.

4. We must always remember that we are not so far removed from those we criticise.

5. We must avoid statements which generalise. Statements which begin with *Women are naturally...* or *Men are usually...* are fraught with the same error as pervades all stereotypes. Qualities like intuition, caring and loving-kindness are not the sole domain or even the propensity of women, just as courage, strength and wisdom are not the penchants of men. We must defemininise and demasculinise the qualities of human character.

6. We must understand the power of words and delete references to the other gender such as *the opposite sex* from our speech and writing. Conceptually, this is very detrimental to gender attitudes. If a man sees himself as having certain qualities, the use of this phrase implies by opposition that a woman does not. Even the use of phrases like *women are different from men* is loaded with psychological implications. This phrase is tautologically redundant; it is obvious that there are two different genders. Whenever the obvious is stated then nuance or innuendo is implied. Aside from the biological distinctions, the person assumes there are also tacit social and psychological differences.

It is important to remember that the syntax we use in everyday language reinforces unacceptable gender attitudes. Linguistically we are forced to mark gender in the words *she* and *he*. What we need is a singular non-gender-specific pronoun for humans. The genderless pronoun *it* is conceptionally unacceptable because there is the social need to differentiate between gender and the inanimate. It is interesting to note that the words *they* and *their* are fast becoming used as singular relative pronouns in vernacular English when they follow a singular non-gender-marked noun. Conceivably, it is possible that people are making an unconscious effort to accommodate this need to degenderise speech.

8. It is an unfortunate quirk of the English language that sex and gender share the same word. We should remember that when we are distinguishing between females and males we should use the word *gender*, and leave *sex* to refer only to sexual intercourse.

9. We must understand the nature of the inherent reciprocity within the concept of rôles and be able to communicate how conceptionally inappropriate it is to think in terms of rôles when it comes to gender. The elimination of gender rôles requires a conscious reshaping of our gender attitudes.

10. We should teach ourselves and then our students that if a social value is found wanting, it should be discarded. Common use is not a valid reason for continued use. Some values are no longer appropriate because the social context has changed, and therefore need to be replaced.

11. It is socially beneficial for children to be instructed formally and informally by both women and men at every stage of their lives. Both parents should share equally in the rearing of children from their earliest days. This should not be restricted to the structure of the nuclear family so prevalent in the Western nations either. All the members of the socially extended family should participate in the moral and social education of the child. Teachers are a part of this extended family. The provisions in the *Kitab-i-Aqdas* for teachers as among the legitimate inheritors of intestate property support this view.

12. We must stop treating sexism as a woman's problem. It is the responsibility of everyone to end gender prejudice. It would be particularly effective if men monitored the social behaviour of their male colleagues and friends and actively endeavoured to educate men so that they could learn new gender attitudes.

13. Perhaps it is time for a compilation of Bahá'í Writings on men and a few conferences for them.

14. Eventually, we must see beyond the present social need to champion the cause of the equal rights of women and feminism, and begin to champion the equal rights of all humans. We should seek equality, justice and truth, regardless of gender.

15. We must stop assuming that social behaviour is natural and decline the use of such phrases as *human nature*. In fact, we must come to understand that ascribing anything to *nature* is tenuous. The perception of nature is a human intellectual artefact.

16. Finally, we must create a new body of literature which is not laden with erroneous social assertions which subtly engender the kinds of gender prejudice which the following examples do: "Time and circumstance, which enlarge the views of most men, narrow the views of women almost invariably." (Thomas Hardy) "We should regard loveliness as the attribute of woman, and dignity as the attribute of man." (Cicero) "Women submits to her fate; man makes his." (Emile Gabouriau) "Man's conclusions are reached by toil. Woman arrives at the same by sympathy." (Ralph Waldo Emerson)

References

1. 'Abdu'l-Bahá, *Paris Talks* (London: Bahá'í Publishing Trust), 1971, p 161.
2. 'Abdu'l-Bahá, *Promulgation of Universal Peace* (Wilmette: Bahá'í Publishing Trust), 1982, p 175.

The Importance of the Arts in the Future Development of the Bahá'í Community

Gordon James Kerr

Introduction

This paper seeks to emphasise the great importance given to the arts in the Bahá'í Writings. It argues that art should be an integral aspect of our approach to Bahá'í education and development. It briefly examines how the arts are related to the growth of individual character and the fulfilment of human potential and argues that arts can and should play a central role in the life of the Bahá'í community.

Whereas the time is not yet ripe nor the Bahá'í community sufficiently diverse or mature to propose the development of a new aesthetic based on the Bahá'í teachings, the relationship of the arts to our search for truth and meaning is a topic worthy of exploration by Bahá'ís. This paper seeks to encourage questions about our understanding of different dimensions of religious experience such as love, joy, vision, meditation, devotion, praise and celebration. Other topics raised include the healing powers of the arts, their contribution to a better balance of the individual psyche and their constructive role in the generation of human happiness. Finally the universality and democracy of the arts are examined in the light of goals to expand and develop the Bahá'í community.

> *Every word that proceedeth out of the mouth of God is endowed with such potency as can instil new life into every human frame, if ye be of them that comprehend this truth. All the wondrous works ye behold in this world have been manifested through the operation of His supreme and most exalted Will, His wondrous and inflexible Purpose. Through the mere revelation of the word "Fashioner", issuing forth from His lips and proclaiming His attribute to mankind, such power is released as can generate, through successive ages, all the manifold arts which the hands of man can produce. This, verily, is a certain truth. No sooner is this resplendent word uttered, than its animating energies, stirring within all created things, give birth to the means and instruments whereby such arts can be produced and perfected. All the wondrous achievements ye now witness are the direct consequences of the Revelation of this Name. In the days to come, ye will, verily, behold things of which ye have never heard before.*[1]

It is interesting to note that, in a subsequent paragraph, Bahá'u'lláh goes on to describe that *in like manner* His revelation has a similar influence on the various branches of science. The significance of this point is that whereas the above quoted paragraph refers specifically to the *arts*, it is almost always used by Bahá'ís when referring to the importance of science. This error suggests a predisposition among Bahá'ís towards the importance of science. This may, in some situations, lead to a prejudiced view of the arts, or at least a failure to appreciate the vital role the arts can play in the healthy development of the Bahá'í community.

Such attitudes, fairly common within western Bahá'í communities in my experience, are often indicated by the bias towards hard science and mathematical subjects in the selection of university courses and careers by young Bahá'ís, especially those from a Persian background, and by a corresponding suspicion of the arts in general. Observers have also noted the lack of respect or appreciation sometimes shown to Bahá'í artists and musicians performing at Bahá'í conferences and gatherings - behaviour which in polite society could only be described as rude.

The challenging task of learning about and building up the institutions of Bahá'í administration can also, if we are not careful, lead to bureaucratic and mainly cerebral forms of communication within the Bahá'í community, which, sapped of spirit, lacks the imagination required for artistic expression. Such prevailing attitudes and mindsets do great harm to the Cause, and so I would suggest we should all seek a more sympathetic understanding of the importance of the arts. This will in turn help achieve a better balance in almost every sphere of Bahá'í life and greatly enrich and deepen our experience of religious faith.

The Importance of the Arts within the Bahá'í Community

In *God Passes By* Shoghi Effendi describes how the formative age of the Faith, which began with the passing of 'Abdu'l-Bahá in 1921, will be characterised by "the crystallisation and shaping of the creative energies released by the Bahá'í revelation".[2] It is our privilege as Bahá'ís to contribute to this revolutionary process and to witness the hand of God at work. With each new development and achievement of the Cause our vision is expanded and our faith challenges us to grow in new ways and in new directions. I believe that one of the most important of these challenges is to bring about a fundamental improvement in the quality of our cultural and religious experience as Bahá'ís. Furthermore, I believe personally, that if *we* are not happy being Bahá'ís - who wants to be one? A greater, general awareness within the Bahá'í community, of the importance of the arts in releasing and channelling the creative energies released by Bahá'u'lláh is therefore, in my view, long overdue.

What do we mean by the arts? Shoghi Effendi explains that there is no such thing as Bahá'í art. Bahá'í art can emerge only as a natural expression of a Bahá'í-inspired civilisation - that is, for a future golden age. Many would agree that there is a growing need for art related to the aims and character of the Faith. For example in 1985, the House of Justice called upon all National Spiritual Assemblies to encourage Bahá'í musicians and artists to give expression through the various arts to important themes related to world peace.

In recent years we have seen the encouraging growth of new associations of Bahá'í artists, and art- and music-based festivals sponsored or run by Bahá'ís in many countries. In the U.K., for example, the Bahá'í Association for the Arts (BAFTA) has begun to have a discernable impact on the life of the community. The exhibition of work by young Bahá'í painters it mounted at a recent National Teaching Conference was impressive. The European Association holds an increasing number of seminars, exhibitions and summer schools creating new networks for support and dialogue between Bahá'í artists working in many media. In North America, special conferences, festivals and newsletters on the themes of art are growing in popularity amongst Bahá'ís. *The Arts for Nature* project, sponsored by the Bahá'ís in the UK together with WWF, was a wonderful example of how a handful of individuals can act as a catalyst for much larger social action.

All over the world the desire of Bahá'ís to communicate at deeper levels can be seen. Only this week I came across a publication from a group of Bahá'ís in Chile - *Oasis*. It's small, homespun but lively. A green, life-giving patch in the desert, full of poetry, short stories and drawings.

Perceptions of Art

Such developments offer hope that the arts are becoming increasingly legitimised within the wider Bahá'í community. Art may have entered the collective Bahá'í psyche, however, only as an advance guard - the battle has not yet been won. In the minds of many, the arts are still mentally compartmentalised as a mere product or device, used to beef up our diet of, sometimes ill-conceived, proclamation and teaching events and even our flagship *educational* programmes - a bolt-on extra.

This attitude sees art simplistically as *entertainment, decor* or even worse as *advertising*. Such dominant attitudes can debase our perception of art and even, dare I say it, lead to its prostitution within the Bahá'í community - something which, as we all know, is forbidden in the Bahá'í teachings. The concept of art as *worship*, repeated and emphasised throughout the Bahá'í Writings, suggests that art is perhaps our most creative response to God and His manifestation. It is, however, as with so many of our Bahá'í teachings, something we may have conceptualised and accepted in principle, but so far been unable to understand.

We are all artists in some way or another, or perhaps it is best to say we are all, by virtue of being Bahá'ís, *potential* artists, in that we have become animated with the spirit of the age. Art in this sense is not just some *other* thing we have to add to the agenda of our busy lives, but something which will give us life, new ways of realising our goals and ambitions, of fulfilling our purpose. The arts have the capacity to change the way we think, feel and act towards one another and the worlds we inhabit. Through art we gain a knowledge of ourselves and of life. Through art we come to know God and the beauty, power, majesty and mystery of His creation. Art in this sense helps fulfill the purpose of Bahá'í education which is to unite souls with their creator. Its central importance should, in my view, become one of the distinctive aspects of Bahá'í education and provide an essential balance to the use of scientific and conceptually based methods of learning. Bahá'u'lláh commands us to use all our faculties and instincts in our search for truth and spiritual knowledge. Art can help us develop these.

The Release of Individual Potential

Through art individuals experience communion with their own being in a much fuller sense emotionally, physically, psychically and spiritually than by thought alone. Art can also help each of us to experience communion with external forces and forms of nature, the elements, the heavens and the earth itself and all its creatures. Each such point of contact with the universe comes with its own message and each represents a unique pathway to God and a form of cosmic union. Art seeks to capture or reflect such points of light and show the way to others.

> *...whatever is in the heavens and whatever is on the earth is a direct evidence of the revelation within it of the attributes and names of God, inasmuch as within every atom are enshrined the signs that bear eloquent testimony to the revelation of that most great Light.*[3]

This mystical dimension of religious experience may be hard for those of us born and bred into modern secular culture, but it is something we need to strive to understand and build into our lives. Without this dimension our faith becomes vulnerable to secular influences and is thereby robbed of its power to heal and transform. There are several who would argue, myself among them, that one of the reasons the Faith has not advanced much in the West in recent decades is because the Bahá'í community has fallen prey to the vulture of secularisation. Art can help us restore the balance. It is an accessible language many of us already understand, a lifeline to the soul which can lead us heavenwards.

There are an infinite number of practical examples of how art can release human potential by engaging the full range of human emotions and sensibilities, thereby demonstrating its capacity to touch all parts of the human psyche. In particular, through the language and practice of art we can bridge the gap between mind and heart. One of the distinctive aspects of Bahá'í education is that it is primarily concerned with the education of the human heart. It has been my experience that our *heart needs art*.

The Power of Imagination

'Abdu'l-Bahá explains that imagination is one of the five inner powers of the human mind, along with comprehension, memory, etc. He describes the mind as the root and the imagination as the branch which bears the fruit of our action and achievement in the world. The distinctive contribution of art to the development of the human soul is that it can feed and inspire our imagination. Art helps us to develop images rather than concepts, which are more the province of reasoning and science. Such images are vital in modelling and managing the process of transformation which is the purpose of Bahá'u'lláh's revelation.

In formal education it is recognised that a period of instruction is necessary before a proper partnership in education between pupil and teacher can be established. Art, I believe, can be a continuous learning process which is not subject to this paradigm shift. It can continue, quite literally, from birth to death and beyond. Some two hundred years after Mozart's death, millions are still moved by his spiritual art. We know that, even before birth, such music has a beneficial effect on the unborn child.

Some of the most memorable and joyful experiences of my life have been working with the severely handicapped and disabled as a counsellor in drama therapy. This involved the use of music, dance, painting and plastic arts and sometimes just pure imagination. No matter how uncoordinated, how messy, how ridiculous we may have appeared to others, those explorations of the world through the medium of the arts revealed, to me personally, the true beauty of the Friend in so many shining faces. So much beauty, so much joy, so much fun, so much learning, so much true education, so much unity. I yearn for such unity with my fellow Bahá'ís.

> *From the exalted source, and out of the essence of His favour and bounty He hath entrusted every created thing with a sign of His knowledge, so that none of His creatures may be deprived of its share in expressing, each according to its capacity and rank, this knowledge. This sign is the mirror of His beauty in the world of creation.*[4]

The great lesson of these experiences for me was to realise the spiritual power of imagination. As a Bahá'í I had been trained to ward off *vain imaginings and idle fancies* and my interest in experimental theatre as a young Bahá'í, if not actively discouraged, was of no interest to my fellow Bahá'ís. I think the mood has changed. Bahá'ís collectively are beginning to realise that we need artists, poets, musicians and actors as much as we do engineers, doctors and teachers. Engineers of the imagination, doctors of the soul and teachers of the heart are, I would suggest, at this stage in the demise of Western society at least, even more important.

Healing Powers of Art

In illness and sickness too, art can be a powerful and sometimes almost the only available tool for the educator and healer. In working with children suffering from autism and post traumatic stress disorders, music, light, dance, sculpture and painting have proved again and again the gateway to communication, contact and learning. The arts thus act as a starting point for conscious expression drawing deeply on the subconscious mind and releasing powerful life forces. In severe cases of psychiatric disorder, art has proved a bridge between heaven and hell, releasing individuals from states of mental and emotional agony.

Music, dance, performance and plastic arts of all descriptions can also aid recovery in physical ailments. The therapeutic influence of art is well documented and constitutes a major element of many treatments, especially within the field of holistic medicine. 'Abdu'l-Bahá in writing to a doctor about the importance of the spiritual aspects of healing said;

> *Matters related to man's spirit have a great effect on his bodily condition. For instance, thou shouldst impart gladness to thy patient, give him comfort and joy and bring him to ecstasy and exaltation. How often hath it occurred that this hath caused early recovery.*[5]

I once worked in a mental hospital. The medicine which everyone agreed had most effect on the patients were the Laurel and Hardy movies. Comedy can be an art too. Laughing is good for you.

The Real Experience

One of the goals of religious education is to communicate the meaning of faith to others. Art can deepen our own religious experience and help to communicate an understanding of faith to those who do not share it.

When we think of our own childhood, we may remember some of the ideas and information forced on us by our teachers and parents but we remember our experiences better. Primary and infant teachers are well aware of the need for learning to be exploratory and fun for children, encouraging personal investigation and discovery. Their sense of wonderment, curiosity, listening, looking, adventure, questioning, their love of action, rhythm, surprise, colour, fellowship and song, are all sensibilities which are bred out of us in our fast paced and oh, so serious secular culture.

Some American lifestyle magazines for the sophisticated have suggested, that we parents, should find ten minutes every day to *be real* with our children. Quality time - time to be real! What are we supposed to be the rest of the time? Why do we forget this so easily as we grow, why do we put on the cerebral straightjacket so easily and so limit the potential and hold back the education of our children and ourselves? Do we not learn from their discoveries? If not, we should, for they inhabit different worlds to our own - worlds which our souls long for but which many of us as adults have forgotten. 'Abdu'l-Bahá emphasises the value of such experiences in the education of our soul. He explains how one of the significant memories of His own childhood was seeing a play about the martyrdom of the Imam Husayn. He was so moved that it had a profound impact on Him for the rest of His life. Rôle play will always be more important for the character training of our children than the speed at which we hurl information, commands and appeals at them. Perhaps, dare I say it, the same is true for adults.

The experiences of art helps our cultivation of spiritual powers expressed as Love, Joy, Vision, Meditation, Devotion, Praise and Celebration. This can have profound effects on the quality of our devotional experience as Bahá'ís. Chanting, singing and the use of music and art can revolutionise the personal and collective worship practised by western Bahá'ís. The sacred and cultural traditions of the West are as important as those of other parts of the world. Such cultural streams of expression are an important part of our individual and collective psyche and a source of transformation and power. We must learn to draw on them fearlessly when we proclaim and glorify the name of our Lord. We know 'Abdu'l-Bahá has said that the stage is the pulpit of the future, and that music is a ladder for the soul. Through communion with Bahá'u'lláh, we are promised that the pictures of the supreme world will appear before our eyes. Now that God has revealed himself to the world in the realm of the spirit, our task is to aquire His attributes and to manifest them in the world. This is what building the Kingdom of God means.

A Unifying Principle

The increased use and exploration of the arts can, I think, help to legitimise a much greater diversity of individual experience and cultural behaviour than up till now has been permitted within the Bahá'í community. We believe in the value of diversity, are sub-consciously hungry for it, but are still afraid of it.

Apart from deepening our own sense of ourselves as spiritual beings and offering every soul its own unique language of expression, the arts offer an infinite range of possibilities for communication between souls. Bahá'ís are committed to the principle of a universal second language. In reviewing the work of Yunus Emre, one of the greatest Turkish poets, Pope John XXIII made the following comment

"Isn't it wonderful that when sincere, all works of art praise God in the same language?"

Learning the language of art serves to increase our sensibilities towards all things spiritual, if, as the Pope says, we are sincere. Proficiency in any art requires discipline and effort. It can also improve our response to spiritual education, if our heart is open to it. 'Abdu'l-Bahá says:

> *I rejoice to hear that thou takest pains with thine art, for in this wonderful new age, art is worship. The more thou strivest to perfect it, the closer wilt thou come to God... What bestowal could be greater than this.*[6]

Consider those words *takest pains...* absorbing hurt, sacrificing for the sake of harmony, beauty, balance and perfection. How different to the pleasure seeking, pain-avoiding indulgence of modern life. Artists by nature are no more moral than the rest of us, sometimes less so, although ironically, they often claim the high ground in matters of truth. In these days of moral relativism, an artist may disassociate himself from his art, in the same way that politicians, corrupt in their private lives, claim a public image without blemish. Double standards are often the product of our western dualism, which separates man from God and nature and consequently, from his fellow man. There is no hiding place even for the Bahá'í artist; we shall all be known by our doings and only God knows our intentions.

Art can aid us to explore meaning and experience, both good and bad. We have mentioned art in healing therapy, it can also be cathartic...it can also be agonising and extremely painful. Art can be light but also fire. Through the domain of art we may find the true testing ground of our soul. A famous writer once said "Only the sincere know the tyranny of a blank sheet of paper!"

Universality and Democracy of the Arts

It is possible to find the art of others painful too, as anyone who has heard me sing will realise. However the beast of prejudice also hides under the mask of *good taste* and comes in many guises. Our attitude towards culturally defined notions of art may be a measure of our real acceptance of diversity. We may welcome all with the light of oneness, but if we then snub or conspicuously suffer the art of our fellows, because it does not conform to our personal taste, then our fellowship is only skin deep. Is this acceptable in the eyes of our Lord? 'Abdu'l-Bahá does point out that music pleasant to some may be offensive to others. It is an interesting point to ponder. Does this mean that we are doomed to *safe art*, e.g. middle of the road popular culture? Serious artists, by definition, often live on the edge of society and question its norms and values. Are Bahá'ís of artistic temperament also to be consigned to the periphery? What will be their role within the Bahá'í community?

Personally, I find the preponderance of *talkers*, *chest beaters* and *bureaucrats* in key Bahá'í positions more of a problem than too much offensive music. I would suggest that we need diversity of temperament and character on our Bahá'í insitutions as much as ethnic mix. Where are all you silent, intuitive types? We need you. Pick up the torch.

Art can be a key to universal participation and can promote equality of access to meaning and experience among members of the community. There are different levels of unity. As Bahá'ís we may be united at the ideational level, i.e. through shared ideas and beliefs and we can also be united spiritually and administratively through the power of the Covenant. There are however, many divisions in the Bahá'í community, and there always will be. Unity is our struggle and it is our task to learn the processes that build unity. In some cases the unity we share is superficial, we may co-exist but we do not really know each other or understand each other. Our life experiences have not equipped us with the tools we need to communicate with other people perhaps vastly different to ourselves. Art can help us out of this dilemma and empower us to communicate with each other on many levels.

Through art we can share vision and excitement about the future. In our conferences and gatherings through music, song, drama and participative forms of learning we can discover the power of unity. Through physical movement, as in dance or games, touching, watching, listening, visualising, sharing, relaxing and laughing can all contribute to a positive experience of unity and community. Through the imaginative and creative presentation of the Sacred Words, stories and teachings of our Faith, our eyes and hearts may be opened to truth in new ways. The western Bahá'í rejection of *churchianity* tempts one to be something of an iconoclast and to reject symbolism of any sort, but symbolic supports are important for every identity including a Bahá'í identity. We can and will create our own symbols, reference points and shared values as we develop the distinctive pattern of Bahá'í life around the world.

Every one of us has an individual psyche rooted in cultural experience. A large part of our personality, our identity, and our creative and spiritual power is derived from that experience. If we deny that experience when we become Bahá'ís, we may throw the baby out with the bathwater. Leave our old world prejudices behind by all means, and cast off the scales from our eyes, but do not lose our soul in the process. In embracing our new rôle as Bahá'ís we run the risk of losing touch with those very forces and instincts that may have led us to the recognition of the Blessed Beauty in the first place. We may become lesser forms of our selves, reminiscing of good times past, and secretly find ourselves rootless and unhappy in our new identity, robbed of our power to transform and heal. We may even forget the language of our heart, which often speaks best without words, expression through art, music, tradition and symbol perhaps. Then we wonder how we fail in our teaching. Teaching is all about expressing to another what is in our heart. We need to speak the language.

Traditional European concepts of *religious art* may be outmoded and innappropriate in a new religious era but I believe as Bahá'ís we could promote the concept and practice of sacred art. Current interests in world art, and the cultural pluralism of contemporary folk art in many forms, perhaps reflect the spirit of the age more than we Bahá'ís realise. We are in danger of ignoring powerful media through which the wonderful healing message of Bahá'u'lláh can be shared. A change in awareness and direction in favour of the arts may have great effects on the expansion and development of the Bahá'í community. It might be fun too! In the words of 'Abdu'l-Bahá:

> *In this great dispensation, art is identical with an act of worship and this is a clear text of the Blessed Perfection. Therefore, extreme effort should be made in art and this will not prevent the teaching of the people in that region. Nay, rather, each should assist the other in art and guidance. For instance, when the studying of art is with the intention of obeying the command of God this study will certainly be done easily and great progress will soon be made therein...*[7]

A Poetic Tradition

One of the artistic traditions which surely has a strong cultural presence in the Faith is poetry. As Professor Bushrui so often reminds us, we are told in the Bahá'í Writings that in rank, after the prophets come the poets. Both the prophets and the poets are engineers of the imagination. Both promote the virtues of the spirit and speak the language of the soul. Poetry gives ideals rather than ideas, it prompts and gives voice to the deepest longings and highest hopes of our inner being. Even the Manifestation of God speaks the language of the poet. Our physical, emotional sensibilities are awakened through the powerful word images of the poet linking the material to the spiritual realm. Thus even within the literary traditions of the Faith itself we may learn the lessons of art and using all our instincts and capacities seek out the truth as our Lord commands.

I leave you with my own modest attempt to express my feelings rather than ideas as a homage to the arts entitled *The Beauty of the Friend*.

The Beauty of the Friend

Did you know we are all musicians,
Can you hear the Divine melody?
Pick up your flute or drum and join the symphony.

You and I are also dancers, moving in harmony.
Together His steps we must follow,
for Lord of the Dance is He.

He has made us players not puppets,
in the Drama of the Kingdom.
Have you taken your place on the stage,
or do you still wait in the wings?
The Fashioner has created a New Race of Men,
Have you become fashionable,
or do you still wear your old clothes?

From water and clay we are moulded,
our image is painted with light.
Can you feel the breath of His Spirit,
Are you held by His fingers of might?

God has once more in this Age,
revealed the Beauty of the Friend.
Can you see His beauty,
Do you have a true artist's eye?
Look into the eyes of your neighbour,
for the face of the Friend is there,
O such Beauty, Blessed Beauty,
Can you see Him in the mirror of your mind?

References

1. Bahá'u'lláh, *Gleanings from the Writings of Bahá'u'lláh* (London: Bahá'í Publishing Trust), 1976, pp 141-2.
2. Shoghi Effendi, *Messages to America* (Wilmette: Bahá'í Publishing Trust), 1947, p 52.
3. Bahá'u'lláh, *Kitáb-i-Íqán (The Book of Certitude)* (Wilmette: Bahá'í Publishing Trust), 1974, p 100.
4. Bahá'u'lláh, *Gleanings from the Writings of Bahá'u'lláh* (London: Bahá'í Publishing Trust), 1985, p262.
5. 'Abdu'l-Bahá, *Selections from the Writings of 'Abdu'l-Bahá* (Haifa: Bahá'í World Centre), 1978, pp 150-1.
6. 'Abdu'l-Bahá, *Bahá'í Writings on Music* - a compilation (London: Bahá'í Publishing Trust), ND, p 8.
7. 'Abdu'l-Bahá, quoted in: *Bahá'í World Faith* - Selected Writings of Bahá'u'lláh, 'Abdu'l-Bahá, (Wilmette: Bahá'í Publishing Trust), 1976, p 377.

Cultural Imperatives of Bahá'í Education in the UK

Stephen Vickers

I bear witness, O friends! that the favour is complete, the argument fulfilled, the proof manifest and the evidence established. Let it now be seen what your endeavours in the path of detachment will reveal.[1]

With this challenge His Holiness Bahá'u'lláh closes the Hidden Words. It is not enough for us to parrot the scriptures, but to "translate what that which hath been written into reality and action".[2] Hitherto the endeavours of the Bahá'í community have largely concentrated upon external goals: taking the Faith to more people and places, building beautiful Holy Places, and raising public consciousness of the oneness of mankind.

There are, however, other fields of endeavour which have not been given the same attention. This paper focuses on one of them. It assumes that there is an urgent need for the identification of what elements belong in a Bahá'í culture, and that our Bahá'í education system, at all levels, is the best medium to assist that culture into being.

In arguing that Bahá'í education should pay attention to culture, I am not making reference to high culture, which varies geographically. By *culture* I mean that network of ideas, sentiments and practices which binds a social group together. There is an interplay between Bahá'í culture and the culture of the outside world, and the relative attractiveness of the two will partly determine whether young people, whether or not they value truth, will espouse the Faith or not. This culture is moreover not primarily an affair of externals, or of how we behave; but of how we feel, and of the common values we espouse. It is about showing our children that the Faith of Bahá'u'lláh is the light for humanity. My references will be largely to the United Kingdom, only because that is the country of which I have the most experience, but I hope that some of my remarks may be relevant elsewhere.

This area of concern is not completely divorced from the *external goals* referred to above. Success in teaching, in PR and in the construction of Holy Places all aid the Bahá'í educator because they raise the awareness of the pupil or student that the Bahá'í Faith is significant and that God's plan really is unfolding. Indeed, the primary aim of education is to teach in the purest way, since it aims to unlock the potential of the human being by means of the word of God and of the spirit. Nevertheless, to be a Bahá'í, as a speaker remarked at the U.K. Teaching Conference in 1978, is like being a stage performer running around keeping lots of plates spinning: due attention must be paid to a large number of conceptually-distinct but, in reality, interrelated issues.[3]

Granted, as the Universal House wrote at Ridván 1990, a single person cannot do everything,[4] but that is not to say that everything does not need to be done. Teaching, for instance, is not merely a question of convincing people of the spiritual or intellectual truth of the Faith, but includes developing the Bahá'í community into an example of a world community, as proffered by the House in its 1985 Peace Initiative,[5] and encouraging oneself and others to develop innate spiritual potential. It is this which makes culture such a vital focus of attention. We cannot yet perceive precisely what Bahá'í culture, or the united world culture, will be like in the future, but we know some of their elements. The whole subject is fraught with danger. So far as possible, the Faith should be at home with every style of thought, every type of music and dance, and a wide variety of human behaviour. The core elements of a Bahá'í culture should include only those things which are essential to the teachings of Bahá'u'lláh. In every other respect, the Faith must be culture-neutral.

In struggling to proclaim what it means to be Bahá'í, and in socialising the young into a Bahá'í culture, three fields in particular challenge the educator, whether he or she be parent, teacher or friend. These fields I have called *Bahá'í attitudes to the Sacred, the sheer force of the dominant culture* and *the lack of cultural provision in the Faith*. I shall look at each of these fields in turn but will show that any apparent problem can be overcome with imagination and faith. In most cases the responses which I have given arise out of five years of experience working as a teacher at a Thomas Breakwell School, but many of the conclusions are I hope relevant to adult seekers as well as to the children of the Bahá'í community.

Bahá'í Attitudes to the Sacred

Attracting the young to the Faith, whether or not their parents are Bahá'ís, is to some extent rendered difficult because the Faith seems hard to make accessible to children and to young seekers. There are four main elements to this.

The first challenge to the teacher is that the Manifestations of God are not portrayed in pictures. This means that there can be no equivalent to Ladybird's book *Stories about Jesus the Friend*[6] entitled, for instance *My Friend Bahá'u'lláh*. The personalisation of the relationship between the believer and the Manifestation, in the attempt to offer hope to humanity, may in some Christian books go further than this (*My Mate Jesus*). The relationship with Bahá'u'lláh cannot be put over in visual terms because to the Bahá'í it is unseemly to make a visual rendition of a Manifestation of God. The relationship between the believer and the Manifestation may seem, to some seekers, an overly-lofty one.

A second challenge is that the Scriptures when translated into English do not scan, making children's songs based largely on them difficult to write or sing.

A third challenge is that the ornate language of Bahá'í Scripture in English seems to provide an increasing barrier to attraction in an age of declining functional literacy in the UK, and of the progressive establishment of basic English as a common second language across the globe. For people brought up on the King James[7] or the Revised Standard Version[8] of the Bible, the Beloved Guardian's translations of the utterances of Bahá'u'lláh are beautiful, and their language appropriately religious, but it is by no means certain that the same holds true for people reared on the *Good News Bible*[9] or *God is For Real, Man*.[10]

A fourth challenge is the variability in quality of collective worship. It is a commonplace that Bahá'í worship has no set forms. At its best this allows the Faith to flourish across the globe, with the friends contributing their own cultural forms. Bahá'í Bhajans in India,[11] and the use of Gospel music forms in South Carolina,[12] enrich the garden of God. At its worst, the absence of set forms to Bahá'í worship can result in a minimalist approach to worship, with a pride in *lack of ritual* leading to the absence of any form of worship but the spoken word. We may find it hard to bring into the Faith, in large numbers, persons reared on very active and musical forms of worship so long as we treat only the spoken word as a legitimate form of worship.

Responses

How, then, can the Bahá'í educator counter these challenges presented by Bahá'í attitudes to the sacred?

The teacher may approach the need for children to picture the central figures in two ways - either by concentrating upon the Master (vide Kalimat's excellent series),[13] or by elaborate evasion of the central figures in drama or pictures. An example of this latter approach is Jack Lenz's play *Midsummer Noon*,[14] when a succession of people recount their experience of the Báb, but the Primal Point Himself never appears.

In relation to the second area of concern, the creation of music appropriate to Bahá'í education and Bahá'í worship can be approached partly by remembering that the hymn is itself a relatively recent form of Christian worship and that anthems of scripture set to music were an acceptable form of worship for hundreds of years. Most medieval church music did not scan, but was nonetheless moving and beautiful.

A Bahá'í musician, Kathryn McGee-Nikjoo, working with a small group of children, has produced some impressive songs using Bahá'í Scripture.[15] Moreover, we do not need to be obsessed with maintaining the wording of Scripture when creating devotional songs. We can write hymns about the teachings or about the central figures. We can simplify Scripture into songs (e.g. "Look at Me, Follow

Me").[16] We can also appreciate that much of a child's learning about God consists of his/her becoming in awe of a loving Father. Many songs which we have in the past treated as specifically Christian do no more than increase our respect for God and His creation (for instance "All Things Bright and Beautiful"),[17] while others remind the child of his/her duty to humanity. There is no reason why these songs should not be used in Bahá'í worship, whether in our educational institutions or in community meetings.

The third problem raised above, the relative inaccessibility of the Writings to persons schooled in the vernacular English of the late twentieth century, needs perhaps to be sub-divided into two.

On the one hand, for some readers, whether believers or seekers, the extended sentences, long words and flowery language may be genuinely too difficult, i.e. require a higher reading quotient than the reader possesses. The solution to this is effort, both with our own children and with our new adult declarants, and an encouragement to attain high levels of literacy. We can also break the Writings up into small pieces. The Universal House of Justice, in its message of Ridván 1989,[18] stressed the need for Bahá'ís to involve themselves in teaching and facilitating literacy in order to help the friends to access the word of God. Moreover contact with the Writings can of itself motivate friends to become literate. Many of us will know Bahá'ís who were semi-literate on first contact with the Faith, and who learned to read well by struggling with their prayer books.

On the other hand, for others the flowery language, the "thees" and "thous", while easy to read, are themselves a barrier to faith. Such words do not speak initially to the hearts of such recipients, because they are unfamiliar. Moreover, one may encounter the accusation that the Blessed Beauty was trying to make something that looked scriptural, an accusation similar to that which Mark Twain levelled at the *Book of Mormon*.[19]

The Bahá'í educator will experience more trouble with the complexity of the Writings than with other challenges listed above. (S)he can explain to his or her children the meanings of scripture, but cannot create simple renditions of his/her own.
Help is at hand, however. With the active encouragement of the International Teaching Centre, Dr Jeffrey S. Grueber, Professor of Linguistics and African Languages at the University of Benin in Nigeria, has produced a glossary of terms and an explanation of principles for simplified texts.[20] It may be that this project will flourish in such a way as to help us, with due reverence, to use simplified texts as a stepping stone to the Writings in their full glory.

With regard to the fourth challenge, the variability in quality of collective worship, the downgrading of music may be a peculiarly English problem, related to the types of people attracted to the Faith earlier in this century. The quietist traditions of Quakers and Theosophists lay little emphasis on devotional music. Whatever the case, things are moving, and the important things are patience and continued hard work. An excellent Bahá'í choir now exists in the south of England, and most Bahá'í Sunday Schools now place an emphasis upon music.

Perhaps a clear, sustained and imaginative use of music, drama and dance within our education system can percolate upwards to practice in the wider communities, and lead hosts to be gradually more imaginative with worship in their Feasts.

The Sheer Force of the Dominant Culture

Challenges

The Bahá'í Faith, as the coming global religion, is only loosely rooted in any single national culture. Anyone coming to it with a baggage of national, regional, local, class and religious assumptions (i.e. everyone) will have a struggle with *some* of the teachings of the Blessed Beauty. Some aspects of teachings strain the Persian, while other aspects strain the Briton.

That being so, in any society the children and youth born into the Faith will find that the wider societal environment reinforces the dominant culture in that society more strongly than it does the Bahá'í culture. This problem is perhaps greater in the West than elsewhere because of the greater sophistication of the visual media and the relatively lower status of parents and grandparents, as compared to other cultures.

There are four elements in the dominant culture in the UK which may tend to undermine children's allegiance to the Faith. These are:

- The youth cult of freedom and unbridled consumerism.
- The xenophobic stance, often unconscious, of the media, in particular the popular press. Much of the UK media tends to report the news from a very UK-centric stance. This tendency was graphically illustrated during the Falklands War of 1982, with *The Sun's* famous headline "Gotcha" welcoming the sinking by a Royal Navy submarine of the Argentine cruiser *The General Belgrano*,[21] while many newspapers have delighted in criticism of the Delors Plan.[22]
- The dominant place in the calendar occupied by Christmas and Easter, and the ways in which their celebration is orientated towards children. Bahá'í festivals lack media and peer legitimation, and in many families neither children nor parents know how to celebrate them so as to make them moving events.
- The poor image which events in the Middle East and Islamic fundamentalism give to Islam, which makes the oneness of religion seem less acceptable.

Responses

How then can the Bahá'í educator tackle the above problems?

The youth cult of freedom and unbridled consumerism: The reaction of the Bahá'í educator to the challenges presented by the dangers of teenage life can be positive rather than negative. Prohibitions and arbitrary authority may work when the parent is around; but when the child goes away to work, or attends college, (s)he will not be protected against inappropriate conduct unless (s)he has internalised the teachings on correct conduct. In many ways, these problems present less of a challenge to the Bahá'í educator than they did in the 1950s and 1960s, since the dangers of unfettered individual freedom are today more recognised by society than they were. The advent of AIDS has dramatically illustrated that a multiplicity of sexual partners is a danger to one's health and can even prove fatal. We do not yet have a similar illustration of any psychological disruption caused by promiscuity. However, Bahá'í views of nonprescribed drugs, of tobacco and of alcoholic drinks are reinforced by respected public figures and by schools in a way that they were not two decades ago.

Thus so long as a youth is not alienated from authority per se, or so heavily immersed in a sub-culture whose authority prescribes self-destructive conduct, we should be able to reinforce Bahá'í standards of conduct in these areas. Bahá'í standards of honesty, courtesy, kindness and humility may prove rather more difficult. Unsavoury revelations about widely-respected public figures and accounts of business success suggest that the rewards for perfect conduct may not be of this world. Courtesy and humility, in particular, receive scant reinforcement from the wider society and the media and perhaps from Bahá'í society. These are areas to which our educators need to give thought.

The xenophobic stance of the press and the media: From the approach of much of the media, one might worry that our children are inoculated by the media against the oneness of mankind. In practice, the reverse is probably true. Firstly, there is happily no longer any identification of nation with race. Children's TV presenters, popular musicians and sportspeople come in many colours, thus that aspect of the oneness of mankind is better understood by children than by adults.

Secondly, the process of European integration, so long the butt of criticism by the popular press, has received an immense boost in prestige from the collapse of Soviet power in Eastern Europe and within the former Russian Empire.[23] These processes, and the constant media exposure which they receive, should have substantially internationalised our children through programmes like the BBC's *Newsround* and ITV's *Wackaday*.[24]

Thirdly, the aid projects launched by people respected by the children, like Band Aid, Blue Peter's Africa Appeal, Comic Relief, etc, and their use of live satellite links with Ethiopian projects.[25] have similarly underlined in the children's minds that there is but one humanity. Also in this category fall environmental programmes like the BBC's *One World* programme.[26]

From these perspectives, our children in 1991 are better prepared for the oneness of mankind than they were in 1981. There is, however, no argument for complacency, since what has become obvious to children in the 1980s, a decade of international change, may not seem so obvious once media attention has moved elsewhere. The task of the Bahá'í educator is therefore to stress world citizenship, as urged in the Peace Statement,[27] using the news of political and environmental events to underline the oneness of mankind. Activism on aid and the environment prove much better motivators than dry words. Nor must this world citizenship be only of the head, but the heart also.

Exposure to the art and music styles of other cultures is something that can be done in the home, but is best undertaken in a non-self-conscious way, so that children come to appreciate a thing of beauty for itself before they stick a mental label on it.
Festivals: One of the biggest pulls which the dominant culture exerts on our children is associated with festivals. Christmas and Easter are each amalgams of Christian and non-Christian festivals, largely Roman and Norse in the case of Christmas and largely Anglo-Saxon in the case of Easter.

The non-Christian elements centre around celebrations of spring and winter, which give the festivals an elemental quality which slots them into the children's calendars. Even the terms at school are organised so as to yield a Christmas holiday and an Easter holiday. The supernatural gangs up to support these festivals, too, with Santa Claus and the Easter bunny. Moreover, primary school activities are dominated by Christmas from the middle of November, as beautiful songs are repeatedly rehearsed and plays prepared. The lure of those festivals is enhanced by the loot on offer, by the mass media and by our children's peers.

The decorations in the shops scream of presents and Easter eggs. In the face of these festivals, the relative appeal to young children of Bahá'í Holy Days may be limited. There are so many of them, and they are bunched during the year. The Ninth and Twelfth Days of Ridvan, in particular, seem hard for children to differentiate.
Although readings at the Holy Day commemoration teach the children the story behind each festival, and although in addition to the religious celebration there may well be children's activities (in my own county of Oxfordshire these have included visits to museums, ice skating, punting, games of cricket, etc.) one festival is very like another. While small my children anticipated Christmas for months in advance, whereas Bahá'í Holy Days hove into view only one week in advance.

What then is the Bahá'í educator to do? Clearly (s)he has to raise the status of Bahá'í Holy Days in the eyes of the children. Much has been done by communities, by means of music, dancing or concerts, to lift the social celebration of a Holy Day from a mere eating competition; while daytime children's events as detailed above can reinforce in children's minds that the Holy Day is a special occasion.

Differentiating Holy Days is more difficult. The fundamental dilemma is this: how do we instil in the children a respect and an anticipation for a particular festival without creating a standard procedure, which might become a *ritual*?

For Naw-Rúz there are 2500 years of Persian culture to fall back on if one wishes - the planting of seedlings, the use of eggs, and special objects on the table. However attractive an option this may be, we do not know how much of this is relevant to the Naw-Rúz established by Bahá'u'lláh. I suspect (although I know of no guidance) that those elements celebrating spring and renewal - the seedlings and the eggs - are relevant, whilst objects on the table sharing a common initial letter are not. The Persian tradition of visiting friends and relations during the Naw-Rúz period is obviously of social value, but should the Bahá'í assume that Naw-Rúz lasts twelve days like Ridván, Christmas or the traditional Persian Naw-Rúz, or should (s)he confine it to one day? If we wish children to associate the giving of gifts with a Bahá'í festival, which one is it to be? Most families I know give presents to children on one or more of either Ayyam-i-Ha (*hospitality and the giving of gifts*) or Naw-Rúz (*"In Iran we ..."*), or the Birthday of Bahá'u'lláh, and surprise children of other Bahá'í families by giving the gifts on what the latter consider the *wrong day*.

Cards are similarly exchanged in a disjointed and uncoordinated way, depriving the Bahá'í community of a friendship-cementing occasion occupying the role played in the secular community by Christmas. While this variety may demonstrate an admirable lack of ritual, it means that there is no reinforcement of Bahá'í festivals by the children giving each other presents or cards, while our relatives who are not Bahá'ís strive in vain to establish when they should send presents and cards.

The lack of differentiation between Holy Day traditions may seem to be of little significance, but one might argue that it is the timetable of Holy Days which gives the shape to the Bahá'í year. This is of great importance, since the UK media emphasis is upon the shape of the Christian year - Easter, Whitsun, Christmas. This accords Christianity a deep legitimacy in children's eyes.

How is the Bahá'í educator to tackle these problems? Unaided (s)he cannot establish how festivals are be differentiated, or how far Persian and Bahá'í cultures coincide at Naw-Rúz, and must await guidance from the Universal House of Justice on this matter. Whatever the case, the educator can ensure that, however a festival is celebrated, it holds both spiritual and social worth for the children.

Not only must the children have an enjoyable time, but the formal celebration must be spiritual and uplifting, preferably incorporating more than the spoken word and the devouring of rice, and must underline the meaning of the Holy Day. Communities wishing to improve their musical presentations for the Holy Days may wish to appoint an Artistic Director or a Musical Director to work on music or drama throughout the year. In my own county, Peter Baldwin has served as Music Officer for three different Bahá'í communities in which he has lived and has played a key role in collecting and popularising songs.

With regard to Christmas and Easter, we must be inclusive, and encourage our children to respect Christianity, but to demythologise some of the magical elements according to the best biblical and historical scholarship which we have available.

The poor press enjoyed by Islam: The fault for the poor press enjoyed by Islam may lie partly with some modern-day Muslims themselves. We must fearlessly uphold the divine station of Muhammad, but in so doing, it would be dishonest and unjust for Bahá'í educators to try to justify behaviour which they would criticise were the perpetrators Westerners. The alternative approach is to free one's children from prejudice by teaching the history both of Europe and of the Middle East. The Crusades, the Thirty Years' War, the Slave Trade, Naziism and Communism will cure the children of any assumption that the Islamic world holds a monopoly of aggression and violence. In addition, one should explain the degradation of Faiths and the seasons through which a faith moves.

The Lack of Cultural Provision in the Faith

This paper began by making a distinction between high culture and culture in its wider sense. However, there must be some place for the flowering of high culture in the service of the Faith. At present the best voices and the best instrumentalists are often conscripted into the service of sacred and church music. One hopes that ways will be found to bring these elements to bear in serving the Faith and in speaking of the Glory of God. Calligraphy, art and poetry have all been used effectively by individuals, but the broad mass of believers has no experience in this area.

Challenges
There are two problem elements in this field, to whit:

There is little art or music in UK Feasts - many Feast programmes have singing (chanting) in Persian but not in English. The *lack of ritual* has in many places thus itself become a *ritual*.

Within the UK Bahá'í community sacred music, choirs etc. are thin on the ground.

Therefore our children train by singing in chapel choirs and in church choir schools.

Responses

With regard to the lack of art and music in Feasts, the Bahá'í educator can perhaps explore with his/her pupils the Writings on Feasts. The child can learn to distinguish what is essentially Bahá'í from what is British tradition. Children may be trained to expect music and drama, and also to offer their own performances to Feasts.

With regard to the paucity of choirs within the Bahá'í world that the children can join, a problem exists. One cannot pioneer and also live next door to the House of Worship. Further, we can hardly impose upon the children a particular style of music. All we can do is to start our own children's choirs, perhaps based around our Sunday Schools. The children would have to be drawn from large catchment areas, but teaching will make Bahá'ís thicker on the ground and choirs more local.

Conclusion

This paper has sought to identify a number of challenges facing the Bahá'í educator in relation to the interplay - between Bahá'í culture - what one might call *new world order thinking*, and the dominant culture - *old world order thinking*. All of the challenges can easily be overcome, providing a sustained and imaginative approach to these challenges is made by the Bahá'í educator, whether parent, Sunday School teacher or deepener.

References

1. Bahá'u'lláh, *The Hidden Words* (Wilmette: Bahá'í Publishing Trust), 1971, Persian, no 82.
2. Bahá'u'lláh, *Gleanings from the Writings of Bahá'u'lláh* (London: Bahá'í Publishing Trust), 1976, p 250.
3. Gerald Warren, a statement at UK Teaching Conference 1978, unpublished.
4. Universal House of Justice, *To the Bahá'ís of the World*, Ridván Message 1990, p 5.
5. Universal House of Justice, *The Promise of World Peace* (Haifa: Bahá'í World Centre), 1985, p 24.
6. *Stories about Jesus the Friend* (Loughborough: Ladybird), 1961.
7. *Holy Bible*, Authorised King James Version, HM letters patent, 1605.
8. *Holy Bible*, Revised Standard Version, Division of Christian Education of the National Council of the Churches of Christ in the United States of America, 1946 and 1952.
9. *Holy Bible*, Good News Bible, Bible Society, 1976.
10. C. Schulz, *God is for Real, Man*.

11. W.N. Garlington, *Bahá'í Bhajans*, World Order, **16** No. 2, pp 43-9.
12. The Louis Gregory Institute concentrates on this and other methods of making the Faith accessible to the people of rural South Carolina.
13. A. Lee, *The Unfriendly Governor* (Los Angeles: Kalimat Press) 1979.
14. J. Lenz, *That Day in July*, performed at the San Francisco Peace Conference, 1986.
15. e.g. "O God, my God, Attire Mine Head...", arranged by Tommy Nikjoo, Alice Vickers and Tom Vickers, unpublished.
16. "Look at Me, Follow Me", song based upon the life of 'Abdu'l-Bahá.
17. "All Things Bright and Beautiful", traditional hymn.
18. Universal House of Justice, *To the Bahá'ís of the World*, Riḍván Message, 1989.
19. Mark Twain, *Roughing It*, (New York: New American Library), 1972.
20. International Teaching Centre, letter of 26 February 1987 to the Continental Boards of Counsellors of Africa, the Americas, Asia and Australasia.
21. *The Sun*, 3 May 1982, p 1.
22. *The Delors Plan* was the name given to a programme presented to the member States of the European Community in 1988, aiming at a single EC market by the end of 1992. Jacques Delors was, and remains at time of writing, the president of the European Commission.
23. Between 1989 and 1991 Communist governments fell in the European States to the east of the Iron Curtain, and the Soviet Union itself divided into a number of new states.
24. "Newsround" was an evening news programme for children which presented international and national news in a way comprehensible to the young. Its presenter, John Craven, won awards for his broadcasting. "Wackaday" was a children's morning programme in which eccentric presenter Timmy Mallett taught children about a different country each week.
25. These three appeals broke new ground, extending the typical Telethon procedure of interviews with the expected beneficiaries to cover interviews of drought-stricken people in Ethiopia. The obvious intelligence of the suffering people, and their command of English, made many viewers feel more humble about "the Third World".
26. "One World" was a series of BBC programmes presented in July 1991.
27. "In keeping with the requirements of the times, consideration should also be given to teaching the concept of world citizenship as part of the standard education of every child." *The Promise of World Peace*, op cit., p 15.

The use of Music, Drama and Art in Bahá'í Education

Alan Woodhurst, John Lester and Carol Khorsandyon

Introduction

It is possible to use drama, art and music in any educational environment, but this paper seeks to identify specific ways in which they can be used for Bahá'í education. Both drama and music are especially attractive to youth, both in the act of delivering and receiving, as witnessed recently by the "Youthquake" group tour where they had declarations in all but one of the places they visited. Art, music and drama can all be used in either a passive or an active manner.

The Use of Drama

We cannot go far in teaching anything without the use of examples and analogies. In the *Seven Valleys*, Bahá'u'lláh Himself tells the story of the night-watchman and the lover to illustrate the meaning of the Valley of Knowledge, whilst in a previous dispensation, Christ had frequent recourse to the parable as a prime means of teaching.
Each story enters a new and more immediate dimension when it is dramatised, and its deeper meanings are likely to have particular point for those involved with the production. There are thus three levels at which an analogy can be appreciated: reading it on a page (illustration), watching it being performed (demonstration) and actually taking part (participation). 'Abdu'l-Bahá gives testimony to the virtues of demonstration:

An actor mentioned the drama and its influence. "The drama is of the utmost importance", said 'Abdu'l-Bahá. "It has been a great educational power in the past; it will be so again." He described how as a young boy he witnessed the mystery play of 'Alí's betrayal and passion and how it affected him so deeply that he wept and could not sleep for many nights.[1]

Drama has traditionally been a potent instrument for teaching. The nativity play, for example, is a commonplace event at schools prior to Christmas, helping to emphasise the significance of that festival. The great tragedies of Shakespeare exemplify such truths as the degenerating effects of regicide (*Macbeth*), the poisonous nature of backbiting and jealousy (*Othello*) and the deadly chaos attendant upon monarchs preferring flattery to truth (*King Lear*). Ben Johnson's

Volpone, though a comedy, points out the perversions brought about by people possessed by avarice. In the epilogue to Shaw's *St. Joan*, Joan (a quarter-century after her burning) is restored to church favour and revered - but the thought of her returning to life brings general consternation. Shaw's message is clear - saviours are more readily recognised once they have safely departed this planet; their presence is too challenging for the establishment when they are here.

The impact of drama is undoubted; to show will always be more effective than to tell. The "Mona" video, with its poignant story of heroism in the face of manifest evil, was far more successful in bringing home to people the persecution of the Bahá'ís in Iran than any number of publications and lists of martyrs. In Bahá'í education little dramas can often be used to demonstrate certain virtues and principles of the Faith (always easier to appreciate in this form than as simple, unpractised abstractions) and also episodes from history (provided no attempt is made to portray the major figures of the Faith). Sometimes enough resources can be mustered to enable a central dramatic production to take place.

The Experience of Drama

Such a venture took place in 1990 when the children of the North East London Sunday School, together with some parents and friends, performed a musical play written by three of the teachers and called *Bahá'u'lláh in Baghdad*. The first performance took place in the presence of the Deputy Mayor of Havering, who (on a later occasion) expressed his enjoyment of the evening. All the children aged over 5 took part and in so doing learnt about the main events of an important period of Bahá'í history (1853-63). There were, however, other lessons to be learnt, not related to the information contained in the scenes and applicable to all levels and ages.

The first of these lessons is responsibility. Each individual in a production has a particular task to perform (lines to say, a song to sing, a piece of narrative, etc.) and the success of the venture depends on the fulfilment of these responsibilities. If the actor playing the teacher who is astounded at the divine penmanship of the dervish in Sulamaniyyih (Bahá'u'lláh) does not turn up or is late, the scene is ruined. The children taking part in *Bahá'u'lláh in Baghdad* ranged from 5 to 15 in age and all of them became aware of their responsibilities towards the overall production.

A cohabitant of responsibility in any production is co-operation. The whole essence of a successful production is co-operation, in fact; each participant becomes a part of the whole, a cog in the wheel, concerned with the success of the whole enterprise and not with any personal glory. Any little problems arising along the way had to be overcome together; any success to be attained could only be achieved together. Each little part had to fit in with another to have any purpose, like pieces of a jigsaw, nonsensical apart but producing a complete picture when combined. When one is a part of something like this the need for co-operation and unity becomes particularly apparent, and so it was for the children (and adults) involved with our production. The fruits of co-operation were the success of the show and the enthusiastic response of the audience.

Both responsibility and co-operation require a high degree of self-discipline, which again was evident during the production of *Bahá'u'lláh in Baghdad*. It is, for example, important that no noise from backstage should filter through to the audience during the show and, despite their excitement, the children did very well in keeping quiet, mutually shushing each other when some chattering did seem about to break out. Learning a part and rehearsing scenes until they are just right also requires self-discipline as well as indicating the need to seek after perfection.

Participation in drama thus enables important Bahá'í attributes to be put into practice as well as enabling the easy learning of material included in the content of the play itself; a double learning process, in short. It may be said that these benefits were not initially recognised by all the parents concerned, some of whom equated lessons with instruction only and felt that participation in drama was not a good use of Sunday School time. Such doubts had drastically diminished by the time of the production.

Drama does not have to be on such a grand scale. Rôle play, for example, can be a successful means of learning at a Teaching Institute (in striking up a conversation with a stranger which will lead to a mention of the Faith, for example) or as part of a summer school workshop. Taking part in a simulated LSA meeting in which each member has been briefed to take a certain rôle (nit-picker, vague idealist, quiet non-contributor, eloquent speaker who tends to dominate, etc.) is not only a frustrating experience but a learning and often chastening one, as one recognises elements present in actual consultations. Rúhíyyih Khánum wrote just such a scene to illustrate her points about how a spiritual assembly should be run, her Mr Boom being a particularly dominant force in need of some restraint. We learn from mistakes, it is said, but better to learn from mistakes in simulation than to commit them during the real thing.

Rôle play is improvised within a basic outline, not scripted, and thus is closer to a real life situation. It is a useful tool for preparing Bahá'ís of whatever age for such situations; an instrument of training rather than teaching (if such a distinction is not too subtle). Simulation can thus be a particularly instructive aspect of dramatic participation.

Drama can thus perform many rôles in Bahá'í education. When observed it can demonstrate many lessons with more effectiveness than can be learnt by simple instruction or reading; when participated in it can both teach those lessons with still more effectiveness and, by its very requirements, teach by action behaviour and virtues that are important for Bahá'í's to attain; lastly by simulation of potentially real situations it can prepare Bahá'ís for actual situations, making them more prepared to cope with these - a potent form of teaching indeed. Teachers requiring guidance in how to use drama could benefit from reading *Making Sense of Drama*.²

The Use of Art

Now we will consider some art forms and how they may help the educational process. The use and study of art in Bahá'í classes is of the utmost importance and should be encouraged and developed at all levels - from reception class: "While the children are yet in their infancy ... let them share in every new and rare and wondrous craft and art"³ to mature students, where its acquisition and perfection is paralleled to the station of worship: "... in accordance with the divine teachings ... the perfection of arts are considered acts of worship. If a man engageth with all his power ... in the perfection of an art, it is as if he has been worshipping God in churches and temples."⁴

Shoghi Effendi, in 1932, stressed the importance of art for its aesthetic value and means of diffusing the spirit of the New Age, and the teachings of Bahá'u'lláh, to a wide audience: "Art can better awaken such noble sentiments than cold rationalising especially among the mass of the people."⁵

Living as we do in a 'media-conscious' society which projects art forms in every possible way through television programmes, commercials, bill-boards, newspapers, magazines, etc. we can see the value of investigating effective, but sincere and dignified ways of presenting material to the public. It is therefore important that we foster respect for art and also stimulate creativity in our young charges. Our duty lies in encouraging them to develop any special talents that they may have and, combined with a deep knowledge of the Faith and immersion in the spiritual teachings, to enable them to use their talents in the future in an effective, pure and demonstrative way. "He (Bahá'u'lláh) ... considers 'arts, crafts and sciences' to be conducive to the exaltation of the world of being,"⁶ 'Abdu'l-Bahá stresses that perfection in art is dependent on one's closeness to God: "Although to acquire the sciences and arts is the greatest glory of mankind, this is so only on condition that man's river flow into the mighty sea, and draw from God's ancient source His inspiration."⁷ Bernard Leach, in the introduction to his book *Drawings, Verse and Belief* points out that "Art, as we endeavour towards perfection, is one with religion."⁸ Therefore we can see that its inclusion on the curriculum of any Bahá'í class is not only relevant but also essential.

The Value of Art

There are two ways in which art, in the broadest sense, may be introduced into the class - in a passive way and in an active way. Passive art is using somebody else's creative thought, be it a sculpture, drawing, painting or other object of intrinsic value, as a starting point for discussion, or as a means of explaining, or exploring a spiritual concept, and which may, or may not, lead the student on to create something of their own. The active use of art demands participation and a contribution from the students, either in a form specified by the teacher, or by allowing the students freely to produce their own interpretation of the subject matter. Both areas are recommended for use in Bahá'í classes, and with students of all ages.

Obviously, when introducing a picture or object stimulus to the children, the discretion of the teacher is needed in deciding whether it has intrinsic value and evokes spirituality. Not all art forms are "conducive to the exaltation of the world of being", as they are products of a society which is desperately seeking a solution to its waywardness and lack of spirituality. However such stimuli could be used in a positive way to elicit Bahá'í solutions to the problems depicted and are therefore of value in the Bahá'í class. One of the joys of art is that it can be permeated into the lesson very easily and used to enhance poetry, drama, music, in a satisfying and stimulating manner. (Hopefully the announcement "Oh, we've got ten minutes before the end of the lesson; here's some paper - just draw a picture or something" will soon become a thing of the past!)

The different forms of art are numerous, and their introduction depends mostly on the dexterity and imagination of the teacher and the availability of a suitable environment and adequate materials. Some topics lend themselves to the creative urge more so than others. The Kingdoms of God and the senses, for example, can be excellently portrayed using (a) collage work in felt, wallpaper or magazine pictures, (b) different textured materials and (c) model-making with clay, play dough or papier maché. Collage work is also an excellent media to use when demonstrating unity in diversity. The children can cut out pictures of flowers and leaves, or use dried flower petals and leaves, and then arrange these on a large sheet of paper, layering and building up a colourful mural. Into the centre of each of the flowers, a small cut out face of each of the children in the class (taken from personal photographs) could then be pasted and the title "We are all the flowers of one garden" printed at the top of the sheet of paper. Flowers can also be collected to dry and then used for Naw-Rúz cards and bookmarks. Different media can be used to create textured paintings e.g. salt, sugar, lentils, rice etc., mixed with paint or adhesive, and then glued to paper, card, plastic boxes etc. When using these dried foods you could talk about the origin of the foods, and the different cultures, how people of different nationalities have diverse tastes because of different resources. When discussing other religions give the children practical examples of the religious customs, e.g. bring in the ingredients for a typical passover meal when talking about the Jewish Faith, and create a passover meal with the children, in class, as part of their lesson.

Teaching the senses to younger children lends itself ideally to practical examples. Tasting the difference between sugar and salt, vinegar and water, etc. and guessing the different foods when blindfolded, help to demonstrate the sense of taste. Similarly, the introduction of different noises, e.g. grating, rattling, shaking, or different smells e.g. pot pourri, orange peel, cauliflower, with the children sitting with their eyes closed, is an excellent way of demonstrating sound and smell.

A practical way of teaching young children about "virtue" is by drawing an outline of a doll on the lid of a cardboard box. Cut a heart-shaped hole in the doll, big enough to enable small slips of paper to be posted into the box. Make up a selection of slips with a good or bad deed written on each, e.g. truthfulness, spitting, helping, arguing etc., and then ask the children to decide which of the slips indicate good deeds and which indicate bad deeds. All of the good deeds are posted through the heart-shaped hole. At the end, the doll can be emptied and the slips counted to see how good she has been that week. This will also help the children to develop their counting skills.

Origami (paper-folding), needlepoint and tapestry are also effective in demonstrating various Bahá'í themes. The level of difficulty would obviously depend on the age group. Aiming at difficult tasks beyond the capability of the child is detrimental as it undermines the child's confidence, and therefore the discretion of the class teacher is important in deciding the level. The art of calligraphy is also recommended to be included on the syllabus as it encourages self-discipline and neatness, and also enables the students to use their creativity in presenting quotations or other forms of written work.

For the younger child, of pre-reading age, art is a crucial means of explaining Bahá'í teachings and of involving the child physically (to encourage manual dexterity and development) and mentally. It also helps them to explore, understand and interpret concepts beyond their mental age. Variety is the key, and suggested activities range from colouring-in line drawings or quotations to finger-painting, paper-folding, cutting and pasting, play dough, model-making, and painting with different media, to name but a few examples.

With the older child, the introduction of art brings imagination, creativity and also self-discipline into the lesson. It allows the students to express their understanding and interpretation of the lesson in a positive but individual way.

The final point, and one of importance to Bahá'í class teachers, concerns the drawing, painting or other interpretations of the central figures of the Bahá'í Faith. Very often a child in class will enquire about the appearance of Bahá'u'lláh or the Báb or 'Abdu'l-Bahá and will express a desire to include Them in a picture. Living in a society which has projected *real* images of the Manifestations of God (Muhammed, Jesus, Buddha, Krishna, etc.) it is understandable for Bahá'í children to express a desire to follow suit. The Universal House of Justice, however, in a letter to a believer in March 1977, explained that we must on no account attempt to portray the central figures of our Faith, or of any other religion, in drawing, painting, model or dramatic medium.

> *The prohibition on representing the Manifestation of God in paintings and drawings or in dramatic presentations applies to all the Manifestations of God. There are, of course, great and wonderful works of art of past Dispensations, many of which portrayed the Manifestations of God in a spirit of reverence and love. In this Dispensation however the greater maturity of mankind and the greater awareness of the relationship between the Supreme Manifestation and His servants enable us to realise the impossibility of representing, in any human form, whether pictorially, in sculpture, or in a dramatic representation, the Person of God's Manifestations.[9]*

The Use of Music

Finally, let us consider how and when music could be used, and the educational implications of its usage. At all levels of education, we should encourage the use of music for its own sake. "Music is regarded as a praiseworthy science at the Threshold of the Almighty..."[10]

There are three aspects of music to consider: composing, performing and listening. Only a few have the gift of composition, rather more are capable of performing music in one form or another, while almost everyone is able to listen to it. In fact we are encouraged to include music at every meeting.

"The element of music is, no doubt, an important feature of all Bahá'í gatherings. The Master Himself has emphasised its importance."[11] Live music is clearly preferable, but when this is not possible then recordings should be used. Sometimes a combination might be appropriate, e.g. if people are reluctant to sing unaccompanied and instrumentalists are not present but a recording of the backing music is available. There are three aspects of education involved here. Firstly we should seriously consider guidance for adults regarding both the desirability of having music at all Bahá'í gatherings and also the variety of forms available and their possible uses. Progress seems slow in some communities, even where much encouragement and plenty of examples have been given; this is probably due to lack of knowledge and understanding, which suitable education could rectify. Secondly we should encourage people, particularly children, to learn how to play a musical instrument. Thirdly we should remember that the human voice is the only source of music allowed in a Bahá'í House of Worship, so unaccompanied singing should be taught at all ages. We had a very successful session recently at which some adults were taught to sing a Naw-Rúz song without accompaniment. "In this new age the Manifest Light hath, in His holy Tablets, specifically proclaimed that music, sung or played, is spiritual food for the soul and heart."[12]

Here we have a good reason for including music at all meetings. It is clear that we may either sing or have instrumental music. We must not, however, assume that all music is suitable. "We have permitted you to listen to music and singing. Beware lest such listening cause you to transgress the bounds of decency and dignity. Rejoice in the joy of My Most Great Name through which the hearts are enchanted and the minds of the well-favoured are attracted. We have made music a ladder by which souls may ascend to the realm on high. Change it not into wings for self and passion."[13]

If words are involved, then these can easily be subject to the same scrutiny as spoken words. There has been a tendency, during the last few decades, towards the production of songs with incoherent and/or unsuitable words. This should be considered part of the 'rolling up of the old world order' and Bahá'ís should not be associated with such songs. For instrumental music, however, the situation is by no means clear. Anyone, who has not given the matter some thought, might well consider that all instrumental music would be suitable. On the other hand, some people are of the opinion that certain styles of music can have a bad influence and should therefore be avoided, while other styles should be particularly encouraged due to their spiritual nature.

"Try, if thou canst, to use spiritual melodies, songs and tunes, and to bring the earthly music into harmony with the celestial melody."[14] Thus we have an obligation to include, as part of the children's education, not only exposure to various types of suitable music, but also discussions regarding aspects of music which might be unsuitable. For young children a combination of recorded and live music is appropriate; they enjoy making movements to music and, with a little patience, can be taught to operate simple percussion instruments at the same time. An early lesson here is that everybody playing when they feel like it results in unsuitable music (a noise, in their vocabulary!), whereas everybody playing his or her part at the correct time results in an overall effect which is pleasant to hear. When the children are older they can participate in discussions about harmony and dischords, etc. Ideally a keyboard would be available for demonstration, but examples of recordings can be used.

Music being used at a meeting does not, of course, have to be at the beginning, but that is when people often use it. Accordingly, we usually start Sunday School with some music. An appropriate type can often help to concentrate the minds on the tasks ahead. For young children it can help prepare them to act in a reverent manner during the opening devotional. While they are learning reverence, it is better to go round and insist on certain behaviour (no talking, folded arms, eyes shut) while introductory music is being played, rather than during the devotional itself. "... consider how much marvellous notes or a charming song influence the spirits! A wonderful song giveth wings to the spirit and filleth the heart with exaltation."[15]

Music can, in fact, help children to learn prayers. Many children learn a prayer more quickly and easily if it is set to music. This may also be true for adults, particularly those who are new to the Faith. Specially composed songs can help both children and adults learn things about the Faith: history, teachings, principles, calendar, etc. This also applies to those who are not Baháí's. For example, guests at a party often join in community singing, especially when provided with printed words. They can learn about the Faith better if actually repeating phrases themselves, but are unlikely to do so if these are just spoken, and repetition of spoken words would be boring. However, a nice catchy chorus like "We are all the fruits of one tree..." can legitimately be repeated by a Bahá'í leading the gathering and guests may soon find themselves singing it too!

Summary

Whereas music can inspire, dramatic presentations can be both entertaining and educational, and the various forms of art are to be encouraged by themselves, yet the ultimate achievement is to combine these into one stage production. "That day will the Cause spread like wildfire when its Spirit and teachings are presented on the stage or in art and literature as a whole."[16] Our musical play, *Bahá'u'lláh in Baghdad*, was more than just a dramatic production. It started as a song composed for a Ridván party in 1989. This song has a lively chorus starting "Baghdad is a nice place for a party" and tells the story of the 12 days of Ridván. The enthusiasm with which the chorus was sung by those present (particularly the children), although they had not heard it before, inspired us to write more songs. Having tried these at the Sunday School, the idea of a full length musical play emerged and the children were invited to help with the writing of the linking dialogue and narrative. They all made a contribution, in writing or verbally, and most of their ideas were incorporated into the script. A hall was booked for a suitable date, and we were very fortunate in being able to arrange curtains and lighting in the hall before the dress rehearsal. There were costumes to be made or obtained, amplification equipment to be organised and stage directions to be added to the script. Last, but not least, three backdrops were made, using painting and collage; this entailed a massive commitment by several people and the monopolising of someone's garage for several weeks! While preparing for, and performing in, this musical play, the children learnt a lot about Bahá'í history, gained confidence, helped to proclaim the Faith, and enjoyed doing it. The script is available and a video was made of the performance. Every encouragement will be given, by the authors, to any group of people who may wish to arrange another performance of this musical play, or part of it, or indeed to write their own.

References

1. *'Abdu'l-Bahá in London* (London: Bahá'í Publishing Trust), 1987, p 93.
2. Jonathan Neelands, *Making Sense of Drama*, 1984.
3. 'Abdu'l-Bahá, *Selections from the Writings of 'Abdu'l-Bahá* (Haifa: Bahá'í World Centre), 1978, p 129.
4. *ibid*. p 144.
5. Shoghi Effendi, quoted in: *Lights of Guidance* (New Delhi: Bahá'í Publishing Trust), 1988, p 98.
6. Shoghi Effendi, *God Passes By* (Wilmette: Bahá'í Publishing Trust), 1970, p 218.
7. 'Abdu'l-Bahá, *Selections*, p 110.
8. Bernard Leach, *Drawings, Verses and Belief* (Oxford: Oneworld Publications), 1988, p 9.
9. Universal House of Justice, quoted in: *Lights of Guidance* (New Delhi: Bahá'í Publishing Trust), 1988, pp 99-100.
10. 'Abdu'l-Bahá, quoted in: *Bahá'í Writings on Music* - a compilation (London: Bahá'í Publishing Trust), ND, p 5.
11. Shoghi Effendi, quoted in: *Bahá'í Writings on Music* - a compilation (London: Bahá'í Publishing Trust), ND, p 10.
12. 'Abdu'l-Bahá, *Selections from the Writings of 'Abdu'l-Bahá* (Haifa: Bahá'í World Centre), 1978, no 74, p 112.
13. Bahá'u'lláh, quoted in: *Bahá'í Writings on Music* - a compilation (London: Bahá'í Publishing Trust), ND, p 3.
14. 'Abdu'l-Bahá, quoted in: *Bahá'í Writings on Music* - a compilation (London: Bahá'í Publishing Trust), ND, p 5.
15. 'Abdu'l-Bahá, quoted in: *Bahá'í World Faith* (Wilmette: Bahá'í Publishing Trust), 1970, p 334.
16. Shoghi Effendi, quoted in: *Bahá'í News*, May 1933, p 7.

Hot Housing: The Way Forward?

John Parris

Introduction

From a Bahá'í perspective it seems clear that parents - particularly mothers - have "the inescapable duty to educate their children".[1] This responsibility falls into three main areas: physical, intellectual and spiritual, and is never greater than in the pre-school years.

This paper examines particularly the area of intellectual development and shows that this is very strongly encouraged by 'Abdu'l-Bahá and the Guardian. Evidence from several influential educationalists demonstrating the current view that cognitive and language development is dramatically affected in the pre-school years by the type of input that the child receives is analyzed. The conclusion is drawn that the "Hot Housing" approach is a useful starting point for considering the stimulation of learning in this age group. A specific example of the use of this technique allied to computers is presented for further consideration.

Physical Development (or Education)

This is described by 'Abdu'l-Bahá as "the progress and development of the body, through gaining its sustenance, its material comfort and ease. This education is common to animals and man".[2]

In the West we are extremely fortunate that in most cases the physical development of most children is probably close to the maximum potential - particularly with regard to neurological development. The progress in nutrition, standards of living, hygiene, public health, control of infectious diseases, medicine, etc. mean that the majority of children reach adulthood in a physical condition superior to that ever previously achieved. It is easy to take these tremendously important advances for granted. There remains, of course, room for improvement. This is probably not to the same extent, however, as that in the other two areas of development.

Spiritual Education

Spiritual education has been defined by Adib Taherzadeh as "acquiring of the knowledge of God and His Manifestations, the understanding of the mysteries of creation, the becoming well versed in the teachings of Bahá'u'lláh, the acquiring of good character, and the becoming equipped for serving the world of humanity".[3]

The emphasis on fostering the spiritual development of children from conception to adulthood is well known and is the most vital aspect of their overall education. 'Abdu'l-Bahá explains that:

> *Divine education is that of the Kingdom of God: it consists in acquiring divine perfections, and this is true education.*[4]
> *Training in morals and good conduct is far more important than book learning. A child that is cleanly, agreeable, of good character, well-behaved - even though he be ignorant - is preferable to a child that is rude, unwashed, ill-natured, and yet becoming deeply versed in all the sciences and arts. The reason for this is that the child who conducts himself well, even though he be ignorant, is of benefit to others, while an ill-natured, ill-behaved child is corrupted and harmful to others, even though he be learned.*[5]

Intellectual Education (or Human Education)

'Abdu'l-Bahá gives the following definition of this third area of development: "Human education signifies civilisation and progress - that is to say government, administration, charitable works, trades, arts and handicrafts, sciences, great inventions and discoveries and elaborate institutions, which are the activities essential to man as distinguished from the animal."[6]

What appears to be not generally well recognised is that almost as great an importance is placed in the literature of the Faith on intellectual development and excellence as on acquiring spiritual virtues. For example the quotation from 'Abdu'l-Bahá[5] above concludes: "If... the child be trained to be both learned and good, the result is light upon light." [7]

The following three passages from 'Abdu'l-Bahá expand this theme further:

> *O loving friends! Exert every effort to acquire the various branches of knowledge and true understanding. Strain every nerve to achieve both material and spiritual accomplishments.*[8]
> *Knowledge is praiseworthy when it is coupled with ethical conduct and a virtuous character; otherwise it is a deadly poison, a frightful danger.*[9]
> *It is clear that learning is the greatest bestowal of God; that knowledge and the acquirement thereof is a blessing from Heaven. Thus is it incumbent upon the friends of God to exert such an effort and strive with such eagerness to promote divine knowledge, culture and the sciences, that ere long those who are school children today will become the most erudite of all the*

> *fraternity of the wise. This is a service rendered unto God Himself, and it is one of His inescapable commandments.*[10]

A letter written on behalf of Shoghi Effendi clarifies the matter further: "It is just as important for the Bahá'í young boys and girls to become properly educated in colleges of high standing as it is to be spiritually developed. The mental as well as the spiritual side of youth has to be developed before he can serve the Cause efficiently.[11]

Excellence (to learn in a month what others learn in a year)

Another implication is that not only should Bahá'í children do well intellectually but in fact *excel* the others. Several passages from 'Abdu'l-Bahá are quite clear on this point: "It is ... my hope that ... the friends may come to excel the others in all things".[12] "It is incumbent upon Bahá'í children to surpass other children in the acquisition of sciences and arts, for they have been cradled in the grace of God. Whatever other children learn in a year, let Bahá'í children learn in a month. The heart of 'Abdu'l-Bahá longeth to find that Bahá'í young people, each and all, are known throughout the world for their intellectual attainments."[13]

Again it is made clear, however, that this should be done with the correct motive in mind (principally helping to carry forward an ever-advancing civilisation) rather than for its own sake. Bahá'u'lláh states: "True learning is that which is conducive to the well-being of the world, not to pride and self-conceit..."[14] "We have decreed, O people, that the highest and last end of all learning be the recognition of Him Who is the Object of all knowledge."[15]

Starting Young

When considering ways of helping Bahá'í children to learn in a month what others learn in a year, it is a sobering thought that progress during the pre-school years is now believed by most educationalists to be one of the major determinants - if not the major determinant - of future intellectual and academic achievement. For example, Professor Edward Zigler of Yale University explains that if he had the choice of running an education programme for children or parents, he would concentrate on parents. "If you want to change children," he points out, "you have to change parents first" as they are those responsible for the long term abilities.[16]

This appears remarkably close to the concept present in the Faith that the education of girls takes precedence over that of boys as they will in turn become the first educators of their children.

Evidence to support the view that intellectual development can be accelerated during the pre-school years and that this acceleration can be maintained throughout late life comes from several sources. This is in contrast to the formerly widely-accepted theories of Piaget and others [17] that it is not possible to accelerate most areas of cognitive development.

Project *Head Start*

Project *Head Start* in the United States has been the largest programme in the world to demonstrate improvements in long term cognitive development by stimulating learning in the pre-school age group. It was commenced in the early 1970s to try and accelerate intellectual progress in under 5s coming from socially disadvantaged backgrounds. This was in an effort to break down the seemingly perpetual cycle of disadvantage witnessed in most Western societies. The long-term results, as reported by David Weikart, demonstrated significant and continuing increase in academic abilities throughout secondary school and college life.[18]

Language Development

One area of cognitive development is language development. A study by Clarke-Stewart nearly twenty years ago provided strong evidence that the rate of a child's vocabulary development during the second year of life was dependent on the amount of time the mother spent talking to the child during the first year of life.[19] Taken together with the now widely accepted view that language must be acquired during a "sensitive period" in the early years or else it will never be mastered, it suggests the supreme educational opportunities presented to mothers.[20]

The Importance of Pre-School Years

Glen Doman, a researcher in the field of brain-damaged children, has calculated that a "child has learned more fact for fact" by the age of three "than he will learn for the rest of his life".[21]

Hot Housing (the idea)

An obvious implication of the above is that the pre-school years are probably the most important *sensitive period* for stimulating cognitive development. The modern concept of *Hot Housing* extends this idea. The name derives from the horticultural concept that if a plant is given the optimal conditions for growth - in terms of water, heat, sunlight, nutrition, protection from strong winds, etc. - it will develop maximally. Two implied points are relevant. Firstly there will always be genetic factors which will specify what the maximum potential is. Secondly, the plant itself grows and develops in response to beneficial conditions: no one can *make* a plant grow beyond its potential.

In an analogous way it is thought that providing the optimal educational environment for children will allow them to develop to their maximum potential. This does not in any way deny that there will be genetically determined or congenital differences.

Factors relevant to providing the best educational environment include:

1. **Physical Factors**: foetal growth and development, nutrition, prevention of disease, cleanliness, etc.
2. **Emotional Factors**: warmth, love and affection, caring parents, a positive, non-punitive and encouraging attitude towards children by the parents, etc.
3. **Social Factors**: stable, warm, home and family environments; protection from detrimental factors such as smoking, alcohol, narcotic drugs, poor diet, bad language, irreligious attitudes, unsuitable television (most of the current output), etc.
4. **Factors Directly Affecting Intellectual Development**: stimulating activities, exposure to language, music, art, games etc.; providing an atmosphere of reverence for and joy of learning, creating an appetite for reading and writing, mathematics, other areas of learning, etc.
5. **Spiritual Factors**: fostering an atmosphere of love of God, love for Bahá'u'lláh and other Manifestations of God, the regular reading of prayers and extracts from the Writings, encouragement of memorisation of the prayers etc.

Standard methods of hot housing assume that the first three sets of factors mentioned will be catered for, and concentrate on the fourth area (factors directly affecting intellectual development). They tend to ignore the spiritual factors entirely.

The above list is not exhaustive. It will also be apparent that the areas are not rigidly defined but significantly overlap. What will be obvious, however, is that Bahá'í homes will as a rule provide a fertile environment for most if not all of these factors. The Guardian's secretary has written on his behalf: "The task of bringing up a Bahá'í child ... is the chief responsibility of the mother, whose unique privilege is indeed to create in her home such conditions as would be most conducive to both his material and spiritual welfare and advancement."[22] 'Abdu'l-Bahá has also written: "Let them [the children] make the greatest progress [in their education] in the shortest span of time."[23]

Hence parents should, in my view, make a conscious decision to nurture the intellectual development of their pre-school children. It is important to note that 'Abdu'l-Bahá specifies that the age at which formal education (outside of the home) should begin is five.[24] The parents (especially the mother) would be almost solely responsible for intellectual development before this age.

Hot Housing (traditional methods)

Several authors have made important contributions by describing traditional methods of hot housing. The best of these methods stimulate an increased *motivation* to learn. This is important because hot housing is often misconstrued as *cramming*. Although this may occasionally occur, most devotees recognise that it is by arousing the child's appetite for knowledge that the greatest long term gains can be made. Any pressure on the child - even that which is very subtle - is almost certain to be counterproductive in the long run.

This touches on a deeper theme: what intelligence is. Sternberg made a study of the views of intelligence between *experts* (mainly developmental psychologists) and laymen. Table 1 summarises some of the different perspectives.[25]

The practical implications of this (assuming the *experts* are right) is that any educational model should attempt to stimulate curiosity and the desire to learn rather than cram in facts. This should really be the acid test of hot housing techniques. Memory is generally accepted to be an important facet of intelligence, but not the *only* aspect.

Critics of the method such as Brian Sutton-Smith seem to have made this fundamental error. "If you get hot housed" he comments "you end up being a rotten tomato - or at least a pallid tomato."[26] His criticisms centre around the pressure to learn facts and the detrimental effects that this could have on the long term development.

Perhaps the best book on conventional hot housing techniques aimed primarily at stimulating a child's desire to learn for him- or herself is Ken Adams' *Your Child Can be a Genius - and Happy!*[27] Despite the rather sensationalist title, a wide range of practical activities for pre-schoolers are described in an easy-to-understand way. Mr Adams himself is a school teacher, and his son John passed his A-level maths after using these techniques at the age of nine while attending an ordinary state school.

A question implied by the book's title is whether children who are hot housed will be happy; also whether the early gains will be maintained. The most celebrated hot housed child - who appeared on television as a prodigy at the age of nine in 1942 - was Professor James Watson. He won a Nobel Prize in 1962 for co-discovering DNA, the reproductive basis of life and undoubtedly one of the most significant advances in biology this century. There can be few greater accolades in any field of endeavour and show that at least in some cases the acceleration of learning can be continued into adult life.

Table 1: Comparing Ideas About Intelligence

Laymen	Experts
Practical Problem-Solving Ability Reasons logically and well Identifies connections among ideas Sees all aspects of a problem Keeps an open mind	Verbal Intelligence Displays a good vocabulary Reads with a high comprehension Displays curiosity Is intellectually curious
Verbal Ability Speaks clearly and articulately Is verbally fluent Converses well Is knowledgable about a particular field	Problem-Solving Ability Is able to apply knowledge to problems at hand Makes good decisions Poses problems in an optimal way Displays common sense
Social Competence Accepts others for what they are Admits mistakes Displays interest in the world at large Is on time for appointments	Practical Intelligence Sizes up situations well Determines how to achieve goals Displays awareness of the world around him/her Displays interest in the world at large

Hot Housing (the role of the computer)

No author has as yet outlined the staggering educational potential for pre-school children of the computer. Excellent programs already exist to aid in virtually all aspects of primary education. These have been designed for older children but can be used equally well in many instances by the under-fives. They have the advantages of being able to hold the attention and stimulate learning by:

1. Direct interaction;
2. The use of sound, music, and moving graphics;
3. Immediate strong positive or weak negative feedback;
4. Variability - most software will change characters, words, etc. each time the program is used, and progress depending on the child's responses; and
5. It is possible to *write* (by typing) without the manual dexterity required for using a pen.

Literally hundreds of programs exist and are readily obtainable. Two caveats need to be mentioned at this point. Firstly, these programs have been designed specifically to aid learning and should not be confused with the fairly ubiquitous arcade type games (which have very little educational potential). The child, on the other hand, will think of them as games. Secondly, no child should be left on his or her own when using the computer. The software provides innumerable opportunities for the parent also directly to interact and encourage the child.

The speed at which it is possible for a child to learn with this approach needs to be seen to be believed. There can be little doubt that computers will play a greater educational role in the future. Anyone who has appreciated what phenomenal progress a child can make of his or her own volition in a short space of time on a computer is filled with an almost missionary zeal to communicate this knowledge to others. It would be no exaggeration to say that the best educational software is the greatest tool to stimulate learning ever invented: it is the hot houser's dream.

Several popular misconceptions need to be explored at this point:

1. The parents need to be computer literate. This is simply not so! The programs have been designed to be used by primary school age children and are always extremely user friendly. No previous knowledge is required.

2. It is expensive. A popular myth. A very good computer to start off with is a Sinclair Spectrum 48k or 128k (because of the very wide and varied range of educational software available). In newspapers these can easily be found secondhand from £25 upwards. If software on tapes is used (rather than the more expensive diskettes) the typical cost would be about £8 - £10 for a tape containing about four programs. Because of the variability mentioned above, children will tend to use the software for longer than any book or toy of a comparable price. A full package of programs to teach a child reading, writing (initially using the keys) and arithmetic/mathematics to an age of 6 would cost around £100. These can be used by other children. A good age for starting on these programs would be from about 2.5 to 3 years. Many programs have parallel books, games, flashcards, etc. giving the advantage and flexibility of a multi-media approach to education.

3. Computers are fragile and easily broken by children. Again a common fallacy. Computers are very robust and can withstand being dropped, trampled on, etc. quite well. The only precaution of note is not to use fluids near them as these are the one thing that can cause irreparable damage. However, given how cheap many secondhand home computers are, it is not really a major concern.

4. A full keyboard is too difficult for a child to grasp. Most people would probably be surprised how quickly children can find their way around a computer keyboard (a typewriter-style QWERTY keyboard). However, all of the simplest

programs utilise the much simpler joystick, or a mouse, thus freeing the child from the need to master the keyboard itself.

5. Educational Software is only available for BBC compatible computers. This is a more sophisticated objection and if the reader does not understand exactly what is meant, it is probably better to ignore this paragraph and move on to the next. Although it is true that the majority of educational software available was designed for BBC compatible computers (primarily BBC B), many of these programmes have later been produced in formats suitable for the common home personal computers - such as the Sinclair Spectrum. Admittedly, a computer which can run BBC software would have the advantage of being able to use the vast wealth of programs available;[28] however, the cost would increase significantly both in terms of purchasing the machine itself and the diskettes required. It is worth noting that many primary schools are currently updating their systems and it is not yet apparent which in the next generation (if any) will ultimately capture the market. Any home computer will have major educational potential even without specialised educational programs. My own son's favourite software is currently the word-processing package used to type this paper! An anecdotal example of the type of result achievable using a computer is my own son, who by the age of 3.5 had a reading and mathematical age of 6-7 and was computer and word processing literate. In the view of the author this could be repeated by most normal children if they were given the opportunity.

References

1. Universal House of Justice, *letter* to the National Spiritual Assembly of the Bahá'ís of New Zealand, 28 December 1980; reprinted in *Family Life* - a compilation (London: Bahá'í Publishing Trust), 1982, p 31.
2. 'Abdu'l-Bahá, *Some Answered Questions* (London: Bahá'í Publishing Trust), 1981, p 8; also reprinted in *Bahá'í Education* - a compilation (London: Bahá'í Publishing Trust), 1987, no 37, p 11.
3. Adib Taherzadeh, *The Revelation of Baha'u'llah*, Volume Three (Oxford: George Ronald), 1983, p 327.
4. 'Abdu'l-Bahá, *Some Answered Questions* (London: Bahá'í Publishing Trust), 1981, p 8; also reprinted in *Bahá'í Education* - a compilation (London: Bahá'í Publishing Trust), 1987, no 37, p 11.
5. 'Abdu'l-Bahá, *Selections from the Writings of 'Abdu'l-Baha* (Haifa: Bahá'í World Centre), 1982, pp 135-6; also in *Bahá'í Education* - a compilation (London: Bahá'í Publishing Trust), 1987, no 81, p 33.
6. 'Abdu'l-Bahá, *Some Answered Questions* (London: Bahá'í Publishing Trust), 1971, p 8; also in *Bahá'í Education* - a compilation (London: Bahá'í Publishing Trust), 1987, no 37, p 11.

7. 'Abdu'l-Bahá, *Selections from the Writings of 'Abdu'l-Baha* (Haifa: Bahá'í World Centre), 1982, p 136, also in *Bahá'í Education* - a compilation (London: Bahá'í Publishing Trust, 1987, no 81, p 33. Also compare "light upon light" with Qur'án 24:35.
8. 'Abdu'l-Bahá, quoted in: *Bahá'í Education* - a compilation (London: Bahá'í Publishing Trust), 1987, no 53, p 20.
9. 'Abdu'l-Bahá, quoted in: *Bahá'í Education* - a compilation (London: Bahá'í Publishing Trust), 1987, no 74, p 29.
10. 'Abdu'l-Bahá, quoted in: *Bahá'í Education* - a compilation (London: Bahá'í Publishing Trust), 1987, no 75, p 29.
11. Shoghi Effendi, quoted in: *Bahá'í Education* - a compilation (London: Bahá'í Publishing Trust, 1987), no 127, p 51.
12. 'Abdu'l-Bahá, quoted in: *Bahá'í Education* - a compilation (London: Bahá'í Publishing Trust), 1987, no 71, p 27.
13. 'Abdu'l-Bahá, *Selections from the Writings of 'Abdu'l-Baha* (Haifa: Bahá'í World Centre), 1982, p 141.
14. Bahá'u'lláh, quoted in: *Bahá'í Education* - a compilation (London: Bahá'í Publishing Trust), 1987, no 17, p 4.
15. Bahá'u'lláh, *Gleanings from the Writings of Baha'u'llah* (London: Bahá'í Publishing Trust), 1978, p 199.
16. Edward Zigler, quoted in: Jane Walmsley and J. Margolis, *Hot House People* (London: Pan Books), 1987, p 32.
17. A good discussion on how the views of Piaget with regard to cognitive development have been challenged is in Alison Clarke-Stewart, M. Perlmutter and S. Friedman, *Lifelong Human Development* (New York: John Wiley), 1988, p 231-7. A useful discussion is also found in Helen Bee, S.K. Mitchell, *The Developing Person: A Life Span Approach*, (New York: Harper & Row), 1984, pp 141-52.
18. David P. Weikart, "*Relationship of curriculum, teaching, and learning in preschool education*" in J.C. Stanley, (ed), *Preschool Programmes for the Disadvantaged* (Baltimore: Johns Hopkins University Press), 1972.
19. K.A. Clarke-Stewart, "Interactions between mothers and their young children: characteristics and consequences" *Monographs of the Society in Child Development*, 1973, **38**, p 82.
20. Helen Bee, S.K. Mitchell, *The Developing Person: A Life Span Approach* (New York: Harper & Row), 1984, pp 190-5.
21. Glen Doman, quoted in: Jane Walmsley and J. Margolis, *Hot House People* (London: Pan Books), 1987, p 42.
22. Shoghi Effendi, quoted in: *Family Life* - a compilation (London: Bahá'í Publishing Trust), 1982, p 31.
23. 'Abdu'l-Bahá, quoted in: *Bahá'í Education* - a compilation (London: Bahá'í Publishing Trust), 1987, no 74, p 28.
24. 'Abdu'l-Bahá, quoted in: *Bahá'í Education* - a compilation (London: Bahá'í Publishing Trust), 1987, no 78, p 30.

25. R.J. Sternberg, "Who's Intelligent", *Psychology Today*, 1982, **16** (4), 30-39. For table see Helen Bee, S.K. Mitchell, *The Developing Person: A Life Span Approach* (New York: Harper & Row), 1984, p 127.
26. Brian Sutton-Smith, *The Hot Housing of Young Children: So Much, So Soon*, Symposium at the University of Pennsylvania in Philadelphia; quoted in: Jane Walmsley and J. Margolis, *Hot House People* (London: Pan Books), 1987, p 45.
27. Ken Adams, *Your Child Can be a Genius - and Happy!* (London: Guild Publishing), 1988.
28. The major company specialising in Educational Software is: Rickitt Educational Media, Ilton, Ilminster, Somerset, TA19 9BR; Tel (0460) 57152. There are two very useful catalogues:
(1) *The Educational Software Directory for Primary Schools* which contains more than 400 programs. This is aimed mainly at teachers.
(2) *Educational Software - A Parents' Guide*. This concentrates on the titles compatible with the most commonly-used home computers in the UK. Both catalogues are an education in themselves in terms of the tremendous range of titles available.

Religiously Integrated Education in Northern Ireland

Edwin Graham, Mahvash Graham

Introduction

There are presently 12 planned integrated schools in Northern Ireland providing education for approximately 2,500 nursery, primary and post-primary pupils. The majority of the schools are already well-established and show all signs of continuing successfully into the twenty-first century. New integrated schools are currently being planned in Bangor, Larne and Derry, while under new legislation the parents of an existing controlled school in Craigavon (Brownlow High) have voted to transform the school into a controlled integrated school.

The Bahá'i community in the Province has given much support to the schools, with a relatively small number of Bahá'ís making a major contribution to the development of the movement for integrated education. The schools have been a source of encouragement to many who have seen them as a glimmer of hope in a divided society. Some Bahá'í parents have welcomed the integrated schools because of the opportunity they provide for the education of their children in a relatively plural environment. Their role in this regard is in sharp contrast to other schools in Northern Ireland which demonstrate almost complete religious segregation.

Many of the Bahá'ís who actively support the integrated schools suggest that the schools are trying to put Bahá'í teaching into practice, and for evidence they would say that the schools attempt to nurture an environment free from prejudice where pupils are treated equally regardless of their religious affiliation and encouraged to develop enquiring minds which independently establish truth.

A very notable aspect of many of the schools is that, because they have arisen as a result of parental initiative, there is an extremely high level of parental participation in all aspects of school life. Some of the schools have responded positively to the challenge of universal participation and have developed creative methods to ensure the optimum use of parents' energies.

Throughout this paper *integrated education* is referred to in the way the Northern Ireland Council for Integrated Education (NICIE) currently uses the term. The current definition of integrated educated in Northern Ireland is:

> *the education together in a school, on a footing of equality, of pupils drawn in equal numbers from the two major traditions with*

> *the aim of providing for them an effective standard of educational provision that gives equal recognition to and promotes equal expression of the two major traditions. The school is Christian in character, democratic and open in procedures and promotes the worth and self-esteem of all individuals within the school community. The school as an institution seeks to develop mutual respect and consideration of other institutions within the educational community. Its core aim is to provide the child with a caring and self-fulfilling educational experience which will enable her/him to become a fulfilled and caring adult in a society which is tolerant, Christian, respectful and protective of human rights and dignity and whose institutions are based on justice and toleration.*[1]

There is little doubt that many of the planned integrated schools have established new standards of educational practice in areas in Northern Ireland where previously little has been achieved. But a number of questions must be asked. The two main questions addressed in this paper are as follows: Will these schools be able to influence the development of education in Ireland? Is there a legitimate role for Bahá'ís in supporting the movement for integrated education in Ireland?

In order to look at the current situation of integrated education it is important to have a broad understanding of the historical development of education in Ireland, and therefore the next section examines the history of education in Ireland. It identifies five distinct attempts at integrated education, four of which have been totally unsuccessful, and provides a background from which it is possible to establish more clearly the viability of the present attempt at integrated education.

Historical Background to Integrated Education

Up until the beginning of the nineteenth century schools in Ireland had been used as a means of proselytising. In 1824 there were estimated to be 8,000 Catholic schools and of these some 7,600 were hedge schools (situated in a hedge and moved regularly from place to place to avoid detection by the authorities). In 1830 it was estimated that the hedge schools provided a better education than their contemporary state schools - such had been the failure of state education in Ireland.[2]

The first attempt at integrated education was made in 1811 when the Kildare Place Society was formed to provide education for Catholics and Protestants together. The society's assistance was to be equally available to "all classes of professing Christians, without any attempt to interfere with the peculiar religious opinions of any."[3] It had a difficult task to overcome the bitterness which had been built up over the previous centuries. A small number of Catholic schools co-operated for a time but soon the Catholic support for Kildare Place schools diminished and the initiative failed. After a debate in Parliament in 1831 the grant to the Kildare Place Society was withdrawn.

At the beginning of the nineteenth century there was a rapid development of Catholic schools. These schools were instrumental in establishing new standards of educational practice in Ireland. They included schools run by the Presentation Sisters, the Sisters of Mercy, the Loreto Sisters and the Christian Brothers.

The Royal Commission report in 1812 had stated a need for "a general plan of education for the lower classes keeping clear of all interference with the particular religious tenets of any and thereby inducing the whole to receive instruction as one body, under one and the same system and in the same establishment..." and further that "...no such plan however wisely and unexceptionally contrived in other respects can be carried into effectual execution in this country unless it be explicitly averred and clearly understood as its leading principle that no attempt should be made to influence or disturb the peculiar religious tenets of any section or description of Christians".[4]

Dr J.W. Doyle, Catholic Bishop of Kildare, gave much support to the concept of integrated education, saying in 1830: "I do not know any measure which would prepare the way for a better feeling in Ireland than uniting children at an early age and bringing them up in the same school leading them to commune with each other, to form their intimacies and friendships which often subsist through life".[5]

In 1831 Chief Secretary E.G. Stanley wrote to the Duke of Leinster explaining his intention "to unite in one system children of different creeds". Stanley's measure met with severe opposition from the Anglican authorities - in 1839 the Church Education Society was formed "for the purpose of affording to the children of the Church instruction in the holy Scriptures and in the catechism and in the formularies of the Church..."[6] In 1854 the Church Education Society took over the operation of all Kildare Place Schools. And then the opposition came from the Catholic ranks. First, in 1859 Archbishop Paul Cullen opposed mixed education, and then in 1864 Pope Pius IX issued an encyclical denying any right by the state to interfere in the education of Catholic children and forbidding the mixed principle. The second attempt at integrated education in Ireland had failed miserably.

The third attempt at integrated education happened after the partition of Ireland when the *Education Act 1923* was passed to attempt to bring together Protestants and Catholics in a single education system. The Catholic Bishops received the *Education Act 1923* with a storm of protest announcing that "the proposed schools are impossible for our children".[7] The Protestant denominations were almost equally hostile. As a result of the opposition the *Education Act 1923* was amended in such a way as to provide for segregated education.

After the outbreak of the "Troubles" there was growing concern from the general public in Northern Ireland about the damaging effects of segregation in society. There were a number of initiatives which began to combat segregation. Among these was a group formed to oppose segregation in schools. One of these, All Children Together (ACT), was formed in 1974 for the development of integrated education by consent in Northern Ireland. In 1978 All Children Together drafted an enabling measure to the Education (NI) Act, allowing existing schools, if the churches requested it, to become integrated schools. The enabling measure was never actioned by the churches. This represented the fourth failed attempt at integrated education.

In 1980 All Children Together prepared proposals for planned integrated schools with private funding, and Lagan College in South Belfast was opened as the first such school in 1981. Lagan soon proved to be successful and there was a rapid succession of similar schools both in Belfast and in provincial towns. The planned integrated schools were soon able to convince the Department of Education in NI of their viability and they received funding as Maintained schools.

With the Education Reform (NI) Order in 1989 the Department of Education was given the responsibility of promoting integrated education. The Order was vigorously opposed by the Catholic Bishops who claimed that it discriminated against denominational schools. To date the Department of Education has failed to give any grant to the Northern Ireland Council for Integrated Education (NICIE) - even though NICIE is the body which gives most support to integrated education. And in 1990, under the new legislation, some integrated schools were prevented from using positive discrimination to ensure the balance between Protestants and Catholics in the schools, creating the fear that the new integrated schools too would become segregated.

Lessons from History

The experience of the past warns us that even the most recent attempt at integrated education in Northern Ireland is vulnerable. The indications of its vulnerability come from two directions:

Denominational imbalance: The schools are not permitted to use positive discrimination to ensure reasonable numbers of Catholics and Protestants and to protect the rights of minorities. In the past when this has happened the schools effectively became Protestant schools. In the present situation many of the schools could through time effectively become Catholic schools.

Lack of protection: Although the recent legislation provides for the Department of Education to fund a central body to support integrated education, the Department has failed to date either to give a grant to the Northern Ireland Council for Integrated Education (NICIE) or to establish a separate body specifically for this purpose. Past history shows clearly how essential such a body would be in ensuring the safe development of integrated education.

Although there is little doubt that the schools will continue into the twenty-first century there must be considerable concern at this stage whether their objectives can continue to be met. The prevention of the schools using positive discrimination is likely to have quite a rapid effect on the extent of religious mixing that the schools will be able to achieve and therefore their primary objective of educating Protestants and Catholics together is called into question.

The secondary objective of integrated education, to establish schools which are "...protective of human rights and dignity and whose institutions are based on justice and toleration"[1] must also be called into question when there is no support for the Northern Ireland Council for Integrated Education to protect the schools or indeed for any other institution to do so. It is all too evident that the forces of society could ensure that the integrated schools end up being little different from other schools.

Bahá'í Support

In recent years there has been considerable support from the Bahá'í community for integrated schools in the Province. This support has been at a number of levels, as follows:

1. As parents of pupils (e.g Forge, Windmill, Enniskillen and Ballymena).
2. Assisting in the planning of schools (e.g Portadown, Windmill, Enniskillen, Ballymena, Omagh and Derry).
3. As members of Trusts (e.g Western Area Charitable Trust for Integrated Education)
4. As members of Governing Bodies of Schools (e.g Enniskillen, Omagh, Windmill and Derry).
5. Representing schools/Trusts at NICIE (e.g Western Area Charitable Trust for Integrated Education, Windmill).

In most cases the support from the Bahá'í community has come from individuals, however more recently the Derry Bahá'ís have as a community given support to the Oak Grove School Project. This has had the advantage that the member of that community who is a member of the project committee is there officially as a Bahá'í representative and not in an individual capacity.

As seen above, the involvement of Bahá'ís in integrated education has been at all levels. And this level of support has come from a very small number of Bahá'ís who have made a very large contribution in relation to their size. The contribution from Bahá'ís has probably made its most important impact on the way the schools have developed their priorities.

In the early years of the movement for integrated schools there was little Bahá'í involvement, and none outside Forge and Portadown. The early schools developed quite a strong Christian identity which tended to be exclusive rather than inclusive (this attitude still prevails in some of the early schools - notably Forge, Lagan and Bridge).
In the later years, and particularly in Windmill, Enniskillen, Omagh, Ballymena, Portadown and Derry, the Bahá'ís involved in these projects were able creatively to ensure that the Christian ethos to which all schools were committed was interpreted in a much more inclusive and open sense.

Furthermore, the involvement of Bahá'ís in discussions on community relations issues, and particularly in discussions on the ways in which religion should be taught in integrated schools, was a very major factor in allowing those schools to go beyond traditional boundaries. The success of such developments at local levels has influenced the Northern Ireland Council for Integrated Education (NICIE) and Bahá'í involvement at that level has ensured that the Statement of Principles currently being drafted by NICIE accommodates Bahá'í views so far as possible.

The Correctness of Bahá'í Involvement

Although there are some individual Bahá'ís and one community in Northern Ireland who have committed themselves wholeheartedly to supporting the movement for integrated education in the Province, this support has not come without much heart-searching and questioning. Nobody has any doubt that it is totally acceptable for Bahá'ís to choose to send their children to an integrated school but what should be our level of support for the movement for integrated education in the Province?

At the heart of this question is the fact that essentially the social development which has provided for integrated education has necessitated a parallel political development. This political development was most evident in 1989 when the Education Reform (Northern Ireland) Order was passed before Parliament. The Order laid upon the Department of Education in Northern Ireland the duty to "encourage and facilitate the development of integrated education."[8]

The scale of this political development can best be seen from the fact that whereas prior to the 1989 Order the Department of Education had no duties or responsibilities in relation to integrated education, the Order laid down 35 Articles defining ways in which the Department should support integrated education. The section of the Order devoted to integrated education was more than one-fifth of the total Order.

Such a significant development did not come without major resistance and it was not possible for those involved in developing schools at that time to do so without influencing the wider political development and to be involved in it.

There are a number of passages from the Writings which give very pertinent indications of the correctness or otherwise of Bahá'í involvement in such matters. Most Bahá'ís are familiar with the statement in *Gleanings*: "Soon will the present-day order be rolled up, and a new one spread out in its stead."[9]

Is this to be interpreted to mean that no matter what we do at this time it will be rolled up with the old world order? Or is it possible that developments at this time will be able to influence the way the new world order is spread out? Is it even possible that we are already beginning to see the new world order being spread out? Shoghi Effendi gave further guidance on this matter:

> *No scheme which the calculations of the highest statesmanship may yet devise; no doctrine which the most distinguished exponents of economic theory may hope to advance; no principle which the most ardent of moralists may strive to inculcate, can provide, in the last resort, adequate foundations upon which the future of a distracted world can be built. No appeal for mutual tolerance which the worldly-wise might raise, however compelling and insistent, can calm its passions or help restore its vigour. Nor would any general scheme of mere organised international cooperation, in whatever sphere of human activity, however ingenious in conception or extensive in scope, succeed in removing the root cause of the evil that has so rudely upset the equilibrium of present-day society.*[10]
> *What we Bahá's must face is the fact society is disintegrating so rapidly that moral issues which were clear a half century ago are now hopelessly confused and what is more, thoroughly mixed up with battling political interests. That is why the Bahá'ís must turn all their forces into the channel of building up the Bahá'i Cause and its Administration. They can neither change nor help the world in any other way at present. If they become involved in the issues the Governments of the world are struggling over, they will be lost. But if they build up the Bahá'í pattern they can offer it as a remedy when all else has failed.*[11]

But it is possible that when the Guardian wrote about 'present-day society' and said that "They can neither change nor help the world in any other way at present" that the statement was specific to that time and that the situation has changed so much that we are being called into action in new ways.

In 1984 the Universal House of Justice called for "...the implementation of a range of activities for their social and economic development which will not only be of immense value for the consolidation of communities and the development of their Bahá'í life, but will also benefit the wider [non-Bahá'í] communities within which they are embedded and will demonstrate the beneficial effects of the Bahá'í message to the crucial gaze of the world".[12]

In the 1990 Ridván Message the Universal House of Justice called our attention to the fact that the situation in the world was changing: "The affairs of mankind have reached a stage at which increasing calls will be made upon our community to assist, through advice and practical measures, in solving critical social problems... it becomes imperative for Bahá'í institutions to improve their performance, through greater conformity to the spirit and form of Bahá'í administration and through a keener reliance on the beneficial effects of proper consultation, so that the communities they guide will reflect a pattern of life that will offer hope to the disillusioned members of society."[13]

It is our feeling that individuals and communities should increasingly be involved in social and economic development projects out of a genuine concern to help society. But those who do become involved in such projects should be very careful to ensure that the projects do not totally eclipse their service to the Faith. Our most important task is teaching and while social and economic development projects can sometimes provide useful teaching opportunities and can help establish credibility for the Faith, our lives - and the Faith - will greatly suffer if we miss the opportunity to be active in teaching projects.

Conclusion

The movement for integrated education in Northern Ireland is facing major difficulties, although the individual schools which have been established recently seem quite secure. The present plight of integrated education, taken with the experiences of four previous unsuccessful attempts at integrated education, indicates that a willingness by a favourable government to promote a particular educational philosophy is on its own insufficient to guarantee results. The willingness by the government must be coupled with widespread grassroots support for the philosophy. This experience could have important implications for the way that Bahá'í education is developed.

Despite the difficulties which have faced the movement for integrated education, the new schools have been able to set new standards for educational practice in Northern Ireland. The most obvious of these are their commitment to foster open and enquiring minds which can independently investigate truth and the determination to encourage universal participation, especially through parental involvement. There are early indications that the benefits of these principles of the integrated schools are being recognised by the Department of Education in Northern Ireland and are being extended to other schools. In this way the extent of change which can be achieved by a very small number of schools has been impressive. There is little doubt that the Bahá'í community in Northern Ireland will also soon be able to exert a disproportionate influence on society.

There are many questions to be addressed around the issue of Bahá'í involvement in the movement for integrated education. This paper has suggested that Bahá'í involvement is legitimate on the basis of supporting a social and economic development project. There are a number of pitfalls which must be carefully avoided if Bahá'í involvement is to be fully productive. Most important is the issue of political involvement but also pertinent is the danger of allowing such involvement totally to eclipse the very necessary teaching work which is so important at present.

References

1. Northern Ireland Council for Integrated Education, *Statement of Principles*, Revised Draft, January 1991.
2. N. Atkinson, *Irish Education, A History of Educational Institutions* (Dublin: Allen Figgis), 1969, p 21.
3. Regulations of the Kildare Place Society, 1811, in *Irish Education*, p 69
4. National Commissioners to Sir John Hardinge, January 1835, in *Irish Education*, p 90.
5. Memo of T.S. Rice, c.1830, in *Irish Education*, p 93.
6. *Roman Church Education Society* in *Daily Express*, 21 September 1859.
7. N. Atkinson, *Irish Education*, p 25.
8. Education Reform (Northern Ireland) Order 1989, Article 64.
9. Bahá'u'lláh, *Gleanings from the Writings of Bahá'u'lláh* (Wilmette: Bahá'í Publishing Trust), 1983, p 7.
10. Shoghi Effendi, *The World Order of Bahá'u'lláh* (Wilmette: Bahá'í Publishing Trust), 1984, p 34.
11. Shoghi Effendi, *Directives from the Guardian*, pp 54-7.
12. The Universal House of Justice, To the Bahá'ís of the World, letter of 2 Jan 1984.
13. The Universal House of Justice, To the Bahá'ís of the World, Ridván Message, 1990.

Towards a Bahá'í Development Model: The Contribution of the Rural Education and Development Programme of FUNDAEC, Colombia

Michael Richards, Sarah Richards

Introduction

FUNDAEC, a non governmental organisation, was founded in 1974 by a group of university teachers, including some Bahá'ís, to explore alternative approaches to education and development. Their "Rural University" model, based on Bahá'í principles, has been successfully replicated in other parts of Colombia, and is being introduced into several Latin American countries.[1,2] A lengthy diagnosis of the development problem led FUNDAEC's founders to conclude that non-formal rural education, combined with appropriate village level structures for consultation, organisation and project implementation, was essential for genuine participation and thus sustainable development.

A rural education programme,[3] officially recognised as equivalent to the country's secondary school syllabus, evolved around painstakingly developed educational materials which attempted to integrate the material and spiritual education of rural dwellers, in so far as this is possible without direct use of the Word of God. The emphasis is on the development of the necessary skills, knowledge and abilities to enable rural youth to investigate their own problems and develop community level solutions. Service to the community as the underlying motivational force is emphasised throughout the programme.

This integration of material and spiritual education by a "secular" organisation goes some way towards a Bahá'í model of development. It has supported and complemented the Bahá'í deepening programme of its sister organisation the Ruhi Institute,[4] and has contributed to a very large expansion of the Bahá'í Faith in the Cauca Valley region of Colombia.

The Evolution of FUNDAEC's Ideas

FUNDAEC, the Foundation for the Application and Teaching of Sciences, is a Non Governmental Organisation founded in 1974 in Cali, Colombia, by a group of university teachers, including several Bahá'ís, disaffected by the lack of impact of conventional education on the development process. Their first task was to make a lengthy diagnosis of education and development in rural Colombia.

It was realised that "development", defined mainly in terms of modernisation and industrialisation, was failing to improve the living conditions of the vast majority of the inhabitants of the so-called developing countries - in fact, very much the reverse: the urban and rural elites got richer and those at the bottom got poorer. Development projects tended to be paternalistically perceived, with development as a product to be handed out. Increased dependency of rural people on projects and "outsiders" was observed to be a major consequence of development projects.

At the same time, in Colombia as elsewhere, alternative approaches to development were beginning to gain ground. The search for new development approaches resulted in greater emphasis on research and diagnosis of problems before action (projects), the increased importance of community participation and of the role of education and training, if development projects were to create anything lasting. The concept of "integrated rural development" gained popularity.

However, the FUNDAEC group observed major limitations in these newer development approaches, and indeed those largely persisting today. Among these problems was that "integrated" did not include the spiritual dimension, and therefore development projects did not touch on the underlying spiritual causes of underdevelopment which relate to the condition of the human soul, and "man's inhumanity to man." In other words, development projects were designed around the concept of man as a material, or at best social, being, rather than around man as having a spiritual reality. Secondly, development was seen as a product (rather than a process) in which the beneficiaries of these projects depend on the initiatives, research and technical solutions designed by outside experts. For example "participation" tends to be limited to elaborate methods of inducing villagers to be involved and participate in projects designed by others, whereas FUNDAEC defined participation in terms of people gaining control over their own destinies, through research, design and implementation of their own development process. The capacity of people to "participate" more fully in the development process depends on their skills, knowledge and abilities.

The formal education system was analyzed both in terms of preparing people for work and life in the rural areas (as a means to an end), and in terms of furthering the intellectual and spiritual development of the individual (an end in itself), and was found to be sadly lacking on both counts. In fact, the *urban biased* education system, with its bias against agriculture and rural life, was clearly exerting a negative effect on the rural development process. An example of this is the attitude of school leavers to farming: their goals and aspirations, which have been partially influenced by the education system, lead them to search for work in the cities. Farming is considered a low prestige occupation, contrary to the statements found in the Bahá'í and other religious writings.

Another important finding was the lack of an organisational base for development. This limited access to vital institutional resources like credit, extension and training to isolated individual initiatives. There was no basis for the vital process of consultation necessary to develop activities, solve problems and mobilise community resources; this consultation was seen by FUNDAEC as vital to real participation. Rural institutions or organisations are not only vital for consultation and participation, they also create the possibility for sustainable development - often to take over when the development organisation leaves off. The destiny of any individual farmer is linked to his neighbours: to progress the villagers need to be educated, to have access to credit, information and technical assistance, and for all this a viable organisation is needed.

The Rural University

Having established that the basic building block was village-based institutions or structures, the second essential element was defined as knowledge. "It could be claimed that a people were in charge of their own development only if they were learning systematically about the changes that occurred in their society, and were consciously incorporating in their continuous learning process appropriate elements from the universe of knowledge."[1] This *universe of knowledge* includes both their own knowledge and that of other peoples and groups in the world facing similar problems. Thus a systematic learning process with access to global knowledge was added to appropriate village structures as preconditions for sustainable development.

On the basis of these ideas, FUNDAEC's founders dedicated themselves to the establishment of an institution that would evolve into the learning institution of a particular region of Colombia - the Valley of Cauca. They called this institution a Rural University, the name itself chosen partly to question the usual university model being used everywhere as an instrument of urban-biased development. The tasks of the Rural University were defined in terms of a series of learning processes among the rural population, designed to set in motion positive integrating spiritual, economic and social forces that would resist and eventually overcome opposing disintegrating forces; for example maintenance of exploitative marketing and credit arrangements by individuals both within and outside the community, which serve continually to widen the gap between the haves and the have-nots.

A spiritual basis to the Rural University
The spiritual basis of FUNDAEC's approach (shared by its sister organisation the Ruhi Institute) to education and development can be found in Bahá'u'lláh's assertion that man is "as a mine rich in gems of inestimable value."

Lack of a proper education has prevented humankind developing spiritual potentialities thereby to enable their true spiritual natures to overcome the darker, more material side of human nature. This conviction led to FUNDAEC's emphasis on the development of an educational programme for the integral spiritual, intellectual and emotional development of rural youth, who, in turn, would constitute the resources for the subsequent programmes of research and action. Thus people were really placed at the centre of the development process, rather than being seen as either obstacles to change, or at best beneficiaries of development projects.

The Rural University was defined as a "social space" in which two systems of knowledge, a modern sophisticated one and a traditional one pertaining to the people of the region, would interact in a healthy way to produce important development processes within the rural population itself. Research and education were to be the two main activities of the Rural University, together with the fostering of appropriate village structures. It was realised that while such actions are necessary conditions for development, they are not in themselves sufficient. Substantial improvements in the lives of rural people will not be made only by changes from within: new spiritually-based values and institutions have to be forged on a world level to allow changes to take place which would dramatically improve people's lives, for example by a massive redistribution of land and through fairer world markets.

It would also be fair to say that the FUNDAEC approach to development is based on the twin Bahá'í paths of individual spiritualisation and building the administrative order. Farzam Arbab, FUNDAEC's first Director, once said that real development was working for these two goals, not the activities of multi or bilateral aid agencies with their development project approach, as these latter were not creating conditions under which sustainable development could occur. Thus any Bahá'í striving to bring waiting souls nearer to God or to build up the Administrative (New World) Order is working far more effectively for development than any official development worker!

FUNDAEC's Rural Education Methodology

In spite of their criticisms of the education system, FUNDAEC's rural education programme seeks not to reject formal education per se, but to change its content and make it relevant to the needs, aspirations and opportunities of rural people. FUNDAEC's System of Tutorial Learning (SAT, in Spanish) has three basic levels at the secondary school level; each level is of approximately 18 months, to two years, duration and, if the student desires, leads on to the next level.

The first level of SAT is that of a *Promoter of Rural Well-being*. Students, mainly youth who have dropped out of the formal school system after primary school, study a series of 28 textbooks developed by FUNDAEC in the areas of agriculture, mathematics, service to the community, including literacy training and preventive health care, language, ideas about society, and descriptions. In these materials knowledge is compartmentalised, so that, for example, when the students study mathematics, examples are taken from agriculture. This is based on the well-established principle that learning occurs much faster when based on subject matter relevant and useful to the student. It is also an example of the unity in diversity principle, and can be a highly motivational system of learning, whereby, for example, positive attitudes to agriculture are developed.

In the tutorial system, the students receive their classes at times convenient for them, often in the evenings or at weekends, so that study does not interfere with work or even formal education. The tutors, who are now mainly graduates of the Rural University (another aspect of its durability), are seen as facilitators rather than teachers. Groups and individuals go at their own pace with their own textbooks, the faster ones being urged to help the slower - part of the service to the community ethic.

Wherever possible the promoters carry out practical *learning by doing projects*. For example, as part of the agriculture course each group of students has to plant and tend a plot in which crops, sometimes new to the area, are tested in different combinations in an attempt to diversify monocultures like maize and cassava, which have caused rapid declines in soil fertility. In the Service to the Community course, each promoter has to give literacy classes and also help neighbouring families diagnose their health problems and improve hygiene. The emphasis all along is on the practical and useful, and on the skills, knowledge and abilities to enable youth to live and work more happily and productively in the rural areas and for the betterment of their communities, rather than join the swelling ranks of the urban underemployed.

The second and third stages of the Rural University are those of the *Practitioner* and *Bacillar in Rural Well-being*, supported by equivalent sets of textbooks developed by FUNDAEC. The Ministry of Education in Colombia has officially recognised these three levels as equivalent to the entire secondary school syllabus.

FUNDAEC has recently begun a four-year university degree in Rural Education. These higher and higher levels of education in the rural areas are necessary to raise the capability of rural people to conduct research, solve problems and implement projects, or in other words, to assume an ever greater control over their own development. At an individual level, rural people have the same right to develop their intellectual as well as spiritual potentials as have urban dwellers. Science and education is the heritage of all.

At the other end of the educational spectrum, FUNDAEC has developed materials with a higher Bahá'í content at the pre-school level and is working towards the development of a stage beneath the Promoter of Rural Well-being level. The need is not quite so great at the primary school level in Colombia, because in recent years a highly innovative and successful rural primary school programme called the New School system has been developed. In other less fortunate countries, however, the need is very great for a primary level non-formal rural education system, for those who do not get beyond the first years of schooling.

The programme of FUNDAEC also covers a number of other vital processes for development: the search for alternative agricultural systems on small farms; the development of a marketing system, based around the village storehouse, a community structure described by 'Abdu'l-Bahá in *Foundations of World Unity*;[5] the development of a Fund for Rural Well-being to which profit-making activities in the village contribute; kindergartens; the setting up of information posts for agriculture and livestock; and the establishment of small businesses and agro-industry.

The Integration of Material & Spiritual Education

The success of any technical or organisational improvement depends ultimately on the spiritual dimension. Since FUNDAEC is a "secular" organisation, which receives its funding from a variety of mainly international sources, it is unable to teach the Bahá'í Faith in a direct way, although one course uses a book called *The Power of Pure Actions*, based on the Holy Writings. However, Bahá'í principles are incorporated at every stage of the education programme: service to the community, the development of spiritual qualities, and unity in diversity all figure very prominently in the materials, and at least half the tutors are Bahá'ís.

Conclusion

The FUNDAEC experience is worthy of study for its theoretical and practical contributions to rural education and development alone. However, its greatest contribution for the future of mankind has surely been the integration of material and spiritual elements into a knowledge system that can enable individuals and eventually entire populations to contribute to the creation of a new world order.

We believe that the FUNDAEC rural education model, which has been implemented in most of Colombia's rural areas with the active and material support of the Ministry of Education and is now being replicated in other countries in Latin America, although by no means a panacea solution, has enormous importance for rural development. More importantly, it provides a prototype model for the future integrated material and spiritual education of mankind. It is the nearest we have to a Bahá'í model of rural development.

Finally, it is interesting to note that this area of Colombia has become a genuine mass conversion area, the apparent result of the two parallel programmes of FUNDAEC and the Ruhi Institute - mankind clearly needs both material and spiritual education, although the former is clearly subordinate to the latter.

References

1. F. Arbab, *Rural University: Learning about Education and Development*. (Ottawa: International Development Research Centre), 1984.
2. F. Arbab, G. Correa, F. de Valcarcel, *FUNDAEC: Its Principles and Activities*, Rural Education Doc - Engl 1 CELATER - FUNDAEC. Cali, Colombia.
3. *A Survey of Basic Education Activities in Selected Bahá'í Communities*. Paper prepared for the UN office of the Bahá'í International Community (Haifa: Bahá'í World Centre), 1988.
4. Fundacion Ruhi, *Strengthening and Systematising the Efforts of Core Groups of the Rural University* (Haifa: Bahá'í World Centre), 1989, submitted to the Office of Social and Economic Development, for approval to be submitted to CIDA and other aid agencies.
5. 'Abdu'l-Bahá, *Foundations of World Unity* (Wilmette: Bahá'í Publishing Trust), 1976.

Festivals and Feasts:
Instruments of Community Development

I.S Narula, J. Jowsey, A. Jowsey

Introduction

Festivals and Feasts have generally been regarded as repositories of the beliefs, traditions and practices of a community, incorporating its manifold manifestations ranging from the religious to the economic. They can also be seen as sensitive indicators of the changing perceptions, consciousness and spirituality of a community.

In the Bahá'í community, the observance of festivals and Feasts are key elements facilitating the evolution of the Bahá'í community life.[1] The Nineteen Day Feast is particularly important, because of its frequency, regularity and its operation at the very heart of the community. It is an instrument that "integrates the spiritual, administrative and social processes of life" and "encompasses all units of human society".[2]

A shift from instruction in a classroom setting to education and training in a community setting, employing the analogy of humanity being the student, is required for expansion and consolidation activities, leading to human resource and community development. The Holy Days provide the content for such training and the Nineteen Day Feast the "arena of democracy at the very root of society"[3] where social and citizenship skills are learned and practised.

The Importance of Experience in Human Resource and Community Development

The Nineteen Day Feast (and to some extent the Holy Day celebrations) "aside from its spiritual significance ... combines an array of elemental social disciplines which educate its participants in the essentials of responsible citizenship".[4]

It is the experiencing of the Feast by the participants, founded on hospitality, that makes it a learning experience where social and interpersonal skills are acquired and tested. The following premises of experiential learning become operational during a well-planned and well-conducted Feast and to an extent during festivals.

Individuals are unique and learn in different ways. Therefore there is a need to provide different approaches to accommodate the many ways in which people learn. People learn as a result of their experiences. People learn best when what they are learning is related to what they want to achieve or accomplish and what they already know in a manner that is enjoyable. People are motivated to learn skills and acquire knowledge when learning activities focus on problems and issues that concern them.

Knowledge and skills acquire a greater meaning if opportunities are provided to apply the knowledge and utilise the skills productively. This implies being able to practise skills.

Origins and Role of Festivals and Feasts

The common perceptions of festivals and feasts in the community at large cannot be isolated from the cultural, social, historical and environmental make-up of its locality. Festivals, invariably, derive their origins from ancient or prehistoric rites and reflect astronomical or agrarian cycles as they impinged on the wellbeing of the community. The primary purpose of a festival or feast is to commemorate a religious (in its broadest sense) anniversary. The individual's part in, and sense of belonging to a community is reinforced. The identity and position of his community in relationship to the society at large, and with the universe and its Creator, are restated and affirmed. With the gradual dissipation of the potent mystical and celestial content of festivals, the prominent spiritual principle is gradually superseded by the rituals and ceremonies, leaving only an enigmatic folk custom of forgotten origins. These folk customs further undergo change with the passing of time, reflecting the evolution of that community.

Some Examples
The culmination of the agricultural year, and the winter solstice in Europe and North America, are celebrated as the harvest festival and Christmas or New Year respectively. These are excellent examples of the relationship of festivals to astronomical and agrarian cycles with superimposed mystical overtones and added religious symbols.

In the UK, the declining agricultural population in what, prior to the industrial and information eras, were largely agricultural communities, has led to a gradual decline in the observance of the Harvest Festival to a point where it appears that it is being abandoned altogether in some areas. On the other hand, the winter solstice, originally an ancient pagan festival, is celebrated as Christmas with the superimposed religious symbolism of Christianity, and as the New Year with its secular symbolism. Easter, also a pre-Christian festival, is linked with the seasonal cycle of spring with its agrarian and celestial origins and is observed as part of the Christian calendar.

Generic Characteristics of Feasts and Festivals

The generic features that characterise feasts and festivals include the following:

1. Special services from a spiritual and devotional perspective expressed as observance of ceremonies and rituals.
2. Suspension of work as a mark of respect and a demonstration of a focus on the spiritual verities underlying the festival.
3. Reaffirmation of the origin of the traditions, rituals and ceremonies being observed so as to derive spiritual sustenance and seek rejuvenation through periods set aside for prayer and the performance of rites.
4. Preparation of special foods reflecting the seasonality and the conditions that attended the original circumstances of the festival.
5. Suspension of normal social conventions during the festival period.[5]
6. The wearing of special forms of dress and personal decorations. Examples include the role of kimonos during the Ubon Festival of the Dead in Japan, or the wearing of hats with flowers and ribbons and dresses by men during the Olive Harvest Festival in Malaga (Southern Spain).
7. Decorations at home places of worship and places where the community gathers, reflecting the spirit and origins of the festival.
8. The giving of gifts and performing acts of philanthropy and charity.
9. Increased levels and intensity of hospitality for friends and strangers, the removing social, class and other barriers which operate at other times of the year.
10. Setting the stage for the generation and exhibition of a wide range of emotional expressions not normally demonstrated,[6] creating a very charged community-wide emotional atmosphere.

The Experience of the Individual and the Community

The two attributes of *increased hospitality*, associated with the preparation and consumption of special foods, and the *display of emotional expressions* are often the only important parts of a festival in many communities. These probably represent the nearest approach to a religious experience average members of a community may encounter in a secular society alienated from its natural surroundings. The putting up of decorations and the wearing of special dresses are practised to a lesser extent.

The creation of a special atmosphere and the preparation that goes into setting the stage for the festival, with the efforts made to get all segments of the community involved, generates a sense of belonging. It also allows for an experience of the collective not easily available to the individual in the course of his or her rather insular existence. In the Bahá'í community, and in some other religious communities, participation in a festival or a feast offers the opportunity to experience the collective, the sense of unity of the community, and a sense of meaningful participation and hospitality, "with all its implications of friendliness, courtesy, service, generosity and conviviality".[7]

Holy Days

Bahá'í Holy Days can be considered as true festivals when applying the above characteristics. One of these, Naw-Rúz, is based on the astronomical spring solstice, while the other eight are associated with events surrounding the Central Figures of the Faith. These Holy Days in themselves represent the guideposts of the Faith, the commemoration of which annually redefines the commitment of the believers to the Faith they have espoused. They also provide, in the lives of its adherents and their communities, a profound mystical experience that links them to their Creator, thus stimulating their spiritual growth and the maturation and development of the communities.
Suspension of work during these Holy Days serves as a further reminder of one's spiritual obligations with the recognition that the material part of our existence is to prepare for the life beyond.

The Fast, the primary engine of spiritual rejuvenation, is situated after the Intercalary Days, days of feasting and giving of gifts. Similarly Naw-Rúz, the New Year Feast, is evidence that Holy Days provide a framework that canalises human expression in its varied forms towards the construction of a new civilisation. Expression takes such forms as courtesy, friendliness, generosity, participation and conviviality.
The encouragement to perform charitable acts and philanthropic deeds during these Holy Days is another characteristic that contributes to the development of the community and the exaltation of the individuals involved in these acts. It also redounds to the intensity and profundity of the spiritual sentiments that motivated such actions. Thus Holy Days provide opportunities to demonstrate the attributes of the higher self. In this sense, the Holy Days provide a curricular framework for a potentially intense experiential learning event.

The Nineteen Day Feast

One of the unique features of the Bahá'í Faith is the relationship of the calendar and the coming together of the community. The Nineteen Day Feast, the microcosm of the World Order of Bahá'u'lláh, embraces "all units of human society; integrates the spiritual, administrative and social processes of life; canalises human expression ...at the very base of society". Functioning at the various collective levels of society, namely "the village, the town, the city," "it is intended to promote unity, ensure progress, and foster joy".[8]

The "Feast may well be seen in its unique combination of modes as the culmination of a great historic process in which the primary elements of community life - acts of worship, of festivity and other forms of togetherness - over vast stretches of time have achieved a glorious convergence". [9] It bestows upon this institution the pride of position as the foremost instrument of community development aided and reinforced by the Holy Day commemorations.

The three parts of the Nineteen Day Feast reflect the primary elements of community life. The acts of worship are reflected in the devotional part. The other forms of togetherness are expressed through the administrative part, the bedrock of which is consultation between the Local Spiritual Assembly and the individual. This has obvious implications for communication between the local community and the national and international levels of administration, for the establishment of the link that connects the local community. It also links dynamically to the entire structure of the Administrative Order; and the operation of collective processes in which the "individuals are free to offer their gifts of thought, whether as new ideas or constructive criticism".[10] Further, it has implications for the education of the participants in the essentials of responsible citizenship utilising an array of elemental social disciplines such as unity in diversity of thought and action, the art of consultation, the attitude of service to others, etc.

The three distinct but related parts of the Feast and the concept of the Feast must be adequately understood.[11] The devotional part of the Feast provides for the religious experience during which connection is established and reinforced between man and his Creator and "entails the recitation of prayers and reading from the Holy Texts".[11] Turning to this same source also contributes to the drawing together of the members of the community in humility, unity and affection. The administrative part "is a general meeting where the Local Spiritual Assembly ... shares news and messages from the World Centre and the National Assembly and receives the thoughts and recommendations of the friends through a process of consultation" meeting "on common ground".[12] Here is the "arena of democracy at the very root of society" which "links the individual to the collective process by which a society is built or restored".

The social part "involves the partaking of refreshments and engaging in other activities meant to foster fellowship in a culturally-determined diversity of forms which do not violate principles of the Faith or the essential character of the Feast." The Feast is "rooted in hospitality", which serves "as the sustaining spirit of so significant an institution" introducing "a revolutionary new attitude to the conduct of human affairs at all levels".[13]

The regularity of the Nineteen Day Feast is in itself one factor that lends to the Feast merit as a tool for community development. The implications of a new solar-based calendar on the economic and social life of mankind are as yet unenvisaged. The attributes as names of the months, attributes that man needs to acquire to become more spiritual, require exploration from a community development point of view. This elucidation of this relationship will require time and experience in much the same way as the evolution of the Feast itself, which has effloresced "as if a symphony, in three movements, had now been completed".[14]

It becomes apparent that the occurrence of such a Feast at the very heart of a community with a regularity resembling its very heartbeat, sustains and nurtures its life and growth. The observance of the Nineteen Day Feast, "this divine festival", in association with the observance of the Holy Days within the framework of a calendar of nineteen months of nineteen days each, with attributes as names of the months and days of the week, presents other communities with a potent instrument to attain the "joy", "agreement and unity", "affection and fellowship" and to lay "the foundation ... for the realisation of so unprecedented a reality", a reality of "world unity which the Central Figures of our Faith laboured so long and suffered so much cruelty to bring into being".[15]

If the Feast is to be properly experienced, preparation of it and the preparation for it must also be taken into consideration. The responsibility for the conduct of the Feast devolves upon the Local Spiritual Assembly and therefore it is pivotal that Assemblies create the necessary infrastructure for the preparation and conduct of the Feast and for the participation of the friends in it.

Since the very essence of the Feast is the education of its participants, every effort needs to be made to ensure that no believer leaves the Feast without having learned something that will inspire and sustain him in the service of the Faith. Careful application of the premises of experiential learning could greatly contribute to this end.
To promote effective participation, it is important to ensure that the believers are informed of the time and place of the Feast. Every effort should be made to make the Feast accessible to all the believers in the community, even if this requires that the Assembly make arrangements to help people reach the Feast.

The Feast should be relevant and its programme content be "culturally determined" so that those attending feel that the Feast was prepared for them. Every member of the community should be made to feel that he or she has something to contribute, even if is only an attentive silence, and to participate such that "all the friends - every man, woman and youth ... demonstrate ... the unified spirit of their association one with another, the rectitude of conduct in relation to all, and the excellence of their achievements, that they belong to a truly enlightened and exemplary community".[16] A sense of anticipation that one is attending a divine festival needs to be generated and sustained.

Talks and related activities could be arranged to entertain and lift the spirits so that "the friends will, once in nineteen days, find themselves spiritually restored".[17]

Conclusion

The importance of feasts and festivals as indicators and vehicles of community growth cannot be overstated. "The winds of God rage on, upsetting old systems, adding impetus to the deep yearning for a new order in human affairs."[18] "The Order brought by Bahá'u'lláh is intended to guide the progress and resolve the problems of society. Our numbers are yet too small to effect an adequate demonstration of the potentialities inherent in the administrative system."[19] The bedrock of this administrative system is the Nineteen Day Feast reinforced by the Holy Day observances. "Since the Administrative Order is designed to be a pattern for future society, the visibility of such a pattern will be a signal of hope to those who despair."[20]

"The affairs of mankind have reached a stage at which increasing calls will be made upon our community to assist, through advice and practical measures, in solving critical social problems. It is a service that we will gladly render."[21] The Holy Day observances and Nineteen Day Feasts are potent learning experiences. The more the believers demonstrate that they have acquired the essentials of responsible citizenship, the greater will be the religious experience that will serve as a magnet attracting others to the Faith. In contemporary society festivals reflect its present state, but in the Bahá'í Faith, feasts and festivals demonstrate the animating power of the Covenant as it galvanises the evolution of its world community.

Festivals and feasts as envisaged and practised (even in their embryonic forms) in the Bahá'í community provide one of the most powerful instruments for its development. Therefore, an effective use and application of the spirit and form of these feasts and festivals can demonstrate to the world at large the accessibility to, and appropriateness of, an effective tool for community development.

References

1. Shoghi Effendi, *God Passes By* (Wilmette: Bahá'í Publishing Trust), 1974, p 214.
2. Universal House of Justice, letter of 27 August 1989.
3. *ibid.*
4. *ibid.*
5. An excellent example of this is the festival of Holi in India where men and women are allowed open social physical contact when applying bright colours to each other's faces and bodies during the celebration (activities not accepted conventionally).
6. For instance the expressions of grief and remorse during the commemoration of Muharram.

7. Universal House of Justice, letter of 27 August 1989.
8. *ibid.*
9. *ibid.*
10. *ibid.*
11. *ibid.*
12. *ibid.*
13. *ibid.*
14. *ibid.*
15. *ibid.*
16. Universal House of Justice, To the Bahá'ís of the World, Ridván Message, 1990, p 4.
17. Universal House of Justice, letter of 27 August 1989, p 2.
18. Universal House of Justice, To the Bahá'ís of the World, Ridván Message, 1990, p 5.
19. *ibid.*
20. *ibid.*
21 *ibid.*

Bahá'í Education for 2½ to 4 year olds

Marion Prentice

This paper is based on the experience of one regional Bahá'í Sunday School nursery teacher who has *grown* with the children, and is written with the hope that the content will help would-be nursery teachers to avoid some of the pitfalls and reap some of the benefits of a most rewarding task.

Preparation

When asked to be a teacher I felt very unsure of my ability, and definitely reluctant. I have experience as a mother and grandmother, but being responsible for teaching other people's children is a different matter!

I went to the library and borrowed some books on primary teaching. There were few which actually addressed the subject of teaching 2½ to 4 year olds, the general assumption being that at this age children only "play". However it was easy to adapt and simplify many of the ideas in the primary teachers' books.

Then I visited several playgroups and nursery schools in the area to see what they do. Many, I noticed, are simply playgroups with no direction. Others were more structured, with little lessons incorporated into the play. All of them had a wide variety of materials, toys, books, etc.

2½ to 4 years old - What is special about this age?

In the writer's opinion this is the most precious age; a clean slate, an empty vessel, sweetly innocent, pure and eager to experience everything. This is the age at which children learn and absorb more than at any other time of their life. Some learning psychologists estimate that by the age of five a child's intelligence quotient is basically established, and that by this age attitudes toward learning and patterns of thinking have settled into one's mind. They see the early childhood years as the time for building the foundations of human intelligence.[1] If this is true, then it is vital that learning at this age is assisted in every possible way through organised play.

The Needs of the $2^{1/2}$ to 4 year old

The Bahá'í Sunday School teacher has precious few hours in which to cover this vast ground, and much of the work overlaps with what the children will learn with their parents at home, and, if they attend them, at their nursery schools and playgroups during the week. The Bahá'í content of the lessons has to be integrated with every new thing they are learning day by day - this will be discussed later.

In a Bahá'í context the needs at this age are to develop a closeness to, and love of, 'Abdu'l-Bahá and what he represents. The Universal House of Justice stated that "the heart and essential foundation of all education is spiritual and moral training".[2] The teacher must then engage the children in activities which help them to develop knowing, willing and loving capabilities, and in a way which helps preserve the innocent qualities which they already possess.

This can only be achieved by establishing a loving and trusting relationship with the teacher. The children need to feel safe, to have the freedom to explore, and above all to enjoy what they are doing. Of course, parameters must be set, and there have to be clear expectations on the teacher's part as to what behaviour is acceptable. Discipline is most effective when an errant child is taken aside and informed of how his/her behaviour is adversely affecting the rest of the class. This method is slightly disconcerting for the recipient and can generate a feeling of responsibility.

In the case of the very youngest a great deal of patience is required, especially where the child is particularly shy and will not communicate, or will not participate, or both. These children must have a great deal of loving encouragement, praise and reward until they feel safe enough to be involved. The more outgoing children must be taught to understand that shyness is not unfriendliness, and in helping the more timid ones the older children can be encouraged to learn a few social skills, such as offering a greeting, "Hello ...", expressing affection, "I like you", or inviting them to play or help with a project. Having said this, at times I have felt that it may be a good idea to have a separate "playgroup" for the 2½ to 3 year olds before they join the class in order to have some experience of communicating with other children, and in fact I noted that one school has actually done this. The reason for saying this is that to teach 2½ to 4 year olds as one group presents the teacher with the difficult task of engineering activities of a group nature which are challenging enough for a nearly five year old with developed skills, and simple enough for a 2½ year old who is virtually still a baby. Then a small voice in my head admonishes me with "if you can't manage this then you should not be teaching!"

However, when examining the pros and cons more closely, my answer is always yes, there should be a pre-nursery school playgroup, if there are enough "tiddlers" to warrant it, and if it does not detract from the main class. I suspect in most cases there are only just enough children of the mixed age group to make up a class (in my case at the present time there are only 7) so the loss of the two smallest ones would make a big difference.

For anyone contemplating being a teacher I would say do not be put off by a "big" class, for it is far easier to manage a class where you have enough children to organise team and group activities than it is with just four or five where two children do not want to be involved in team games!

Faced with the problem of integrating the babies with the older children, with the shy ones, with the ones who are not motivated to do anything physically, one has to find ways of inducing some communication, and I have found that making puppets and using them for enacting a play is a very successful way of triggering normally silent children into articulation. One child who had not uttered a word for six weeks suddenly became very vociferous by adopting a different identity and talking through her puppet.

My overall vision for the class is to lay down the foundation of excellence in all future stages and create an environment in which even the smallest of the children can become everything that 'Abdu'l-Bahá would wish them to be. The desired outcomes could be listed as follows:

>   Improved ability to communicate
>   Improved self-confidence
>   Improved ability to work with others
>   A strong sense of love for 'Abdu'l-Bahá
>   A personalised relationship with 'Abdu'l-Bahá

The Needs and Resources of the Teacher and Parent

The physical needs are good premises, having a clean, light and airy room with plenty of space and from which potentially dangerous objects can be easily removed, a power point, and easy access to water and toilet. It is unfortunate that most Bahá'í Sunday School nursery teachers are at a great disadvantage in not being able to set up equipment and leave it on the premises, as would happen in a regular nursery school. This rather limits the type of material and equipment that can be used, and rules out bigger items such as climbing frames, sandpits, etc. However, with a little inventiveness and ingenuity one can usually overcome these limitations by either scaling down or compromising.

At the Thomas Breakwell School (South-East) the Management Committee, recognising that a great variety of materials were needed for the nursery class, generously allotted £50 per term, and we have gradually built up a small stock of standard items which are taken to the class weekly. These include pictures of 'Abdu'l-Bahá, a story, powder paints (4 colours), non-spill paint pots each with a separate brush, and three plastic pinafores. A Nobo board serves as an artist's easel, and children can paint whenever the urge takes them. We also maintain a stock of coloured construction paper, glue, several pairs of children's scissors, cotton/string, and anything useful for collage such as bottle tops, macaroni, sequins, wool, etc.

Other essential materials are computer paper (very useful for drawing round prostrate figures to measure height and size - they can be filled in with eyes, nose and mouth and pinned on the wall), home made play dough with rolling pins and pastry cutters and any other objects that feels good in dough. We also have a number of games for 3 year olds obtained from the Early Learning Centre (shape game, matching game, colour identification game, picture and word matching game, dominoes for counting, and bean bags for throwing and catching), balloons for use in games, music tapes for young children - Red Grammer especially useful, and percussion instruments. (For a list of recommended books and tapes see Appendix A.) Most important are some tissues, a bowl of water, several clean rags, and some soap. In addition to the props to demonstrate the particular lesson for that day, all these things are brought to the lesson each week.

Apart from the physical things, the teacher needs parents who are supportive but not interfering, and a well-organised management within the School. This latter aspect can be very important, as a visitor who wanders into the class with a day-visiting child can be very disruptive. This also applies to any visitor who comes into the class without pre-arrangement; to have someone walk right into the middle of an important story which is the basis of your lesson can have a disastrous effect and lose the concentration of the little ones immediately.

Parents and teachers alike, therefore, need to know that the smallest children in the school are taken very seriously, and that their support is required to help the class run smoothly. The teacher needs to know the full names, ages, and birthdays (so that they can be celebrated) of the children, and the Registrar or Director helps enormously by providing the teacher with these details. Discipline is needed in fetching children to and from class to prevent them going astray, and a reliable Assistant is absolutely essential because inevitably there will be the occasion when a child has to be taken to the toilet, or there is some minor mishap when the teacher has to leave the room to fetch a parent (in many of the playgroups and nursery schools visited there was a ratio of one adult to four children).

The parents need to know what is happening to their children on Sunday mornings, and to this end an explanatory note when the child begins school is useful, as well as an end of term report. The parents are also encouraged to leave the classroom as soon as possible for two reasons: (a) several parents in a classroom almost always chatter together and forget the children and (b) the presence of a parent inhibits the process of forming a close teacher/child relationship.

Aims and Objectives

1. That the children may foster love for 'Abdu'l-Bahá, may recognise His picture, say His name, know who He is.
2. To have the children attain the virtues of 'Abdu'l-Bahá; polite, obedient, loving, generous, giving, willing, considerate, compassionate, respectful, tolerant, patient, cooperative, forgiving etc.
3. As well as having high regard for others, the children would have self-esteem, be able to relate to each other and cooperate, laying the foundation for the teacher of the following age group.
4. A strong awareness of Bahá'í identity and of being a member of a world family.
5. Some understanding of God and the connection between themselves and Creation.

At the end of term the children like to receive a picture certificate acknowledging them for their best attributes. A certificate with lots of writing will have little meaning for a little one who can't read, but a picture depicting the quality/attribute with the child's name written in large letters will be something to be proud of. This is also a good exercise for the teacher as it focuses attention on aspects of each child's progress and ability.

The first term of the writer's experience was an exploratory one: getting to know one another and overcoming our shyness. This was done by a great variety of activities so that each child could explore what he/she really enjoyed doing, and for the teacher to find out what each child's strengths and weaknesses were and what skills had already been developed. After that first exploratory term, the following examples have become the regular activities, varied in different ways to maintain interest.

Skills

The skills gradually introduced are: The Five Senses, Measuring, Language Development, Prereading, Understanding Relationships, Sorting and Classifying, Counting and Problem-Solving, Exploring, Creativity, Self-Esteem.[3]

Practical Examples

Over several weeks we explore weights and measures, words, opposites, comparisons, using every kind of material that it is practicable to bring into the classroom. This includes non-Bahá'í material. For instance, at the end of one term we demonstrated much of what had been covered with the story of "Goldilocks and the Three Bears". This, of course, envelops the concepts of *hard, medium, soft, hot, warm* and *cold*, and of a naughty girl who entered someone's house without being invited, stole food, vandalised a chair and took many more liberties! Dressing up in teacher's hats, shoes, cast off dresses, etc., the children enacted the story, which reinforced their concept of the more practical things, and gave them an opportunity to discuss what Goldilocks did, why it was wrong, what the bears felt, if Goldilocks should be punished, and what the punishment should be.

In this way, and through other stories such as this, one can usually find a Bahá'í context. The writer feels that for children of this age it is important to have a link with the "world outside"; that Bahá'í education cannot be allowed to be a "cocoon" but must be applied to the world we live in.

If we are talking about the people of the world, and the world being round, the child must first have a concept of roundness to understand what we are talking about. There have to be many experiences of real, round things such as balls, apples, wheels, rings, pebbles, peas, etc., so games and projects using these things were introduced, and the word "round" included in the dialogue.[4]

It is important to help children verbalise what they think and feel. To this end the story is told to the children about the man who had only his stale bread and 'manky' fruit to send as a gift to 'Abdu'l-Bahá, who upon receiving it immediately laid down His palatable meal, ate some of the gift and broke it into pieces to share with the friends. To demonstrate the story more vividly, a piece of stale bread and a very tired apple are tied up in a cloth for the children to open and share. They are asked to talk about how the man must have felt, and why 'Abdu'l-Bahá received it so graciously.

The statement of the Universal House of Justice that "the heart and essential foundation of all education is spiritual and moral training" made the writer wonder how she was to convey to a little person who cannot yet read that one's purpose in life is to attain virtues. Finally, to help the children understand what a virtue is, a doll was made with a hollow body (in this case a small cardboard carton with a picture of a heart and slot like a letter-box, but it could be a rag doll with a heart-shaped pocket on her dress). Then small cartoon pictures depicting good deeds and bad deeds were drawn on cards to fit into the slot.

Every other week each child is given a handful of cards and asked to identify whether the cards are virtues (good deeds) or bad deeds. If they are virtues they are posted into the dolly's heart. When the posting is finished the virtues in the doll are counted (an incidental counting exercise), to see how good she has been that week.

The children are eager to look at the pictures, and after two weeks several children identified the pictures with the word "virtue".

To demonstrate the difference between spiritual food and physical food, the teacher purchased a very pretty gift box in which she placed a small prayer book and some sweets.

Before opening the box it is explained to the children that there are two different kinds of food: one that is good for our bodies and one that is good for our minds. When the box is opened they are asked to guess which is the food for the body and which for the mind. Someone is invited to say a prayer they may have learned at home.

After the prayer one child is invited to hand around the box and then, of course, they get to eat the sweets! One week we made photo frames. The frames were made of cardboard with a cardboard backing, the "glass" was pre-cut heavy duty clear plastic. The pictures of 'Abdu'l-Bahá were good quality photocopies already cut to fit. The children decorated the frames with paint and stuck sequins all around. Ribbons were attached to the top so that they could hang them in their rooms and have their very own picture of 'Abdu'l-Bahá to look at each morning. The results were surprisingly lovely.

Group Work

Later we introduce group work and team work: to demonstrate the meaning of "we are flowers of one garden and leaves of one tree", we talk about how gardens contain many different varieties of flowers and how people are like flowers. Then together we draw lots and lots of leaves and petals and colour them in bright colours. (The children in the next class happened to come in at the end of one class and eagerly fell in to help us). The leaves and the petals are then all stuck onto a big piece of blue backing paper, and a trunk is drawn for the tree and grass for the garden. The teacher takes photographs of the children meanwhile, and cuts out the faces of each child, including herself and her assistant, and the faces are stuck in the centre of each flower. The result is a garden of beautiful child flowers.

Another example of our teamwork: we take a large square of material about tablecloth size with a balloon in the middle. The children each take up a position holding the cloth with both hands, one child at each corner and the rest around the edges. After a count of three, not letting go of the cloth, the children pull it in an outward and upward direction tossing the balloon in the air. The aim is then to catch the balloon back on the cloth. This only works if the children all toss at the same time and move in the same direction to catch it.[5] It has proved extremely popular, with shrieks of laughter and delight, and with several weeks' practice the children are getting better and better at working together.

Later still we have "testing" games to explore our willing and loving capabilities. An example of this is two children holding the ends of parallel garden canes with a balloon balanced on top, then walking, one backward, the other forward across the room. Of course, the child walking backward has to trust the forward walking child to give directions and stop him bumping into anything.

Another example of "testing" is to give the children a variety of gaily wrapped presents of varying shapes and sizes. They are invited to choose a present and sit in a circle. They each choose the present that attracts them most, then, when sitting in the circle they are asked to give their present to the person sitting next to them. They are then asked how they felt about giving away their choice. Of course, they are invited to open and keep the presents they finish up with.

Class Management

The class needs to be carefully thought out, with everything prepared well in advance with props and materials all in place before the class starts. If presents or rewards are involved it is a good idea to have one or two extra for the unexpected happenings, and to have them well hidden until needed, or they are not a surprise.

The lesson always begins with the children sitting in a tight circle close enough to touch. Each child takes the hand of the person sitting on the right, raises the hand, and says "this is my friend ... (eg Shiva) ..." and so on, until everyone has been introduced.[6] Then the teacher says *good morning* by name to each child in turn (including any adult visitors present). Then the class says *Alláh-u-Abhá* in turn. Some children will not want to hold another person's hand, some will not want to say anything at all. However, if this little lesson is repeated every week, one day the excruciatingly shy ones will whisper your name and the reward is truly great!

A picture of 'Abdu'l-Bahá is then produced (a different one each week) and the children are asked if they know who it is. They practise saying *'Abdu'l-Bahá*. One week, to help them remember Him in a pleasant way, teacher explained that 'Abdu'l-Bahá loved to sprinkle rose water on His guests and we passed round a bottle of rose water and sprinkled each other with it. The class then made little pot-pourris of rose petals enclosed in white net and drawn up with narrow pink ribbon to give to mummy for her drawer.

Then they are told a story about the life of 'Abdu'l-Bahá, or perhaps a story which depicts one of His qualities. After the story the project for the day begins. During the story there must be a certain number of physical things to look at, props with which to demonstrate a point, things to feel and touch. A book which is merely read to a very small child will not hold his/her interest for very long. Picture books containing morals are very hard to find, and if all else fails one can write the story and draw the pictures; however poor the artistic talent of the teacher, they will be well received.

A sitting down activity after another sitting down activity would not be appropriate because there must be "steam" time in which the more effervescent members of the class can divest themselves of some of their energy.

Generally after the story the need is for something more physical, and music and dancing are welcome. The percussion instruments have recently been introduced and the class practises banging out a rhythm whilst marching round the classroom into the next room and trying to stay in line.

After break the children can choose what activity they would like to do from the variety set out on the tables. Those who want to do something individually are helped to do so, whilst those who would like to play a game with someone else are encouraged to do that. When a team game is played everyone is invited to join in, and whilst not all of them do at first, when they see what fun is going on they generally choose to participate.

The lesson, while being organised, has to be flexible and the teacher must be prepared to seize opportunities for teaching each one individually. Children of this age have a very short concentration span, and ten minute activities are usually about the limit to hold their interest. Anything longer will result in the very smallest losing interest and disrupting the play. Therefore each activity needs to flow from one to the other without interruption, with some in reserve, for once there is a break in the continuity control is lost and pandemonium results.

It can happen that when the children are engaged in an activity an opportunity will arise to explore something that had not been planned for that day, and the chance can be seized to expand upon it. Alternatively, the children will organise themselves, as happened one Sunday; the background music motivated one little girl to dance. She was quickly joined by another until the whole class had formed a ballet troupe and Sugar Plum Fairy was the order of the day. The next five minutes saw teacher and the whole class expressing what the music inspired them to do, counting the beats and enjoying a feeling of unity.

Evaluation

Evaluation can be made at two levels: what the children can recall from previous lessons and how long they remain absorbed in the current activity. The former is not very reliable, for one can ask a child a question about a detail of a previous lesson, but if that child is not prepared to tell you at that particular moment he/she will not come over with the goods!

However, you might get the answer quite spontaneously at break-time, or going home several weeks later! An example of this was when, after many weeks of stories about the kindness and generosity of 'Abdu'l-Bahá, and how he had sent his bed to a sick person and his lunch to a starving man, the writer's small granddaughter was turning out the toy box to send toys to children in Romania. After packing the last toy she declared that "they can have my bed, and my lunch as well".

Evaluation of lessons as one goes along is a more obvious method, as the intensity of the attention of the participants will let you know if the activity is interesting. As soon as one or two start fidgeting it is time to draw the lesson to a close. The lesson, therefore, must be short, sharp, and interesting. There must be an element of "revealing a secret" that holds the interest to the end and questions that lead one to another.

Weekly repetition is vital for little ones to learn, but to avoid boredom the subject should be presented in a different way each time. When answers to questions become trite it is the signal that the message has been absorbed, and it is time to move on.

To move on to a different activity, the teacher needs to gauge the mood of the class and to use his/her intuition about which one it will be next.

At the end of the class it is good practice to overview the lesson as a whole and jot down what was actually taught that day, because although you planned your lesson carefully, you may have quite spontaneously covered several new areas. The end of the lesson is a good time to make notes for next week while the ideas for continuity are still fresh in the mind.

The classes are like a journey. They are planned to a certain level, you start the ball rolling, but the children will take you to many new places, and it is interesting and challenging to let them lead you to new pastures while gently steering the moral and spiritual course of knowing, willing, and loving.

References

1. Jean Marzollo and Janice Lloyd, *Learning Through Play* (London: Unwin Paperbacks), 1972, p 3.
2. Universal House of Justice, *Letter to all National Spiritual Assemblies* (Haifa: Bahá'í World Centre), Aug. 1976.
3. Jean Marzollo and Janice Lloyd, *Learning Through Play* (London: Unwin Paperbacks), 1972, p 7.
4. Terry Orlick, *The Cooperative Sports and Games Book* (New York: Pantheon), 1978, p 23.
5. Jean Marzollo and Janice Lloyd, *Learning Through Play* (London: Unwin Paperbacks), 1972, p 5.
6. Terry Orlick, *The Cooperative Sports and Games Book* (New York: Pantheon), 1978, p 10.

Appendix A

Recommended Books

1. *Tablet of the Heart* (Wilmette: Bahá'í Publishing Trust), 1987.
2. *Let Thy Breeze Refresh Them*, Bahá'í Prayers and Tablets for Children (London: Bahá'í Publishing Trust), 1976.
3. Jacki Mehrabi, *Stories of 'Abdu'l-Bahá* (London: Bahá'í Publishing Trust), 1984.
4. Jacki Mehrabi, *Stories for Children* (London: Bahá'í Publishing Trust), 1985.
5. Nina Scott and Dawn Staudt, *My Bahá'í ABC Book* (Co. Louth, Rep. of Ireland, self-published), 1986.
6. Irene Taafaki, *Thoughts* (Oxford: George Ronald), 1986.
7. Peggy Godin, *Raising Children as Peacemakers* (Los Angeles: Kalimat Press), 1989.
8. *Blessed is the Spot* (Malaysia: Bahá'í Publishing Trust), 1990.
9. *Blessed is the Spot* (Wall chart) (London: Bahá'í Publishing Trust), 1990.

Recommended Tapes:

1. Red Grammer, *Teaching Peace* (New York: Smilin' Atcha Music), 1986. A collection of songs created to help children and their parents break down the "big" idea of World Peace into the individual daily actions that will make it a reality.
2. Red Grammer, *Can You Sound Just Like Me?* (New York: Smilin' Atcha Music), 1983. Songs, fingerplays and imagination games that touch the heart and the funnybone.
3. *We Are Bahá'ís* (Toronto: Kosinec/Lenz Music Corp.), KLC-01.

What Can Bahá'ís Offer Religious Education in Schools?

George M. Ballentyne

This paper responds to a question put by Professor John Hull to a conference of teachers, administrators and representatives of faith communities meeting to consider a new religious education syllabus for Leicestershire schools. The question, which he described as the central issue for consideration by members of any denomination involved in religious education, was, *What can we, as a faith community, contribute to the moral, spiritual and religious education of the ordinary school student?* A Bahá'í response is offered and key points of that response discussed.

How do other faith communities respond to this type of question? I have listed five responses which I consider typical. I acknowledge that I am not writing as a member of any of these faith communities and that the responses which I, as an outsider, have listed may be described by the insider as unimaginative. Nevertheless, I am prepared to present them as frequent examples which can serve as useful generalisations for the purposes of this paper.

Normally, those members of faith communities who are aware of the needs of RE see themselves as resource banks for schools and respond to the demands of students and teachers in a number of ways, namely:

1. Offering visits for students to Mosque, Gurdwara, Temple, Church or Synagogue.
2. Offering audio-visual resources to schools, e.g., videos, slide sets, posters.
3. Offering ritual objects to schools, e.g., menorah, illuminated calligraphy, statues of gods and goddesses, and offering to unpack their symbolism and significance.
4. Offering students an introduction to distinctive aspects of ethnic culture associated with their religious community, e.g., dress, music and dance, food.
5. Offering speakers to classes.

Can the Bahá'í community match these responses?

There are no Bahá'í Houses of Worship in the UK, and only a few Bahá'í centres. Those that do exist are of very little interest for students and teachers of religious education, as they are not maintained as places of worship. They are simply not interesting enough, and the Bahá'í community has not generally recognised the potential of these centres for this purpose.

There are very few Bahá'í audio-visual resources, and even fewer suitable for school use. Most resources of this type are not produced by the faith communities themselves, but by educational publishers who identify common needs in schools, and decide what to supply on a commercial basis. There are at present not enough Bahá'í children in schools (or Bahá'í RE teachers) to convince the educational publishers that it is worthwhile to produce such materials on the Bahá'í Faith.

What *ritual objects* have we to offer? A print of the Greatest Name? A picture of 'Abdu'l-Bahá? Even at the basic level of symbols, one of the simplest means by which teachers and students try to begin to study a religion, there is confusion in the Bahá'í community over the *symbol* of our Faith.[1] We certainly have to pass on this one!

Many of those responses typical of faith communities throughout the UK depend more on culture than on religious beliefs and do not differentiate between the two. Indeed, religious education does not, as a rule, distinguish between them, as can be seen clearly in the way in which Holy Days and festivals are studied in the classroom.

Bahá'ís deliberately seek to separate their religion from any dominant culture, and take pains to prove that their religion is not *Persian*. What cultural dimensions would we like to introduce to students? The multi-cultural nature of the Bahá'í community appears to be more of a hindrance than a help in this category of response, which requires a clear focus on a small number of specifics, suited to the limited time allowed in the classroom.

Offering a speaker is virtually the only one of the standard responses which Bahá'ís are able to match. Even then, it depends on the existence of a sizeable Bahá'í community and of the availability of appropriate speakers locally.

If we remain with this list of standard responses, we would have to come to the conclusion that Bahá'ís cannot make a suitable response to Professor Hull's question, *What can we, as a faith community, contribute to the moral, spiritual and religious education of the ordinary school student?*

I believe that if we try to match those responses which I have identified as *typical* we certainly will fail to meet the needs of students and teachers, and will deny ourselves the opportunity to make a very distinctive and valuable response, which can highlight the value of the Bahá'í Faith as a component in religious education.

Since we do not have the same material resources as other faith communities, and do not wish to identify ourselves with particular cultures, I would contend that Bahá'ís have to offer a response based on distinctive elements of our beliefs. To this end I have selected a few such elements, chosen on a purely personal basis.

One of the best-known quotations from the writings of Bahá'u'lláh provides a key to the kind of response which I contend Bahá'ís can offer: "Let your vision be world-embracing, rather than confined to your own self."[2] As religious education struggles to justify its place in crowded school timetables, and to redefine its function in an increasingly pluralist society, our world-embracing vision is surely our greatest asset to put before educationalists. The Bahá'í viewpoint is particularly relevant and enlightening in the area of global issues, which demand a supranational, multi-faith and multicultural perspective, such as the environment, international relations, cultural imperialism, and others. Our interpretation of *progressive revelation* provides a uniquely positive basis for the study of religious pluralism and inter-faith relations.

In *The Promise of World Peace,* the Universal House of Justice offers the Bahá'í experience as a model for study if it "can contribute in whatever measure to reinforcing hope in the unity of the human race".[3] The Bahá'í community is a unique model of that unity in action - of interracial, multicultural co-existence, which can play a useful and positive role at this time in the development of our pluralist society in the UK, and in the context of an exploding world culture.

Further to our desire to reinforce hope, our certainty that permanent and universal peace on earth is inevitable is unique among the established religions and is a healthy counteragent to the energy-sapping pessimism and life-destroying cynicism which pervades so much of the debate in the classroom about the future of humanity. (This raises questions about the possible relationship between the Bahá'í contribution to religious education and certain other subjects, such as history, geography and social and personal studies, but that is outwith the scope of this paper).
All of the elements of the Bahá'í response which I have outlined depend on having entrée to the classroom to present them, either in person or in printed or audio-visual media. So, how do we go about gaining this entrée?

I would contend that this is a duty which devolves equally on Bahá'í institutions at a national level and on Local Spiritual Assemblies and on Bahá'í parents at the local level. At the national level, the Bahá'í Information Office, the Bahá'í Publishing Trust, a radically-strengthened Religious Education Committee of the National Spiritual Assembly, and other agencies of the National Spiritual Assembly responsible for conducting the public relations activities of the Bahá'í community must actively, persistently and resolutely court the attention of decision-makers in education and in educational publishing, and present them with a clear picture of the benefits to their students (or consumers) of the Bahá'í Faith's being part of their religious education. This is one critical and potentially fruitful aspect of the current focus of the Bahá'í community on "fostering cordial relations with accomplished and distinguished figures, with people of capacity and with those occupying prominent positions in society",[4] with the purpose of making them friends of the Faith, of "dispelling any misconceptions they may have and unfolding before their eyes the vision of world solidarity and peace enshrined in the teachings of Bahá'u'lláh".[4] In seeking their positive attention for the Faith, we must adopt the posture not of *supplicants*, but of *applicants*, who know the value of what we have to offer, and who are convinced that others will find it worthwhile.

At the local level, Spiritual Assemblies must step forward and actively seek representation on agencies of their Local Education Authorities, such as SACREs[5] and ASCs,[6] so that the Bahá'í community and the Bahá'í viewpoint are positively and accessibly represented. At the grass roots level, Bahá'í parents should be actively involved with their children's schools at suitable levels, whether as members of the Board of Governors, or of Parent/Teacher Associations, or simply as concerned parents.

Of the material currently available to support our claim that study of the Bahá'í Faith is an attractive proposition I would recommend liberal use of *One Country*, the quarterly publication of the Bahá'í International Community, and the new series of videos, *The Bahá'í Newsreel*, but such resources are as yet little known amongst the Bahá'ís themselves and are shamefully under-used.

To conclude, I would contend that the Bahá'í community can make a distinctive and positive response to Professor Hull's question, and that the best basis of our response is not our current level of material resources, but our positive and hopeful global vision. However, in order to make this response, we have to re-examine how we can convey that vision enshrined in the teachings of Bahá'u'lláh to those who make decisions about the content of religious education in schools.

References

1. "Strictly speaking the five-pointed star is the symbol of our Faith, as used by the Báb and explained by Him." From a letter written on behalf of Shoghi Effendi to an individual believer dated 28 October 1949, published in *Lights of Guidance: A Bahá'í Reference File* (New Delhi: Bahá'í Publishing Trust), 1988, p 110.
2. Bahá'u'lláh, 'Tablet of the World', published in *Tablets of Bahá'u'lláh Revealed After the Kitáb-i-Aqdas* (Haifa: Bahá'í World Centre), revised edition, 1982, p 87.
3. The Universal House of Justice, *The Promise of World Peace*, (London: Bahá'í Publishing Trust), 1985, p 24.
4. Secretariat of the Universal House of Justice, from a letter dated 28 September 1990 to all National Spiritual Assemblies.
5. Standing Advisory Council on Religious Education. Each Local Education Authority (LEA) must convene a SACRE, under the terms of the *Education Reform Act 1988*. Certain categories of interest must be

represented, but Bahá'í representation is *not*, unhappily, mandated in the law. At time of publication there was Bahá'í representation on around 20 of the 108 SACREs in England and Wales.
6. Agreed Syllabus Conference. Each Local Education Authority is required by the Education Reform Act 1988 to convene a Conference representative of a range of faith communities to establish a syllabus for the schools in that LEA.

Racial unity: The most challenging issue in spiritual education

Mahzad Mazloomian

Everywhere we look today, in South Africa, in America and in Britain we can see the long traces of racism reaching across the centuries into the present time. Racial dominance suffered by millions of people has wounded generations deeply, and it will take a long, long time to get rid of its scars.

It is only recently that many multicultural societies are struggling to find a solution to their racial problem. They have realized that the world has become like one country, that people have to live together and work together, and that it is essential that they put their racial prejudices aside.

This recognition of the problem has not however provided an answer, although one exists. As Shoghi Effendi, the Guardian of the Bahá'í Faith, writes in a letter to the West:

The whole of mankind is groaning, is dying to be led to unity, and to terminate its age-long martyrdom. And yet it stubbornly refuses to embrace the light and acknowledge the sovereignty and authority of the one Power that can extricate it from its entanglements, and avert the woeful calamity that threatens to engulf it.[1]

Race issues have been discussed at many conferences since the first Universal Race Congress, held in 1911 in London. Thinkers such as Dr Martin Luther King have brought this matter to the attention of the people of the world as the "moral imperative of our age" and "the most challenging of issues". The great American scholar W E B Du Bois, writing in 1903, placed racism on the social agenda of the twentieth century. He writes "The problem of the twentieth century is the problem of the colour-line - the relation of the darker to the lighter races of men in Asia and Africa, in America and the islands of the sea."[2]

What no one has apparently appreciated is that a matter as significant and as deeply rooted as this requires a spiritual remedy which can transform the hearts of the people, rather than a quick and superficial one. It is my contention that in order to combat racism we need new guidance and new education to prepare us for a new age in which racism plays no part.

Education according to the principles of Bahá'u'lláh's teachings will enable people to understand the barriers to racial unity and multicultural progress and help them find a way to build a multicultural society based on harmony and justice. "Man is the supreme Talisman. Lack of a proper education hath, however, deprived him of that which he doth inherently possess... The Great Being saith: Regard man as a mine rich in gems of inestimable value. Education can, alone, cause it to reveal its treasures, and enable mankind to benefit therefrom."[3]

One of the gems of inestimable value in humans is the capacity to develop love for their fellow human beings and the ability not only to understand racial unity but also to celebrate it throughout their lives, thus letting the whole of mankind live in peace and harmony.

I believe that these abilities and capacities in all people only develop through recognising the Manifestation of God for the day and by following His teachings.

The coming of Bahá'u'lláh has released a special power in the world which can develop those capacities in human beings which enable them to understand the necessity of unity and the oneness of mankind. For although the world has developed its material civilisation, it cannot solve its spiritual problems without spiritual guidance and spiritual education. As 'Abdu'l-Bahá writes: "...no matter how far the world of humanity may advance in material civilisation, it is nevertheless in need of spiritual virtues and the bounties of God. The spirit of man is not illumined and quickened through material sources. It is not resuscitated by investigating phenomena of the world of matter... Material development may be likened to the glass of a lamp whereas divine virtues and spiritual susceptibilities are the light within the glass."[4]

We can begin to understand something of the intrinsic unity of the human race by developing our spiritual susceptabilities and acquiring virtues. These we achieve through our love for God and for His Manifestation.

Human beings all have shortcomings. Thus the only way to love one's fellow human being is through loving God. The first step therefore in achieving racial unity is to learn to love mankind through the love of God. 'Abdu'l-Bahá has emphasised the importance of the love of God and its effect on human life: "In truth, the fruit of human existence is the love of God, for this love is the spirit of life, and the eternal bounty. If the love of God did not exist, the contingent world would be in darkness; if the love of God did not exist, the hearts of men would be dead, and deprived of the sensations of existence; if the love of God did not exist, spiritual union would be lost; if the love of God did not exist, the light of unity would not illuminate humanity; if the love of God did not exist, the East and West, like two lovers, would not embrace each other; if the love of God did not exist, division and disunion would not be changed into fraternity; if the love of God did not exist, indifference would not end in affection; if the love of God did not exist, the stranger would not become the friend. The love of the human world has shone forth from the love of God and has appeared by the bounty and grace of God."⁵

Therefore, appreciating the love of God is a primary goal of spiritual education. Such an education will bring forth a new race of men who will love their fellow human beings regardless of race, creed or gender. Through Bahá'í education, which stresses this goal, the world of humanity will gradually come to understand and celebrate racial unity.

The achievement of racial unity is a beautiful goal, but the question remains how do we achieve it? Bahá'u'lláh commands: "It is incumbent upon every man of insight and understanding to strive to translate that which hath been written into reality and action."⁶

Thus in the Bahá'í Community, each person is responsible for the education and wellbeing of the community: individuals, parents, teachers and the institutions. The eradication of racism requires the attention and the work of the entire community. 'Abdu'l-Bahá says: "The attainment of any object is conditioned upon knowledge, volition and action."⁷

To work on eliminating racism, we need to have knowledge of the problem and knowledge of the solution. In other words, to work on the solution we need first to address the problem. The problem stems from an ignorance, a lack of knowledge and an inability to recognise and admit this.

A gradual awareness and acceptance of one's deeply-rooted prejudices will come from the Writings of Bahá'u'lláh. To move on from this awareness of the problem, one must strengthen the resolution by deepening further on the Writings.

In order to acquire knowledge of the problem and thereby a knowledge of the solution one must, as Bahá'u'lláh says: "Intone, O My servant, the verses of God that have been received by thee, as intoned by them who have drawn nigh unto Him... Though he may, at first, remain unaware of its effect, yet the virtue of the grace vouchsafed unto him must needs sooner or later exercise its influence upon his soul."⁸

Therefore it is through volition and action of individuals that things start to happen, and people begin to see and realise that it is possible to change when they immerse themselves in the ocean of the knowledge of God.

One must have a vision that it is possible to achieve racial unity. 'Abdu'l-Bahá is the best example of the courage, volition and action required to overcome racism:

> *While in the United States (1912), 'Abdu'l-Bahá's every act seemed to be calculated to demonstrate the Bahá'í Teachings on*

> *the supreme importance of love and unity between all members of the human race, especially blacks and whites. Perhaps at no other time and place during his visit to the United States did 'Abdu'l-Bahá demonstrate in so dramatic yet so characteristically gentle and unassuming a way the Bahá'í teachings and principles of racial unity, than at the luncheon held in his honour in Washington DC. The luncheon had been arranged by two Bahá'ís, Ali-Kuli Khan, the Persian chargé-d'affaires, and Florence Breed Khan, his wife. Some of the guests were members of Washington's social and political elite. Before the luncheon, 'Abdu'l-Bahá sent for Louis Gregory, a well known black Bahá'í. They chattered for a while and when lunch was ready and the guests were seated, 'Abdu'l-Bahá invited Louis Gregory to the luncheon. The assembled guests, including the Bahá'ís were no doubt surprised not only at 'Abdu'l-Bahá's inviting a black person to an upper class social affair but even more by the affection and love shown by 'Abdu'l-Bahá for Gregory when he gave the latter the seat of honour on his right... A biographer of Louis Gregory writes of this event: "Gently yet unmistakably 'Abdu'l-Bahá had assaulted the custom of a city that had been scandalised only a decade earlier by President Roosevelt's dinner invitation to Booker T Washington.[9]*

These historical stories can form a part of the early education of a child and instil concepts about the value and worth of each race. But more than this, Bahá'í education starts with the parents at home, where the children learn by example, by deeds not by words, that all mankind is one.

Children need a multicultural Bahá'í community in which to grow, so that they can witness the positive effects of different cultures and nationalities interacting together. They will develop a new eye and see the beauty of other nations' cultures and races. 'Abdu'l-Bahá helped some children to develop their "new eye" during His visit to America in 1912:

> *While 'Abdu'l-Bahá was visiting the Bowery Mission area in New York, some poor boys visited him in His room. 'Abdu'l-Bahá greeted each one. The last boy who entered the room was the only black in the group; he probably felt that 'Abdu'l-Bahá and His host would not accept him. But as an observer reported, when 'Abdu'l-Bahá saw him, His face was lightened up with a heavenly smile. He raised His hands with a gesture of princely welcome and exclaimed in a loud voice so that no one could fail to hear, that here was a black rose. The room fell into instant silence. The black face became illumined with*

happiness and love hardly of this world. The other boys looked at him with new eyes. The boy had been called many things, but never before a black rose.[10]

Another aspect of Bahá'í education is in helping people to understand unity in diversity. 'Abdu'l-Bahá sent a message to the Universal Race Congress in London in 1911 in which He explained the importance of the diversity of the human family and compared humankind to a flower garden adorned with different colours and shapes each enhancing the loveliness of the other. The next year, 1912, He spoke at Howard University, the premier black university in Washington DC. As he looked at the racially mixed audience He was overjoyed and said, "Today I am most happy, for I see here a gathering of the servants of God. I see white and black sitting together."[11] On another occasion He said, "A meeting such as this seems like a beautiful cluster of precious jewels - pearls, rubies, diamonds, sapphires. It is a source of joy and delight."[12]

'Abdu'l-Bahá also encouraged intermarriage of black and white. He was very pleased when Louis Gregory, an American black, and Louisa Matthew, an educated English Bahá'í, were married. He described their marriage as "an introduction to the accomplishments of good fellowship between blacks and whites."[13] Contrary to what people anticipated, their marriage lasted four decades until the end of their lives.

In addition to practical deeds, Bahá'í education requires parents to teach the words of God to their children every day in the morning and in the evening, and to help them to memorise the words of Bahá'u'lláh from an early age. By doing so, the children have the treasures of admonishments and guidance of the Blessed Beauty in their hearts for ever, the treasures that will guide and support them throughout their entire lives. As a result, their behaviour will reflect the Bahá'í teachings and create a new race of men which is neither eastern nor western, but from God.

To conclude, racial unity is a very important and challenging issue. The people of the world, including the Bahá'ís, have a "long and thorny road... to travel." As Shoghi Effendi explains, "White and Negro, high and low, young and old, whether newly converted to the Faith or not, all who stand identified with it must participate in, and lend their assistance, each according to his or her capacity, experience, and opportunities, to the common task of fulfiling the instructions, realising the hopes, and following the example of 'Abdu'l-Bahá. Whether coloured or non-coloured, neither race has the right, or can conscientiously claim, to be regarded as absolved from such an obligation, as having realised such hopes, or having faithfully followed such an example. A long and thorny road, beset with pitfalls, still remains untravelled, both by the white and the Negro exponents of the redeeming Faith of Bahá'u'lláh."[14]

Racial prejudice has cost humankind potential scientists, musicians, philosophers and others who could have contributed so much to the world of humanity. As the Universal House of Justice, the international governing body of the Bahá'í Faith, explained in its Peace Statement in 1985, "Racism retards the unfoldment of the boundless potentialities of its victims, corrupts its perpetrators, and blights human progress."[15]

Education, spiritual and practical, is the most effective way to combat racism. Educating children to understand that mankind is one, to know about the love of God, to learn to love the manifestation of God and as a result to love humankind, is a most urgent task. The Writings of Bahá'u'lláh can be used as a basis for such education. 'Abdu'l-Bahá says:

> *Behold a beautiful garden full of flowers, shrubs, and trees. Each flower has a different charm, a peculiar beauty, its own delicious perfume and beautiful colour. The trees too, how varied are they in size, in growth, in foliage and what different fruits they bear! Yet all these flowers, shrubs and trees spring from the self-same earth, the same sun shines upon them and the same clouds give them rain.*
> *So it is with humanity. It is made up of many races, and its peoples are of different colour, white, black, yellow, brown and red - but they all come from the same God, and are all servants to Him... Bahá'u'lláh has drawn the circle of unity, He has made a design for the uniting of all the peoples, and for the gathering of them all under the shelter of the tent of universal unity. This is the work of the Divine Bounty, and we must all strive with heart and soul until we have the reality of unity in our midst, and as we work, so will strength be given unto us.*[16]

References

1. Shoghi Effendi, *World Order of Bahá'u'lláh* (Wilmette: Bahá'í Publishing Trust), 1976, p 201.
2. W.E.B. Du Bois, *The Souls of Black Folk* (Chicago: A.C. McClung), 1904, p 13.
3. Bahá'u'lláh, *Gleanings from the Writings of Bahá'u'lláh* (London: Bahá'í Publishing Trust), 1978, pp 259-60.
4. 'Abdu'l-Bahá, *Foundations of World Unity*, pp 58-9.
5. 'Abdu'l-Bahá, *Some Answered Questions* (Wilmette: Bahá'í Publishing Trust), 1981, p 301.
6. Bahá'u'lláh, *Gleanings from the Writings of Bahá'u'lláh* (Wilmette: Baha'í Publishing Trust), 1983, p 250.
7. 'Abdu'l-Bahá, *Foundations of World Unity*, p 101.
8. Bahá'u'lláh, *Gleanings*, p 295.

9. G. Morrison, *To Move the World - Louis G Gregory and the advancement of racial unity in America* (Wilmette: Bahá'í Publishing Trust), 1986, p 63.
10. Howard Colby Ives, *Portals to Freedom* (Oxford: George Ronald), 1934, p 65.
11. 'Abdu'l-Bahá, *The Promulgation of Universal Peace* (Wilmette: Bahá'í Publishing Trust), 1982, p 44.
12. *ibid.* p 56.
13. G. Morrison, *To Move the World* (Wilmette: Bahá'í Publishing Trust), 1986, p xxvii.
14. Shoghi Effendi, *The Advent of Divine Justice* (Wilmette: Bahá'í Publishing Trust), p 34.
15. The Universal House of Justice, *The Promise of World Peace* (Haifa: Bahá'í World Centre), 1985.
16. 'Abdu'l-Bahá, *Paris Talks* (London: Bahá'í Publishing Trust) 1976, pp 52-4.

The Children Act 1989 and the Bahá'í Faith

Kathryn C. McGee

Introduction

When the level of changes in our perceptions are considered as well as the will of the people of this country and the world, the last 150 years has been dramatic, but even more so these last few decades. These changes are pervasive in some ways, such as the popular views of issues such as the environment, international peace and universal education, and dynamic in terms of the political arenas of Eastern Europe. In these Bahá'ís are able to see the clear influence of the Will of God as expressed by Bahá'u'lláh. One of the most significant of these changes in Britain is framed in the *Children Act 1989* which came fully into force on the 14 October 1991.

The effect of this was that on 14 October 1991 a new concept was applied to child care, both in law and in practice. In order to understand the full significance of this Act it is necessary briefly to describe the law which was in operation before that date. The law regarding children in civil matters (i.e. not criminal) covered three main areas: family matters (divorce), care cases (local authority) and adoption. As adoption is to be addressed in a future Act and the *Children Act 1989* deals only with the two former areas, we need only concentrate on these.

Family law was previously practised in three jurisdictions, the Magistrates Court, the County Court and the High Court. It dealt with questions of custody of and access to children upon the breakup of marriage, and also gave putative (unmarried) fathers the ability to apply to be guardians of their children in exceptional circumstances (e.g. the death of the natural mother).[1] This area of law is known as Private Law (i.e. between individuals), but the local authority could intervene in both family matters and guardianship applications when it was thought that to do so was in the best interests of the child.[2]

Public Law relates to all other times when the local authority acts in accordance with its statutory duty to safeguard the interests of the children in its district. It was also practised in the three above mentioned jurisdictions and was formed by a number of Acts, such as the *Children and Young Persons Act 1933*, the *Children and Young Persons Act 1963*, the *Children and Young Persons Act 1969*, the *Child Care Act 1980*, the *Matrimonial Causes Act 1973*, the *Guardianship of Minors Act 1971* and *1973*, and the *Family Reform Act 1969*, all of which give specific duties and by the inherent jurisdiction of the High Court in Wardship. Briefly, this meant that a child could come into care by care proceedings in the Magistrates' Court,[3] by intervention in Family Proceedings,[4] by order of the High Court in regard to a warded child or by a voluntary process which did not appear before a Court.[5] By all of these methods custody of a child was removed from the parents and vested in the local authority. By this the parent ceased to have a say in the future or day-to-day life of the child. The requirements in regard to evidence varied between the courts. This was regarded as an unsatisfactory and patchwork frame in which to work, and was further exacerbated by the multiple Acts coming into force piecemeal (i.e. section by section at different times). *The Children Act 1989* addresses all these matters and brings into one piece of legislation all Private and Public Law which relates to children, save adoption, and did so substantially on one day, the 14 October 1989.

The Children Act 1989

It is important to note that the *Children Act 1989* is not a response to the events in Cleveland which resulted in a major enquiry into methods of investigation and the assessment of child sexual abuse and establishment of good practice, or to the deaths of children such as Jasmine Beckford, Kimberley Carlisle and Tira Henry, where questions were raised regarding Social Services' response to children identified as needing protection. Rather, it began in about 1984 when the House of Commons Social Services Committee recognised the differing jurisdictions and varying grounds present in the legislation. A review of Child Care Law was commissioned. At the same time a fresh look was being taken in respect to children in private law. The result is the *Children Act 1989,* which was not a Tory bill, but the product of cross-party support and cooperation.

The significance of the Act is further seen in the two-year delay in bringing it into force. The Act requires the Social Services Division of a local authority to practise its statutory duties in ways which are more *family oriented* than previously. Good practice had always been to support families so to maintain children with their parents, but this has now become a requirement of the local authority.[6] Even child protection issues are viewed so as to include turning to the family to find ways to protect the child. It also has ramifications for the education and health services as well as for the funding of resources. Two years were required to allow for training and reorganising of the ways in which the various services will respond.

The philosophy which underpins the whole of this Act is that a child is presumed to be best looked after by his or her own family.[7] Parents have responsibility and duties in regards to the child, and no longer have a Victorian-type *right* in the child. This concept is termed "parental responsibility"[8] and is a completely new legal term. It is defined as "all the rights, duties, powers, responsibilities and authority which by law a parent of a child has in relation to the child and his property".[9] A parent owes a duty of care to the child to raise the child to emotional and physical health which is the basis for all the authority held in respect to the child.[10] It is this concept which I believe is a reflection of the Bahá'í principles of child care:

> *It is incumbent upon every father and mother to counsel their children over a long period, and guide them unto those things which lead to everlasting honour.*[11]

Another feature of the Act is that parental responsibility is not affected by the separation of the parents or by a care order. The intent behind this is that a parent will remain responsible for his child and can neither divest himself of his duties nor be excluded by the other parent, as has so often happened in maintenance/access disputes. This is reflected in the types of Court Orders which are available in respect to children in family proceedings. These are known as Section 8 Orders,[12] and include Residence Orders and Contact Orders. The familiar, old concepts of custody and access are abolished by the Section 8 Orders, which are extended in availability beyond parents to any person who can satisfy the Court of his "...connection with the child".[13] This includes relatives, such as grandparents, for the very first time. It also requires a local authority to consider placing the child within the extended family as a first choice for alternative care when the parents are unable to look after the child.[14]

Parental responsibility is gained in the following ways:[15] When a child's father and mother were married to each other at the time of his birth, they each have parental responsibility, when the parents were unmarried at the time of the child birth, the mother will have parental responsibility[16] and the father only gains it by having entered into a written agreement (in the prescribed form) between the couple or by court order.[17] A third person will gain parental responsibility by becoming a recipient of a guardian upon the death of the parents of a child;[18] or by the making of a Residence Order.[19] It will be shared with the local authority upon the making of a Care Order.[20] Once parental responsibility is gained by a parent or guardian it is binding and may only be broken by death or adoption.[21] It ceases upon the discharge of a Residence Order[22] or for the local authority upon the discharge of the Care Order.[23] It is capable of being "shared" between several people, but each person may exercise the responsibility alone for the child.[24] As an example, this means that only the immediate carer having parental responsibility for the child need give authority for a medical operation to take place on a child.

These features of the Act also strike me as compatible with the Bahá'í belief in the special spiritual relationship between natural parents and their children on the one part, and the concept of the collective community described as "a single social organism, representative of the diversity of the human family"[25] on the other. Furthermore, this profound enlargement of the common perception of the family to the community has a number of implications for the treatment of its members by its members. This is arguably the basis of the Public Law duties of local authorities. *The Children Act 1989* places a general duty on every local authority to:

> a) *safeguard and promote the welfare of children within their area who are in need; and*
> b) *so far as is consistent with that duty, to promote the upbringing of such children by their families, by providing a range and level of services appropriate to those children's needs.*[26]

A child is in need if:

> a) *he is unlikely to achieve or maintain, or to have the opportunity of achieving or maintaining, a reasonable standard of health and development without the provision for him by a local authority...*
> b) *his health or development is likely to be significantly impaired, or further impaired, without the provision for him of such services; or*
> c) *he is disabled.*[27]

Implications for the Community

It is my desire that the entire population of Britain be made aware of this Act and the wider implications it has for the entire community, not only for the professional services and the individual parents. However, this paper is addressed to the Third Symposium of the Bahá'í Education Committee, and consequently, I am primarily sharing my thoughts on the implications with the Bahá'í community.

I must firstly express the basis upon which I believe it is necessary for individuals to support this Act. *The Promise of World Peace* clearly points out the Bahá'í community as an example to the world.[28] It indicates that there are influences in the world which are driving us towards peace, with all its ramifications.[29] These influences can be interpreted as the workings of God's Will as expressed by Bahá'u'lláh. It is then, arguably, incumbent upon the adherents of Bahá'u'lláh's Faith to demonstrate their belief by outward actions which support those examples which are believed to be the result of God's Will. One of the areas in which action is required is contained in the *Children Act 1989*.

Another feature of the Bahá'í Faith is the emphasis placed on individual service for the benefit of the human family. It must be recognised that most services will only affect a small proportion of this family, but are no less important for that restriction.

Two of the goals of the Six Year Plan for the Bahá'ís of the United Kingdom are concerned with family life. The Six Year Plan calls for Bahá'í families to consider fostering or adoption.[30] This is probably the most direct and personal service a family can perform together. There is a national shortage of foster carers and this is a service which is most desperately needed for the successful application of the intentions of *The Children Act 1989*. A feature of the Act is that it requires Social Services to promote the primary position of parents in caring for children, which will mean the increased use of short term and relief care with the aim of returning children to their family. This means that foster carers will work more directly with the natural parents of a child to accomplish this aim, and that parents will have a greater involvement in decision-making in regard to their child while their child is being accommodated by the local authority.[31]

Another factor which makes it so important that potential foster carers come forward is that *The Children Act 1989* is the first piece of legislation to define a child in need so as to include disabled children.[32] The effect of this Act is that parents will be encouraged to look after disabled children in their own home, with support from Social Services. One of these supports will be increased use of relief carers who will work over a period of years with a family to ensure a child may remain in her or his family.

However, fostering is not the only service available. There are many ways in which individuals may serve the community. *The Children Act 1989* requires better care of children after school and during school holidays. Here the creative spirit and many talents available within the community may be used to care for both able bodied and disabled children, and also adults. There is further legislation which requires care for disabled persons to be carried out in the community. The result of this is that many long-term hospitals have closed, forcing expatients into the community for community care. While the institutionalising of individuals in long term hospitals was not good, it is believed that the closures have caused a rise in homelessness with the accompanying problems of poverty and disease. This is a complex problem which requires a high level of organised service, which may best be met by joining with like-minded groups in the wider community.

Another group some of whose members would benefit from friendly, consistent service are the ever-growing numbers of elderly people in our population. The opportunities to serve our fellow beings are limitless.

Conclusions

There is a world of people needing attention. There is a world itself needing help. These needs are calling for the committed service of people. Bahá'ís are taught that we manifest our belief in God and in Bahá'u'lláh by our attitude of service to mankind. This is a concept we try to instil deeply into our children. There is no better way to teach than by example.

References

1. *Guardianship of Minors Act 1971* s9.
2. *Matrimonial Causes Act 1973* s43, *Guardianship of Minors Act 1973* s2 (2) and (3).
3. *Children and Young Persons Act 1969* s1.
4. *Matrimonial Causes Act 1973* s43.
5. *Guardianship of Minors Act 1973* s2, *Family Law Reform Act 1969* s7(2).
6. *The Children Act 1989* s17(1)(6).
7. *ibid.* s1(5).
8. *ibid.* s2.
9. *ibid.* s3(1).
10. ibid. s1 and s31(2).
11. 'Abdu'l-Bahá, *Selections from the Writings of 'Abdu'l-Bahá* (Haifa: Bahá'í World Centre), 1978, p 134.
12. *The Children Act 1989* s8.
13. *ibid.* s10(9)(b).
14. *ibid.* s23(6).
15. *ibid.* s2(1).
16. *ibid.* s2(2)(a)
17. *ibid.* s4(1).
18. *ibid.* s5.
19. *ibid.* s12(2).
20. *ibid.* s33(3)(a).
21. *ibid.* s2(9).
22. *ibid.* s12(2).
23. *ibid.* s33(3).
24. *ibid.* s2(7).
25. The Universal House of Justice, *The Promise of World Peace* (Haifa: Bahá'í World Centre), 1985, p 24.
26. *The Children Act 1989*, s17(1).
27. *ibid.* s17(10).
28. The Universal House of Justice, *The Promise of World Peace* (Haifa: Bahá'í World Centre), 1985, p 24.
29. *ibid.* p1.
30. National Spiritual Assembly of Bahá'ís of the UK, *Six Year Plan*, 1986.
31. *The Children Act 1989* s22(4)9b).
32. *ibid.* s17(10).

SunWALK: A Model for Moral and Spiritual Education

Roger Prentice

This paper presents SunWALK, a Bahá'í-inspired model of learning, and discusses issues in the management of Bahá'í education. In defining Bahá'í education the discussion has been confined to three categories: *the student group*, *outcomes* and the *organising principles in curricula*. The term *Bahá'í education* is used in two different senses. Firstly, there is Bahá'í education arranged so that members of the community can become more literate and able to express their beliefs. Such expression would include the ability fully to enjoy and exercise their *citizenship* within the Bahá'í community and to teach the Faith effectively to others. Secondly, there is the sense of education that is influenced by or inspired by the Bahá'í Faith and its teachings. In the first sense the *consumers* are members of the community. In the second the *consumers* can be any individual or group. Bahá'í-inspired education might be used in full-time schools, such as the Maxwell School in Canada,[1] or in a social and economic development service project, helping a national government develop moral education such as FUNDEAC in Colombia.[2]

At this stage of development both education for Bahá'í communities and Bahá'í-inspired education are likely to use principles and materials from the wider community as well as those drawn from or inspired by Bahá'í teachings. Therefore monitoring the field of education for ideas that are in tune with Bahá'í teachings is almost as important as seeking to understand what the Writings would have us do.

To take the process of definition a step further, we will have to ask what the *outcomes* are likely to look like if desired learning within Bahá'í education has taken place. For Bahá'ís the individual's purpose in life is to acquire virtues. Possession of such virtues, in action, is the criterion of success.

Given that the purpose of Bahá'í education is primarily the development of virtuous character, the *organising principles* in curriculum development must comply. For example, we cannot be satisfied with knowledge as information, important though that is, since it is quite easy to produce people who know a lot but who are morally cretinous. At this our civilization has become adept. Perhaps it was this that Mahatma Gandhi had in mind when he answered the question, "What do you think of Western civilization?" The great man is reputed to have said something to the effect that, "I think it would be a good idea!" Nor can we be satisfied with the demonstration of skills, important though they are, since again deception, self and otherwise, can occur. The organising principle must be the process toward becoming most fully human. This, from a Bahá'í perspective, is the same as becoming spiritualised, which in turn is the same as acquiring virtues. In Bahá'í education skills must be the servant of being, and knowledge as information must be the servant of skills. In the wider UK community the shift is just taking place from knowledge as information to possession of skills in the form of such initiatives as National Vocational Qualifications. Bahá'í education should be the cutting edge combining our best reading of the Bahá'í Writings and the best the educational sciences can offer.

In my view this emphasis on the process of *virtuous becoming* is the clear principle in many statements in the Bahá'í Writings that relate to education. We cannot fully become our true selves without a foundation of moral and spiritual education. The Bahá'ís' supreme *authority*, the Universal House of Justice, says "...resources of the Faith in the field of education should be concentrated on spiritual and moral training."[3]

A second form of *authority* is scientific - the advice of the best thinkers and practitioners in the educational sciences. We need to bring together discovered truth and revealed truth in a process of continuous dialogue and development.

Consideration of the student group, of the desired outcomes, of the organising principles in curriculum development and of guidance received can yield a working definition of Bahá'í education. From these perspectives Bahá'í education is spiritual and moral education - learning which leads to feelings, thought and behaviour which serve unity, peace and human development - as envisaged by Bahá'u'lláh. The value of this definition is that it provides a model of Bahá'í education for everyone - not just induction, initiation or development for Bahá'ís. More broadly, we can say that Bahá'í education is any range of activities consonant with Bahá'í teachings that create learning experiences and which support the development of Bahá'í qualities and Bahá'í behaviour within individuals or groups.

The first definition might lend itself more to work in social and economic projects with the wider community and the broader definition to education within the Bahá'í community. However, neither case need be exclusive.

Definitions help expose what we really believe, and can therefore give greater control over the teaching that actually takes place. How we instinctively reply to the question *What is Bahá'í education*? will shape what we actually do in the classroom, or wherever it is that teaching takes place. If we use one of the above definitions we are compelled to accept a great diversity of kinds of learning as constituting education from a Bahá'í point of view; that is, formal and informal learning, learning in the family, at school or work, in the local community and in the wider community.

Such a definition and such consequent diversity is a good thing since there is a tendency for untrained, and sometimes trained teachers as well, to build the worst aspects of their own formal education into their own attempts at Bahá'í education. In practice, the above definition would validate the arts and outward bound courses, to name just two less commonly used modes of education within the Bahá'í community, and would prevent Bahá'í education being interpreted as simply book learning.

We know, however, that merely possessing a definition, or good materials, good conditions and good intentions, is no guarantee in itself of good educational practice. Clearly such elements as developing teacher *reflectivity*, providing good in-service courses and developing specific skills can help greatly. Definitions, like teaching materials, are not teacher-proof and the bottom line is, "what does the teacher really believe about the whole process of learning and teaching?" Deeper than definitions, then, so I am suggesting, are the *images of belief* we hold as to what education is. What images of belief are creating the educational experience actually being delivered?

Commitment to self learning by the teacher is vital since it can be transmitted as a model via enthusiasm, reflectiveness, willingness to struggle and so on. Similarly struggling for self-understanding is vital for the teacher since her or his decision-making is based on beliefs, values and attitudes - understanding the beliefs that have stuck with us is vital because we see and behave in accordance with what we believe. Therefore, the term *images of belief* is suggested here to describe the fact that at deep levels we hold metaphors of the life processes in which we are involved - teaching, parenting, learning and so on. We act out what we believe. We also learn and communicate in differing ways as shown, for example, in the descriptions provided by Neuro-linguistic Programming, which teaches how to adjust your communication to the style of the person you are with.

We might do well to seek to discover the images that we each hold, consciously or less than consciously, about teaching, about learning, about the processes of learning, and about those to whom we seek to bring learning. This could be a highly informative activity because these *images of belief* influence the thinking we do and therefore the kinds of decisions that we are making - they also, I suspect, contribute to the music between words, the vibrations we give out, of compassion or hostility or likeableness and so on. In another context, that of organisational development, we find, in *Images of Organisation*,[4] images not of life in general or the process of education but of how individuals picture the functioning and development of organisations with which they are associated. Morgan[4] found that, commonly, organisations were pictured as machines, as organisms, as brains, as cultures, as political systems, as psychic prisons, as flux and transformation, as instruments of domination! What images do we hold, deep down, about family life or Bahá'í administration or the processes of Bahá'í education?

In particular, these images that we hold are highly relevant to the idea of curriculum and the principles we use to organise our curricula. What is the difference if we see our task as transmitting information, or if we see it as nurturing seeds with the teacher being thought of as a gardener? A gardener, of course, has only partial control over the processes in gardening. Some processes he or she sets in motion, others occur through nature. Given that the teacher has only partial control, the teacher's contribution consists in the main of creating the most nurturing and stimulating environment.

These and other such *images of belief* greatly influence the kinds of decisions that we make, and therefore the way that we try to create learning. Through these images and their attendant beliefs a curriculum can be, for example, information to be transferred, it can be faithful replication of what I know, it can be process and performance of skills, it can be arranging different kinds of activities to nurture the uniqueness of the individual, or an amalgam of more than one notion.

What kind of teacher did 'Abdu'l-Bahá model for us and which of His many relevant statements most inform our thinking about education? Thinking of 'Abdu'l-Bahá - how far does what actually takes place in the teaching for which we are responsible correspond to the image of the tender and wise gardener arranging the most effective environment for each plant or group of plants?

If we are to change a prevailing culture we have to change behaviour. If we are to change behaviour we have to change attitudes. If we are to change attitudes we have to change beliefs. Looking at and reflecting on deep images might help because we are what we believe, and our beliefs are images of how we believe reality is and how life works. But how, once we've started, do we know that what we are doing is Bahá'í education - what characteristics would we place uppermost, at least for the years ahead? Clearly education is culturally relative, and I speak from within the Western and European context - however, the characteristics I have chosen, have to a reasonable extent, general relevance.

Some Characteristics of Bahá'í-inspired Education

What characteristics would we hope to see in a Bahá'í-inspired class? The more sharply we can answer this question, the more effectively we will be able to evaluate the process of Bahá'í education. If we don't evaluate, we can't know if we were successful; and if we don't know what the characteristics should be, we can't evaluate!
Good evaluation is a combination of formative evaluation, evaluating as the lesson or course goes along, and summative evaluation, evaluating after the lesson or course has ended. Consequent to effective evaluation are abilities: to do course corrections (as in navigating), to clarify vision and objectives, to clarify the suitability and range of types of content, to clarify suitability of methods, to assess the effectiveness of management tools, to use resources better, to plan better and to tune the process of Bahá'í education, through rapid feedback, much more

effectively. All of these elements are also subject to the cultural milieu in which the learning is taking place. The argument, then, is that the planning, evaluation and adjusting of the stages of course development, Vision, Aims, Content, Methods, Management and Evaluating, should always be set up as a continuous feedback loop. This need not be sophisticated - the experienced teacher does it automatically, just like the automatic adjustments made by the experienced car driver.

Clearly there are more characteristics than can be discussed here. I have chosen those that I believe educational planners and writers should emphasise now and in the years ahead: focus on language and the Word of God, focus on metaphor as a key to unlock the world of the spirit, focus on the ability to enable students to connect to make Bahá'í-inspired meaning of the whole of their lives and to read what they see and experience from a Bahá'í point of view, thereby strengthening sense of purpose and identity, focus on spiritual education as a corrective and counterbalance to all of the wider society's materialistic influences, focus on the heart as well as the head, focus on problem-solving including conflict-resolution. All such characteristics have as their aim the creation of independent learners in whom virtuous capabilities of mind, heart and will are continuously developing in service to others. No doubt colleagues might want to add other characteristics.

The Importance of Language, the Word of God and Understanding of Metaphor

With *images of belief* comes language; we speak according to our beliefs as well as see according to our beliefs. We are dependent on the Word of God for all of our development. It not only reshapes belief but also energises our cognitive and affective selves. One way to contribute to this energising or enlargement of our consciousness is through memorisation of the Writings, whether we are very young or not so young.

Language and the development of thought go hand in hand. Within language metaphor is the central key to understanding spiritual realities. A metaphor is a use of words to indicate something different from the literal meaning as in such everyday expressions as, *I'll make him eat his words*! or *He has a heart of stone*! Metaphor is also the essence of poetic expression and of our understanding of the world of the spirit. The teaching of metaphor must be a central concern for all Bahá'í educators because understanding and use of metaphor is the key to the language of the world of the spirit. Central to such work is the idea that the physical universe is a metaphor for spiritual reality and as such is a classroom which God has provided for our intellectual and spiritual growth.[5]

Metaphor in Moral and Spiritual Education

Moral education is a way of experiencing all other subjects. In fact, in focusing on spiritual and moral education we are providing keys to understanding reality, keys to motivation and action, keys for meaning and purpose, perspectives and life-planning, keys for transformation and rising above the limitations our past and our beliefs have imposed on us, keys for cherishing harmony in diversity, keys for applying spiritual principles to social and economic needs, and keys for enacting loving unity. For this whole process we need to study metaphor, within a general study of language and the Word of God, as the major key to understanding spiritual realities, and thereby as an enhancement for learning in general.

Learning, of course, takes place all through the waking day - one Marshall McLuhan used to say that, given the power of television, children go to school as a break in their education! One challenge we face as Bahá'í-inspired educators is to provide appropriate links for *all* the domains in which learning takes place - between Bahá'í school, home, school or work and the wider community. In this, characteristically, we will assist the process of making sense of life, in the light of Bahá'u'lláh's teachings.

Reading Our World - Fragments or a Whole?
Another way of describing this essential role of Bahá'í education is to say that in a world of fragmentary, even atomised, experience Bahá'í education must assist the pupil or student in making a meaningful and purposeful whole of all the different kinds of experience she or he undergoes or participates in.

The purpose of nurturing a holistic understanding of life is not that the pupil can reduce stress or excel academically, although these might be highly desirable benefits. The purpose is that the process of reflection, behaviour and further reflection can strengthen the individual's sense of identity and commitment to the purpose of life, which is to know and love God, primarily through service to others. In this respect the pupil is led to read his inner and outer life effectively, not with ready-made answers but with a command of the spiritual principles to be applied. We then see with our own eyes and not with those of another. Bahá'í education should also characteristically be a corrective, a counterbalance to the materialistic and other excesses of the wider community.

As a counterbalance, Bahá'í education should give primacy to the feminine, the nurturing, the cooperative, to the heart rather than the head. Someone said that the longest journey in the world is from the human head to the human heart and the shortest journey in the world is from the heart to the head - it is not surprising, therefore, that God reserved for Himself out of the whole of creation, our hearts! We should, consequently, in our Bahá'í education be more heart-centred. What are the implications for the education we create of the statement that the heart is the seat of revelation?

If knowing involves judging and discriminating then it leads to making choices, which in turn engage the individual's values in many ways. The laws of Bahá'u'lláh and their purpose are the standards embedded in our teaching and our understanding of them is later activated according to our perceptions of choice and the profile of caring responses that are elicited from within us. In turn, our willingness is a product of the history of our actions, and attempted actions, as well as the product of our caring responses and our judging and discriminating perceptions.
What we've arrived at is a model which says that Bahá'í education is about the acquisition of virtues and the development of moral capability, and that moral capability is about judging, caring, willing and acting - toward the solution of the problems/challenges that we face in contributing to unity and peace.

The moral-development problem-solving model implies that we see students as progressively independent and learning to become, in the psychologist Maslow's term, self-actualised human beings who see through their own eyes and not the eyes of others. That is, that they see themselves as progressively having the means to mastery, and not the converse of seeing themselves as victims. With inner mastery they can be masters of external reality, however chaotic or antipathetic.

The Universal House of Justice in the *The Promise of World Peace* gives us a model of spiritualised problem-solving which combines outer and inner realities:

> *There are spiritual principles, or what some call human values, by which solutions can be found for every social problem. Any well-intentioned group can in a general sense devise practical solutions to its problems, but good intentions and practical knowledge are usually not enough. The essential merit of spiritual principle is that it not only presents a perspective which harmonises with that which is immanent in human nature, it also induces an attitude, a dynamic, a will, an aspiration, which facilitate the discovery and implementation of practical measures.*[6]

One kind of problem-solving is conflict-resolution. We need to study conflict-resolution at all levels from the personal and interpersonal to the national and international. One useful approach to conflict-resolution involves increasing a point or points of unity or seeking to increase the domain of unity on which both sides of a conflict agree - ideally this shared domain is increased to the point where the points of conflict disappear - most often it is done until a compromise agreement can be reached.

Problem-solving and conflict-resolution along with project management need to be built into Bahá'í education from the earliest years - initially, in simple forms via rôle play and simulations.

It seems that it is a sign of God's mercy that teachers do not carry full responsibility for their students' behaviour and knowledge. Were the responsibility complete, then teachers, like very conscientious mothers, would feel suicidal much of the time!

The education of community members is not the sole responsibility of teachers of Bahá'í education. Indeed, the Bahá'í teachings suggest that, at latest from the age of maturity, each individual has the responsibility to manage her or his own learning and development as an independent and dedicated life-long student. There are many opportunities to enhance our experience as independent and life-long learners - in the Writings, laws and teachings and their application. These opportunities include reading the sacred Writings, prayer, meditation, consultation, problem-solving, working together on projects and others. Formal and informal learning blend into one another. It is important early on to instil the idea of being in charge of one's own learning and to have the desire to be given opportunities to learn - in groups as well as on one's own.

In discussing a selection of characteristics it is intended to imply that discovering the essential nature of Bahá'í education is a continuous process of looking back and forth between the Writings, the actual process and the educational sciences.

Some feel that the shortage of time and the power of a materialistic education, and other negative influences in the wider society, mean that we have to find or create a kind of education that is distinctive at least in that it is intensive, challenging and highly effective in helping solve the problems of today. In doing this, as with other areas of life, we need to lay aside the important in favour of the most important. We must look for the yeast, the catalyst, the quintessential. It is not too early to think of Bahá'í education as an identifiable process in much the same way that Montessori or Tai-chi are identifiable and deeply shaping forms of education. If such a degree of urgency does not apply within the Bahá'í community it certainly applies to the contributions we can make in the wider community, which is increasingly asking for our assistance.

One approach to evolving, discovering or assembling a distinctive form of education would seem to lie in evaluating the best of what we have in the wider community in the light of the Revelation of Bahá'u'lláh, and in particular in the light of His teaching that spiritual and moral education is the foundation of all learning. This is what I have started in the SunWALK model - but clearly it is a task for many people networked together. Of the existing moral education programmes the one that is most brilliantly developed and, to my mind, wholly consonant with Bahá'í teachings, is *Philosophy for Children*.[7]

Accepting that diverse people will come up with diverse teaching, are there essential characteristics and core elements? If we do not have embryonically a distinct process, then alternatively Bahá'í education is simply education in a Bahá'í context. The distinctive nature of Bahá'í education at any one time will be in the harmony of the correctly chosen elements or characteristics, some of which are *eternal verities*, and some of which will always be time and place specific. But what seems to be the heart of the matter and what kind of core model could we use?

Moral and Spiritual Education using SunWALK

'Abdu'l-Bahá says, "the heart and foundation of all education is spiritual and moral training".[8] My rediscovering this statement combined with other coincidences in my life to lead me towards the SunWALK model.

What is Spiritual Education?
Spiritual education enables the development of spiritual qualities. It is seeking to enable the students to develop divine or virtuous qualities evident in thought and love and will - and expressed in loving service to others. The totality of these virtues is exemplified in the being and life and Writings of 'Abdu'l-Bahá.

Enablement is a key concept that implies that a teacher serves, at a conscious level, his or her student's struggle to learn. Such a teacher might say, "I don't teach" her or him in the sense of transmitting the knowledge I have gained, so much as I serve by creating the environment of her/his learning process. Through this nurture both shared and uniquely personal learning can take place. At a deeper level, the being of the student vibrates to the quality of the spiritual relationship she or he has had with the earliest teachers, including parents. We only have to know of work with abused children to see the reverse truth of this. Someone said that children are a projection of the unconscious reality of their parents - in other words, they are shaped by our deepest truest selves not our public selves. With young children the teacher is like a parent, and vice versa, and as the bonds between them deepen the children will vibrate to the resonances of the teacher's own spiritual and moral makeup.

We also need to pay particular attention in spiritual and moral education to the balance between process and content, method and information, the experiential and the cognitive. We don't, for example, most effectively encourage the growth of desirable virtues by simply teaching about 'Abdu'l-Bahá per se. We encourage that growth by asking the student to experience, or imagine experience, in which in his or her heart or head they can make reference to the knowledge they have of 'Abdu'l-Bahá. That is, gaining real knowledge must be a personalised meaning-making process. What do you think 'Abdu'l-Bahá would have done? What would you feel like if you were a prisoner with Bahá'u'lláh in the Most Great Prison? Would you have felt happy or sad? In such imaginative *entering into* the drama and, coincidentally or subsequently, into the solving of problems and moral predicaments the student learns to develop resources from the whole of her/his being. In such use of simulation the student engages all three sets of the soul's powers, knowing and loving and willing and can act or simulate action.

What is Moral Education?

Morality is about choices enacted against a set of standards. New standards are set with the coming of a Manifestation of God and are to be seen in His life and teachings and in the heroic lives of early believers. By definition, morality, we suggest, must involve thought, feeling and action. With the gradual acquisition of virtuous qualities we become spiritualised and our frames of reference for moral action advance. Upon the quality of the spirit depends the quality of the decisions we enact since it is the light that illumines thought. Reciprocally spiritualised feeling, action and reflection inform each other.

Hersh *et al*[9] reviewed a range of moral education programmes available in the US and came to the conclusion that moral education was education in judging, caring and acting, and that morality could not exist where all three elements were not present. It will not escape Bahá'ís that this conclusion concurs with models implicit in statements by 'Abdu'l-Bahá - for example, that achievement is dependent on knowledge, volition and action.

In the light of such teachings it seems reasonable to look at *willing* as a set of capabilities of the human soul separate from *loving* (caring) and from *knowing* (judging) - certainly it deserves separate attention because of its importance and because it is a neglected area. (Substance abuse and sports psychology are two of the few areas to concern themselves with volition). Consequently, I have put forward here the notion that actions or behaviour, including spiritual and moral actions, are products of the mixture and interaction of knowing, loving and willing capabilities as observed in the flow of behaviour.

As teachers, we need to be aware that children's focus of attention and engagement with the reality that we or they see constantly switches back and forth, and indeed, we should seek to activate all three areas of the soul through providing appropriate activities (as well as simply *keeping* their attention). These ought to include actions in which they have to test themselves, including knowledge that they have to use in various ways, and activities that engage their loving and caring abilities. Rôle play and group work are of course very useful in providing simulated reality, with content and method being grist to one mill - the development of spiritual and moral capabilities sown as seeds for the future or quickly shown in current behaviour.

Examples of spiritual and moral teaching include asking young children to show that they care and love the community of which they are part by serving the biscuits or sweets at a Nineteen Day Feast, inducing caring attitudes towards animals at a very early age simply by saying "Ah! Nice Doggie! Stroke the doggie" or whatever. In such small acts in the early months and years human and divine qualities are encouraged.

Similarly, from an early age by learning to ask appropriate questions, we develop the foundations of an enquiring mind - developing our questioning capabilities is vital for parents and teachers as well as pupils. As children get older, rôle play and group work are major means for simulating spiritual and moral experiences. Within the family *sacrifice*, i.e. making sacred all the activities needed for spiritual and physical parenting, might include adopting a sport such as sailing which serves not only family unity but also challenges the development of qualities in the daughters or sons. A family I know who did this sailed through their children's adolescence - literally and metaphorically! Thinking about practical ways to enhance the development of virtuous qualities is vital and we should work on this with friends in the wider community.

Taking spiritualisation to be the development of divine qualities (the acquisition of virtues), and moral education as the development of the ability to enact choices that have been thought out against a set of values, beliefs, and standards; we have much toward a model of human nature and human learning, understanding of which is vital for a teacher of moral and spiritual education. The clearer our understanding of the Bahá'í view of human nature, the reality we are trying to influence in the light of Bahá'u'lláh's Revelation, the better equipped we will be in making all those decisions that make up the process of teaching. Central to our view of human nature is the teaching that humankind's essential nature is spiritual, each individual is a soul, and that in addition to thought, the characteristic of the human level, each can choose to reflect the divine qualities of her or his Maker. The soul then in its existence and in its life-journey possesses three sets of qualities or powers; knowing (potentialities and capabilities), loving (potentialities and capabilities), and willing (potentialities and capabilities). From combinations of these three, we are suggesting, our actions flow and our true personality is made up. Teaching is enabling potentialities to become capabilities, the latent to become manifest. Similarly in Bahá'í administration the Auxiliary Board Members and their Assistants arouse and release the power that is in all of us potentially, and that power is directed toward goals that the assemblies authorise.

From this view of the spiritualising soul travelling through life with its Teacher (Bahá'u'lláh, Jesus, the Buddha, etc) came the SunWALK model of spiritual and moral education. The name SunWALK is a mnemonic, an aide memoir, a single word through which to remember the issues discussed in this paper.

In our lives and in the education of our souls we walk with Bahá'u'lláh and 'Abdu'l-Bahá (Christians with Christ, Buddhists with the Buddha, etc). We walk in the heat of the love and light of the knowledge brought by Bahá'u'lláh with capable souls demonstrating Willing Action through Love and Knowledge - *WALKing*. These sets of capabilities of the soul give rise to the virtues with which moral and spiritual behaviour are endowed. Bahá'í education therefore is about understanding how the *WALKing*, that is developing the Willing, Acting, Loving and Knowing capabilities, can become imbued with the qualities of the *Sun*, the Teacher and His life and teachings. From our Teacher and His teachings we learn of the attributes or virtues to be developed. From a range of these virtues I have constructed *The Sunburst* curriculum model, which provides an outline curriculum for both family education and for Bahá'í community schools.

The main framework of the curriculum consist of a range of target virtues within the Bahá'í months of the year plus Nineteen Day Feasts and Holy Days - the pattern of religious observance for the individual and for the community. To give a single example, *Justice* could be studied as a personal quality and as a need within society. It could be studied as something expressed in different ways in the different religions.

Some of the positive points of the *Sunburst* curriculum model include: the essential simplicity of the study of virtues within the framework, based as it is on the rhythm of months, Feasts and Holy Days; the model can be used year after year providing the teachers find stories and other materials that are progressively demanding and providing they frame tasks that are progressively demanding in terms of thought, feeling and will; the simplicity of the outline is helpful to the new teachers; the curriculum concentrates on developing virtues and capabilities; and consequently skills and information content take their rightful place as *servants* and not *masters* of the curriculum development process.

For me there is an unresolved issue concerning the will. Ought *will* really to be considered separately or is it a function of love and knowledge? I suspect the latter, however I choose to build it separately into the model because *will*, *volition* and *character* belong to such a neglected area in educational thought and writing. Of course, traditionally, sport, games and outward bound courses were supposed to build character. More recently, character-building leadership work has been done in management development courses. Our ongoing concern, however, is progressively to throw light on how education for will/volition/character relates to education for developing thinking and loving capabilities within the framework of a model of spiritual and moral education. Many questions can arise here. For example: what activities best develop will? how far is *will* a given (ie genetically determined)? what special attention needs to be given to the earliest years? what kind of thinking skills best support the development of volitional qualities? and so on.

Managing the Spiritual Process

National and Local Assemblies have to manage their systems of Bahá'í education through their Bahá'í education committees. Bahá'í schools have to manage the process within their institutions and the teacher is also a manager - but what does she or he, ultimately, manage? What do we think we are actually doing when we are *conducting* Bahá'í education? What is the medium with which Bahá'í teachers, as artists, work? What raw material or medium do they use? A painter works with paint, a sculptor with stone, a writer with words and ideas. It seems to me that Bahá'í educators, as all true educators, work with the human spirit, along with intimations of the Divine Spirit that we would like to see reflected in the holistic development of human spirit. We are managing spirit through spiritualised management, writing with light, making meaning in the human heart or, as the students get older, we are serving more and more the individual in his or her process of doing those things.

As teachers then we are also managers. We manage our own spiritual and moral tenor. We also manage our input to the process of others' learning - indeed the whole process of teaching, from the teacher's point of view, can be looked at as a series of interventions. To achieve high quality learning interventions for the learners, high-quality thinking, feeling and willing action by teachers and teacher-educators is required. Managing that process is usually the task of a national Bahá'í education committee.

We also manage our Bahá'í schools and we manage our Bahá'í education system and the community as a whole. We need spiritualised management in the management of spirit, because that human spirit, reflecting or motivated by the breaths of the Holy Spirit is the energy through which to achieve all development. The power to achieve plans rests with the rank and file, so we are told by 'Abdu'l-Bahá. The release of that power, individually, is, of course, dependent on our own volition as expressed in prayer, meditation, religious observance and general behaviour. Communally the arousal and release of that power is dependent on the appointed arm of the Faith and authorisation and direction of the use of that power comes from the assemblies. Power, release of that power and direction of the use of that power - these are the three elements in the dynamic of Bahá'í administrative and community life. Education is also about managing the arousal and release of potentialities and of directing their development toward goals defined for us by Bahá'u'lláh and the Universal House of Justice. The teacher manages the key learning environment in which the spirit of the student learns the essentials with which to deal morally with life and, if the parents and teachers have done the job well, the student comes to master his inner spiritual environment and thereby his outer material environment. As teachers, of course, we should never forget that we also are empowered in many ways - by those we teach.

Closely linked with spirit, as previously noted, is language, and central to language with which to study the spiritual is metaphor - the teacher's command and appropriate use of language and metaphor, for example in questioning techniques or task definition, are also vital to the process of managing student development in moral and spiritual education.

The statement of the House of Justice that spiritual and moral training is the foundation of all education is intriguing for a number of reasons. In the early years we are seeking to shape in a desirable way the process of formation - the desirable way being to the manifestation of spiritualised moral behaviour, behaviour which flows from caring, thinking and willing capabilities. As children grow toward youth and adulthood, the process of transformation becomes the process that we are trying to influence. As formation gives way to transformation, the child is progressively given more responsibility for her/his own learning as well as correction of behaviour since, in most, imperfections as well as perfections become apparent.

It seems that spiritual and moral education are the heart of education because they are the processes which centre on the wellspring of human reality, the soul of man from which knowing and loving and willing capabilities flow and to which they return - in unity. The single source of these three sets of qualities or capabilities is the deep level from which the soul manifests truth, knowledge and beauty - yet in outward expression we perceive it as predominantly either thought or love or will rather than the single reality. The three sets of powers become separate realities when they flow out from the heart of man and when we, as observers, focus on one mode, in knowing, loving or willing so as to distinguish the various qualities and capabilities. With this acknowledgement of unity at the root of the soul's sets of powers, we can go on to start to understand how love affects knowledge and knowledge affects love or will and so on. I see understanding more about these dynamic and reciprocal relationships of cause and effect as vital to understanding more about how to arrange effective spiritual and moral education.

When we are teaching children spiritual and moral realities, we are not, as we have said, teaching an extra subject: we are teaching the way they experience all other subjects. As such, the foundation of all other learning can also be seen as a set of keys with which the child *reads* or unlocks the realities of all other areas of her or his life. These *spiritual tools* give perspectives, connectedness and the ability to weigh the worth or rightness of any thing. Possession of such *spiritual technology* is true empowerment.

We are thus teaching spiritual core skills that are at the heart of the thinking, feeling, willing and acting in all other *subjects* - as air, water, food (vitamins minerals and trace elements?) are essential to physical capabilities. We are teaching caring, judgement, discrimination, and the skills through which these capabilities are expressed and a perspective, a framework of reference from which they view and can assay the ever- changing world in which they live. Each small element in the efforts of Bahá'í education teachers has the potential to illumine and shape all the areas of that student's life and through them to illumine humanity.

We are seeking to connect them to a knowledge and reality that underpins everything. We are providing a set of keys with which the child unlocks truer realities of the subject and experiences that he or she studies. Geography is invested with additional meaning because through it he or she learns more about the family of man that Bahá'u'lláh has come to unite. Vocational training is invested with additional meaning because it is the means to travel teach or pioneer. We are providing sources of motivation for that child to achieve in all domains throughout his or her life. We are providing capabilities to love and be loved. Above all, we are working with a reality from which these three sets of capabilities flow and to which they return. This is a locating experience, a focusing experience, a rooting experience, a connecting-up experience and one that is denied to all those that are not in touch with the Manifestation of God.

For those of us who are struggling with transformation, teaching (proclamation, expansion and social and economic development, as well as consolidation) will, as we become more skilled, enable each individual student to add meaning and purpose - to past experience as well as present. A great deal of Bahá'í education is about adding meaning and showing purpose and the connectedness of the otherwise chaotic flow of our experience. In the process of discovering these truths we can see how it is that the true status of teachers is so high. If creation was created for the true believer, how could the station of teachers be anything other than truly great? We provide the means for students to feel as Bahá'ís, to think as Bahá'ís, to care as Bahá'ís, and to resolve and carry out service as Bahá'ís.

Bahá'í teachers are language teachers teaching the language of the human spirit seeking to help bring about reflections of the Holy Spirit.

Conclusion

The assertion within this paper is that the true model and curriculum for Bahá'í education is always the optimum use of all available resources to create learning that advances spiritual development and moral behaviour. Spiritual and moral growth takes place through active engagement with challenges to solve problems toward unity and peace, using skills that emanate from our knowing, loving and willing capabilities.

In seeking to become more and more efficient in creating the learning that produces Bahá'í feelings, thinking and behaviour we need progressively to make use, through the unity of networked effort, of the principles in the Bahá'í Writings and the knowledge developed in the educational arts and sciences.

In all of our efforts we are inspired by the Central Figures of our Faith and the Revelation of Bahá'u'lláh brought by Him to effect the greatest of educational programmes - the spiritualisation of the human race to establish the Kingdom of Heaven upon earth.

References

1. For a more detailed exposition of the aims and methods of the Maxwell School, see Johnson, this volume.
2. See Richards and Richards this volume.
3. Universal House of Justice in *Bahá'í Education* - a compilation (London: Bahá'í Publishing Trust), 1987, p v.
4. G. Morgan, *Images of Organisation* (Beverley Hills: Sage), 1986.
5. John Hatcher, *The Purpose of Physical Reality* (Wilmette: Bahá'í Publishing Trust), 1987.
6. Universal House of Justice, *The Promise of World Peace* (Haifa: Bahá'í World Centre), 1985, pp 15-16.
7. *Philosophy for Children* is a moral education programme developed by Professor Matthew Lipman at The Institute for the Advancement of Philosophy for Children, Montclair State College, Upper Montclair, N.J. 07006, USA.
8. 'Abdu'l-Bahá, quoted in: *Bahá'í Education* - a compilation (London: Bahá'í Publishing Trust), 1987.
9. Hersh, Miller and Fielding, 1980, in *Models of Moral Education - An Appraisal*.